The Scapegoats

The Scapegoats

THE EXODUS OF THE REMNANTS
OF POLISH JEWRY

BY

JOSEF BANAS

TRANSLATED BY
TADEUSZ SZAFAR

EDITED BY
LIONEL KOCHAN

HOLMES & MEIER PUBLISHERS, INC.
IMPORT DIVISION
IUB Building
30 Irving Place, New York, N.Y. 10003

First published in Great Britain by
Weidenfeld and Nicolson Ltd,
91 Clapham High Street, London sw4
1979

English translation copyright © 1979, Josef Banas

ISBN 0 297 77563 4

Printed in Great Britain by
Butler & Tanner Ltd,
Frome and London

In Memory
of K.

I wish to thank Mr Jerzy Ros of Tel Aviv for his kindness in putting at my disposal his manuscript 'The Jews and the Armed Struggle Against the Nazi Occupiers in Poland 1939–45: Anti-Semitism and the Rule of Law in Poland'.

J.B.

Contents

THE anti-humanitarian essence of totalitarianism finds its expression, *inter alia*, in its inimical, sometimes even outright hostile attitude towards minorities which, in extreme cases, may take the form of physical extermination.

The main aim, however, of every totalitarian movement is to seize power in its own country and to subjugate its own people. That is why these people – in whose name and for whose sake the persecution of minorities is or was ostensibly carried out – have to pay the ultimate price for the misdeeds of their totalitarian rulers.

J.B.

1 . It Might Have Happened

From our East European Affairs Correspondent
Vienna, 21 March 1953

Nine eminent Soviet physicians were sentenced to death, and four to life imprisonment, after pleading guilty to assorted crimes of high treason, murder, terrorism, espionage, sabotage, 'wrecking', etc., in the first major show trial held in Moscow since that of Bukharin, Rykov and others in March 1938. The trial, which opened on 18 March before the Military Collegium of the Supreme Court of the USSR in the October Hall of the Trade Unions' House, lasted four days, and was attended by a small audience consisting of plain-clothes security officials, hand-picked representatives of large Moscow factories and ministries and a handful of foreign journalists, representing mostly Communist newspapers.

The defendants admitted that they belonged to a terrorist group of doctors 'connected with the international Jewish bourgeois nationalist organization "Joint" (American Joint Distribution Committee – AJDC) established by American intelligence allegedly in order to provide material aid to Jews in other countries', but which in fact, 'under the direction of American intelligence, conducts extensive espionage, terrorism and other subversive works in many countries, including the Soviet Union'. Several of the defendants also admitted to being 'veteran agents of British intelligence'.

The Victims

The indictment, which was fully confirmed by the defendants' confessions, included charges of having precipitated the death of A. A. Zhdanov, who, until 1948, had been considered Stalin's heir-apparent, by 'incorrectly diagnosing his illness and concealing an infarct of the myocardium'. They were also charged with having precipitated the death of General A. S. Shcherbakov in 1945 by 'incorrectly utilizing strong drugs in his treatment', and of having plotted the murder of prominent military leaders, including Marshal A. M. Vasilievsky, Marshal L. A. Govorov, Marshal I. S. Konev, General S. M. Shtemenko, Admiral G. I. Levchenko and others. Although no party or state officials were listed among the intended victims, and the Generalissimo's name was never mentioned, it was the common belief – a belief assiduously fanned by a whispering campaign – that 'the Jews wanted to poison Stalin'. Although

3

only four of the thirteen defendants were identified as Jewish, while two other Jews, listed in the official TASS communiqué of 13 January 1953, were reported dead – presumably the result of torture inflicted during the investigation – the court proceedings were conducted with a distinctive anti-Jewish bias, a bias reflected by the mass media.

The Defendants

The case of the 'Kremlin doctors', or 'murders in white gowns', began with this communiqué, which listed among the participants of the terrorist group such luminaries of Soviet medicine as the therapeutists Professors M.S. Vovsi, V.N. Vinogradov, M.B. Kogan, B.B. Kogan, P.I. Yegorov, Ya.G. Etinger and G.I. Maiorov, the otolaryngologist Professor A.E. Feldman, the neuropathologist Professor A.M. Grinshtein, 'and others'. Six of the nine bore easily recognizable Jewish names; Professors M.B. Kogan, and Ya.G. Etinger were missing from the dock, where the original seven were joined by six other professors of presumably Russian or Ukrainian nationality – V.K. Vasilenko (who was arrested on his return from China, where he had treated Mao Tse-tung), V.F. Zelenin, B.S. Preobrazhensky, N.A. Popova (the only woman among the defendants), V.V. Zakusov, and N.A. Shereshevsky. 'The Jewish Connection' was stressed in the bill of indictment by a quotation from Professor Vovsi's confession. Vovsi admitted that he had received from the USA, through the 'Joint' organization, orders to 'wipe out the leading cadres of the USSR'. One of his intermediaries had been the well-known physician, Dr Boris Shimeliovich, formerly director of the Botkin Hospital in Moscow (one of the largest and best in the Soviet Union), and former member of the Jewish Anti-Fascist Committee; a second intermediary had been his cousin, 'the well-known Jewish bourgeois nationalist', Solomon Mikhoels-Vovsi, a brilliant actor and director of the Moscow Yiddish Theatre. Shimeliovich was arrested in the autumn of 1948 together with other members of the Jewish Anti-Fascist Committee, which was then disbanded under the pretext of having fostered 'Jewish bourgeois nationalistic tendencies' and under suspicion of espionage; he presumably died, or was murdered, in prison. Mikhoels, chairman of the Committee and member of an official delegation which in 1943 had visited the United States and Great Britain in order to rally support for the Soviet war effort, was killed in Minsk (the Byelorussian capital) in January 1948, under mysterious circumstances (there were hints of a road accident or violent robbery), which gave rise to suspicions that he had been murdered by secret police.

A Hitch

All the defendants pleaded guilty as charged. When one defendant at-

4

tempted to retract the self-accusatory deposition he had made during the investigation, the prosecutor called for a short recess. When the court resumed, the defendant admitted his guilt and meekly explained he had been so ashamed of the crimes he had committed against the Soviet Fatherland, that he had 'automatically' (*mashinalno*) tried to deny them. According to reports by eye-witnesses, although the defendants bore no visible traces of physical ill-treatment, they looked old and emaciated. Questions put by the prosecutor, judges and defence counsel were answered promptly, but coldly and cautiously, as though previously learned by heart and rehearsed many times. This impression was enhanced by the fact that both prosecutor and members of the court followed the depositions as though verifying their accuracy against a typewritten script lying before them; several times they even corrected the defendants who had apprently strayed from the prepared text. Such admonitions were invariably accepted with gratitude by the accused, and their testimonies proceeded without further hitches. 'We were working for the aims of the Anglo-US Imperialists and of the aggressive bloc of US and British Imperialists, these aims being the restoration of capitalism and a new world war, which is today being prepared by the imperialists' was a typical confession.

The Wire-Pullers

According to the bill of indictment,

'the US monopolists make extensive use for their odious purposes of Jewish Zionist organizations, including the international Jewish bourgeois nationalist organization "Joint", which acts at the orders and direction of American intelligence. Zionism has become the tool of the American-British warmongers. Relying on a group of Jewish bourgeois nationalists, the wreckers and murderers of the "Joint" have been criminally active in our country.... The monstrous crimes of these base agents of American and British intelligence ... evoked the indignation of the entire Soviet people. Executing the will of their masters, the imperialists of the USA and Britain, this despicable band of wreckers, which posed as learned doctors, sought to cut short the lives of public figures in the Soviet Union ... to undermine the health of leading Soviet military cadres, put them out of action, and thereby weaken the country's defence.' The indictment dwelt at length on the 'Trotskyite-Titoist-Zionist' conspiracy against world peace and socialism in the USSR, organized by the American and British imperialist warmongers who made use of their subordinate espionage agencies – those of Israel and Yugoslavia. The 'Joint' was described as 'one of the most important branches of the American Intelligence Service: murderers, spies, and saboteurs who are members of this organization carry out the vilest assignments of Wall Street, without shrinking from any, even the most inhuman, means. US imperialist circles generously finance their Zionist Agency', while the Israeli Legation in Moscow served as a recruiting post for spies and saboteurs, and a clearing-house for anti-Soviet intelligence.

The Indictment

'Never yet have our people's courts had to try such criminals as these who sit before us in the dock today, and on whom you have to pass judgement', the prosecutor began his final address. 'This is the abyss of degradation! With the exception of high treason, there is no more monstrous crime than the betrayal of a patient's faith; there is no criminal more abominable than a murderer dressed in a doctor's white gown.' The prosecutor went on to describe the world-wide conspiracy against peace and the Soviet Union, a conspiracy which, he claimed, was in the interests of US imperialism and world domination. He recalled in this connection the spy-ring led by the Field brothers, and the recent cases of Laszlo Rajk in Hungary, Traicho Kostov in Bulgaria, Rudolf Slansky in Czechoslovakia, Wladyslaw Gomulka and Marian Spychalski in Poland. In all these cases the threads led to the 'Titoist fascist clique' and to the Zionist spymasters – Henry Morgenthau, Bernard Baruch and Judge Frankfurter in the US; the Rothschilds, Konni Zilliacus and Herbert Morrison in England; Mosha Pijade in Yugloslavia; and the leaders of 'The American protectorate – the so-called State of Israel',

David Ben-Gurion and Moshe Sharett. Those whom they were able to recruit through the 'Joint' posing as a charitable organization became traitors to their countries on account of their Jewish bourgeois nationalism. Trotskyism, Titoism and Zionism were thus lumped together as an anti-Soviet fifth column, but 'the Soviet people wrathfully and indignantly condemn the criminal band of murderers and their foreign masters. They will crush like loathsome vermin the despised hirelings who sold themselves for dollars and pounds sterling. As for those who inspired these hired murderers, they may rest assured that vengeance will not pass them by but will find a way to them....'

Shadows of the Past

Passing to specific charges, the prosecutor reminded the court that the defendants' crimes were not unprecedented. In the trial of Bukharin in 1938 two physicians – Professor D. Pletnev, aged sixty-eight, previously framed by the NKVD for alleged indecent assault on a woman patient, and a Jew, L. G. Levin – were convicted for the murder of two senior Soviet dignitaries, V. R. Menzhinsky and V. V. Kuibyshev, as well as of the writer Maxim Gorki and his son Maxim Peshkov. Two of the present defendants, Shereshevsky and Vinogradov, were on that occasion called to give evidence as expert witnesses for the prosecution, and their testimony had contributed to the

6

death sentences; while three more of the defendants had signed violent resolutions attacking their erstwhile colleagues. At the recent (November 1952) trial of the 'anti-state conspiratorial Centre' in Prague, Rudolf Slansky, former Secretary-General of the Communist Party of Czechoslovakia, admitted having instructed his personal physician, Vladimir Haskover, 'a Zionist and Freemason ... from a hostile environment and with a murky past', to shorten the life of President Gottwald by withdrawing proper medical care. This, too, had been done on orders of the 'Joint'. The links between the defendants and their alleged victims were, however, rather coincidental: Shcherbakov died in 1945, apparently of natural causes, and his attending doctors had not been named at the time. The death certificate of Zhdanov (who died on 31 August 1948) was signed by five doctors, all of them non-Jewish; four of them (Vinogradov, Yegorov, Maiorov and Vasilenko) were now in the dock.

Law: An Algebraic Formula

As all the accused, after prolonged interrogation, admitted their guilt and confirmed it in court, neither the investigating officers nor the prosecutor needed to recall the main principles of Soviet jurisprudence, as set down by Andrey Vyshinsky, Prosecutor-General during the great Moscow trials of the 1930s and recently Soviet Minister of Foreign Affairs: namely, that a court cannot aspire to absolute truth and must accordingly be satisfied with some degree of probability; the evaluation of evidence is based only on inner conviction; the law is an algebraic formula, which is corrected in the process of application by the judge; an accomplice must bear responsibility for all the activity of the group to which he belongs; finally and most significant, in cases involving crimes against the state the confession of the accused is sufficient proof.

Heroine-Unmasker

Among the prosecution witnesses, special interest was aroused by the testimony of Lidia Fedoseyevna Timashuk, a doctor employed as a radiologist in the Kremlin health service, and widely believed to be a secret-service informer. Timashuk was credited with having written directly to Stalin in order to draw his attention to the fact that many eminent physicians, professors and academicians were intentionally applying incorrect or in some cases directly harmful methods of treatment. Having been awarded the Order of Lenin Timashuk became an overnight celebrity throughout the Soviet Union; *Pravda* even published column after column of fan-mail praising her Soviet patriotism and Communist vigilance. According to the press, she 'had fought as one combats enemies of the homeland – heedlesss of the danger to her life', and thus 'has become near and dear to the hearts of millions of Soviet people'. Similar sentiments concerning a 'heroine-un-masker' were expressed by the presiding judge who, when summing up, praised this 'simple, rank-and-file Party member' and appealed to all Communists to follow her example; 'sometimes, ordinary people come closer to the truth than some high institutions', he remarked.

Beria – The Target?

Among well-informed observers in Moscow, Timashuk's evidence and the judge's summing-up provoked widespread rumours. The original TASS communiqué announcing the 'unmasking' of the 'murderer-doctors, who became monsters in human form, trampling the sacred banner of science and desecrating the honour of scientists, and were enrolled by foreign intelligence services as hired agents', was accompanied by a *Pravda* editorial. Under the headline 'Miserable Spies and Assassins Masked as Professors of Medicine', *Pravda* stated, *inter alia*: 'The fact that a group of despicable degenerates from among men of science were able for some time to engage in their machinations with impunity, shows that some of our Soviet agencies and their officials lost their vigilance and were infected with gullibility. The agencies of state security did not discover the doctors' wrecking, terrorist organization in time.' Even worse, Timashuk's evidence implied criminal negligence on the part of the security services: even after her letter had alarmed some officials in the Ministry of State Security (MGB), the minister (Abakumov) had supposedly ordered the Head of the Investigation Department, Ryumin, not to investigate the letter and had had him arrested. Stalin himself, it is said, then ordered Ryumin's release, dismissed Abakumov, and appointed Ignatev (from the Party's Central Committee apparatus) Minister of State Security, thus taking personal charge of the investigation. If confirmed, these rumours would strengthen reports that Beria's position had lately become precarious: Abakumov was reputed to be *his* man, whereas Ignatev, later appointed Secretary of the Party's Central Committee, was allegedly Khrushchev's protégé.

Information concerning Beria's imminent disgrace dates from the so-called 'Mingrelian affair' – a purge of his followers among the Mingrelian minority in the Georgian SSR in the Caucasus. The purge had begun in November 1951 and continued throughout 1952. Beria, since 1938 the all-powerful head of the security apparatus, and therefore directly responsible for the premature death of Zhdanov and Shcherbakov, was also closely implicated in the activities of the Jewish Anti-Fascist Committee during the war, and had approved sending its leaders, including Mikhoels, to the West. According to Moscow gossip, Beria might himself have been part Jewish, having changed his name from Berman or Berenson.

8

Struggle for the Succession

Anti-Semitic overtones had been clearly discernible in official Soviet propaganda since at least the 1948 campaign against 'rootless cosmopolitans'. The anti-Semitic campaign culminated in the disappearance, and presumed slaughter, of virtually all the leading Jewish writers and intellectuals, and led to the current daily vilification in the press of profiteers, racketeers, black-marketeers, hoarders and 'wreckers', most if not all of them with clearly Jewish-sounding names. If this smear campaign is indeed linked with the struggle for the succession among Stalin's closest collaborators, then not only Beria but by implication his closest ally and reputed heir-apparent, Malenkov, would seem vulnerable on this count. Kaganovich, one of the last 'Old Bolsheviks', is well known to be Jewish, and his brother was lately rumoured to have committed suicide. Molotov's Jewish wife, Paulina Zhemchuzhina, has apparently been exiled from Moscow for having a brother living in the USA, and for the excessive warmth of the greetings accorded the first Israeli diplomatic envoy, Golda Meir. Thus only Khrushchev, whose reputation for Jew-baiting is second to none (with the possible exception of Stalin himself), would be left in the field.

The Purge

The 'Kremlin doctors' plot', preceded almost immediately by the Slansky trial in Prague and the rupture of diplomatic relations between the USSR and Israel, has given a tremendous boost both to Soviet anti-Semitic propaganda (thinly disguised as anti-Zionism or anti-Israelism), and popular Jew-baiting. While reports from the provinces on anti-Jewish outbursts or even pogroms, especially in the Ukraine and in Moldavia, are difficult to confirm, both the central and the local Soviet press have intensified their drive against the Jews. It is reported that the accusations appear to be generally accepted by the public, who desperately need a scapegoat for their continuing misery. In Moscow Jewish officials and employees have been arrested in several major industrial plants – the *Dynamo* factory, the Stalin automobile works, the Metro administration, etc. – charged with belonging to a Jewish counter-revolutionary organization, whose aim was allegedly to blow up Moscow. In the Party Central Committee, the Moscow City Committee, the *raion* committees, editorial boards (including *Pravda*), Ministry of Internal Affairs, Procurator's office, courts, military administration, Soviet Information Bureau, Radio Committee, ministries, and other state offices, the remaining Jews are being systematically purged without any attempt to find pretexts for their dismissal. At the height of the witch-hunt against the Jewish 'doctor-poisoners', the Russian mass-circulation satirical weekly *Krokodil* published on its front cover a caricature of Mikhail Romm, the leading Soviet film director. Romm was portrayed with crudely exaggerated Jewish facial features, reading a work by André Gide (an obvious pun on the vulgar Russian word 'zhid' [yid], a coarse anti-Semitic insult strictly prohibited by Soviet law).

foreign accent! In fact you can't really speak any language properly – neither Russian nor Ukrainian. You are a typical rootless cosmopolitan! And you claim to belong to the great Russian state!

A Quaint Sense of Humour

In the course of the 'Kremlin doctors' trial', anti-Jewish jibes by the prosecutor and the court were reported at length in the Soviet press. Here is a typical interrogation of a defendant (member of the Soviet Academy of Sciences):

JUDGE: What is your nationality?
DEFENDANT: Russian.
J: Are you certain?
D: (No reply).
J: What language did your parents use at your home?
D: Yiddish, but that was sixty years ago...
J: (*interrupting him*): You mean the jargon?
D: I suppose so...
J: Where were you born?
D: In the Ukraine.
J: Do you speak Ukrainian?
D: I did as a child.
J: Can you speak Russian well?
D: Yes.
J: Do you want an interpreter?
D: No.
J: You can understand the questions and you will be able to reply in Russian?
D: Yes.
PROSECUTOR: But you speak it with a

The Witnesses

To illustrate the links between American intelligence and the 'Trotskyite-Titoist-Zionist' terrorists, the prosecutor called as witness a certain S.D. Gurevich, an old-time Trotskyite and allegedly an agent of foreign intelligence services, who had grown up in a Menshevik home and had been a member of the Jewish Socialist *Bund*. Western journalists in Moscow had known a man of this name, and regarded him as a person authorized to maintain contact with foreigners. Another witness for the prosecution, the eminent cardiologist, Professor Davidenko, formerly Zhdanov's personal physician, gave evidence especially incriminating the defendants: nobody dared to point out that as a prisoner of war in Germany, Davidenko's son had volunteered for the Vlasov army, and had been captured after the end of hostilities. Since then the cardiologist had been blackmailed by the Soviet security services.

Counsel for the Defence

The defence counsel, all of them appointed by the court, did not question their clients' guilt as set forth in the bill of indictment; on the contrary, they stressed the irrefutability of the evidence against the accused and drew attention to the fact that each of the defendants had made a total confession. Indeed, the defence claimed 'extenuating circumstances' – in the case of the Jewish defendants, this was invariably based on their bourgeois or petty-bourgeois origins, Jewish-nationalist upbringing, lifelong connection with the 'Judas-Trotsky', religious or sentimental attachment to the State of Israel, the fact that they had relatives abroad, chiefly in the USA, and their 'inherent cosmopolitanism' – or pure greed – which had been skilfully exploited by their spy-masters from the 'Joint' organization, American or British intelligence services, and the Israeli Legation in Moscow. Both counsel and defendants in their final plea demanded severe and just sentences which would furnish the guilty men with an opportunity to expiate their crimes against the Soviet Fatherland.

Liberalism Abused

As if wishing to forestall criticism, and in particular charges of anti-Semitism, the presiding judge said in his summing-up that the Soviet people despised anti-Semitism; this fact was, however, abused by various Jewish racketeers and terrorists. 'Our people know that our Party will never give up its proletarian internationalism, and

that the defendants in this trial are anti-Soviet traitors and murderers, international Zionist terrorists, highly important spies and agents of Western imperialism.' The judge even quoted from an interview granted by the Chief Rabbi of Moscow, Schlieffer, who claimed that 'it was inconceivable that questions of race or religion could play any part in accusations made against anyone in our country'; Schlieffer added that 'Zionism, which the Soviet people are now being told to regard with the utmost suspicion, is not associated with religion or race'.

Panic

All available reports agree that the doctors' trial had aroused widespread anxiety bordering on panic among the Jewish population of Moscow and other Soviet cities. The fate of the former members of the Jewish Anti-Fascist Committee, including the wartime Deputy Foreign Minister, Solomon Lozovsky, and over twenty Yiddish writers and well-known scholars, is widely known there, though never revealed in public. In the summer of 1952 they were put on trial charged with attempting to sever the Crimea from the Soviet Union, and have not been heard of since. But now it is suspected, though rarely said, that Stalin has embarked on another round of mass purges reminiscent of the late 1930s and euphemistically referred to as the 'Yezhovschchina'. While directed against all or some of his close collaborators, such a witch-hunt could on this occasion resort to open anti-Semitism in order to discredit political opponents, divert attention from the genuine issues, or curry favour with the masses, who are conditioned to despise the Jews. This anti-Jewish feeling is the result of an age-old tradition, Nazi propaganda in the occupied Soviet territories, and the recent Party campaign against 'rootless cosmopolitans', 'tribeless vagabonds', 'strangers to the people and its national culture', Trotskyites and Zionists. Anti-Semitism might also occur as a corollary to the internecine struggle for power after Stalin's demise. Hence the various rumours and speculation around the question, against whom was the Kremlin doctors' plot staged, and whether the notion of 'collective guilt' will be used against the two and a half million Jews who have survived in the Soviet Union.

Such fears are by no means far-fetched, as the fate of the Volga Germans, Crimean Tatars, and Kalmuk, Balkar, Chechen and Ingush inhabitants of the North Caucasus has recently demonstrated. Soviet Jews fear exile *en masse* to the Arctic or the Far East. This will result either in response to the 'people's demands' that the accomplices of the traitors be punished, or as a preventive measure to 'defend' the Jews against attempts by the masses to take the law into their own hands.

*　　　*　　　*

Well, that did *not* happen. . . . The trial of the Kremlin doctors was indeed due to open on 18 March 1953, but providence intervened like the classical *deus ex machina*: on 6 March Josef Vissarionovich Stalin died under circumstances which to this day perplex serious historians and Sovietologists. A 'collective leadership' replaced the late dictator, whose antics in the last years of his absolute rule frequently verged on paranoia. Malenkov, Beria and Khrushchev, as well as a number of lesser worthies, all took up positions in the inevitable fight for succession. The 'doctors' plot' seemed all but forgotten until a month later, on 4 April, the Party newspaper *Pravda* published on its second page a brief communiqué 'from the Ministry of the Interior'. Startled readers were told that there never had been a conspiracy of 'murderers in white gowns', and that the maligned doctors were innocent and had subsequently been rehabilitated, two of them posthumously. 'It had been established', *Pravda* reported, 'that the depositions of the accused, which supposedly confirmed the accusations made against them, were obtained by workers in the investigative service of the former Ministry of State Security by investigative methods rigorously forbidden by Soviet laws.' A very short item, tucked away under a lengthy article on fruit trees, announced that the Supreme Soviet had annulled the decree conferring the Order of Lenin on Lidia Timashuk.

Although, as in previous official pronouncements, there was no reference to the anti-Semitic aspects of the affair, the mass media began condemning 'all propaganda of racial or national discrimination'. Solomon Mikhoels, the brilliant actor and Chairman of the wartime Jewish Anti-Fascist Committee in the USSR, murdered in Minsk in January 1948, had re-emerged five years later on the pages of the satirical weekly *Krokodil* (30 January 1953), depicted as a hypocrite who, 'for thirty pieces of silver', had sold himself to American imperialism and personally trained the Kremlin doctors (including his cousin, Professor Vovsi). Now posthumously rehabilitated, the Jewish actor became once again 'this honest citizen, this great artist of the people of the USSR'. The text of an appeal to the Jewish people 'requesting' mass resettlement in Siberia and Central Asia, which had awaited signature by several distinguished Soviet scientists and cultural leaders of Jewish origin, had to be scrapped, together with resolutions already passed by workers from several large-scale factories on the eviction of Jews from major Soviet cities.

The projected trial of the Kremlin doctors had a dual function. The first was to introduce the Soviet version of the solution to the Jewish question as they did with the people of Karachai, Chechen, Ingush, and Crimean Tatars and Volga Germans. Khrushchev said, in his 'Secret Speech' to the Twentieth Congress of the Communist Party in 1956:

We refer to the mass deportations from their native places of whole nations, together with all Communists and Komsomols without any exception; this deportation action was not dictated by any military considerations.

Thus, already at the end of 1943, when there occurred a permanent breakthrough at the fronts of the Great Patriotic War benefiting the Soviet Union, a decision was taken and executed concerning the deportation of all the Karachai from the lands on which they lived.

In the same period, at the end of December 1943, the same lot befell the

whole population of the Autonomous Kalmuk Republic. In March 1944 all
the Chechen and Ingush peoples were deported and the Chechen-Ingush
Autonomous Republic was liquidated. In April 1944 all Balkars were deported
to faraway places from the territory of the Kabardino-Balkar Autonomous Republic and the Republic itself was renamed the Autonomous Kabardinian Republic.

The Ukranians avoided meeting this fate only because there were too many
of them and there was no place to which to deport them. Otherwise, he would
have deported them also. (Laughter and animation in the hall.)[1]

The second function of the projected trial was to justify (as did Kirov's
murder in the thirties) a new wave of bloody mass purges throughout
the Soviet establishment. This trial did not, however, take place after all:
the report from 'our East European Affairs Correspondent' is obviously
apocryphal.[2] But although millions of sorely afflicted Jews, both in the
Soviet Union and throughout the Communist-ruled empire, might heave
a sigh of relief, it soon became apparent that even if they had been spared
the worst, political anti-Semitism in the USSR had only temporarily been
put aside for reasons of expediency – it had by no means ceased to be
considered a legitimate weapon in the Communist ideological armoury.

This unpleasant truth was borne out by the aftermath of the 'Kremlin
doctors' plot': the communiqué on their rehabilitation was issued not
by the Soviet government nor the Party Central Committee, but by the
Minister of the Interior, Beria, thus clearly pointing to differences of
opinion, or even internecine struggles, inside the new 'collective leadership'. The denunciation and punishment of the perpetrators accordingly
followed a curiously selective pattern. While *Pravda* raged against 'spies
and diversionists, bearers of bourgeois ideology and degenerates', and
reminded its readers that 'against these true enemies, open and recognized, of the people, these enemies of the Soviet state, it is always necessary to keep our powder dry' (6 April 1953), virtually the sole man put
forward as responsible for the affair was the former Deputy Minister of
State Security Ryumin. Even his immediate superior the former Minister
and Central Committee Secretary, Ignatev, Khrushchev's protégé,
escaped with a short spell of disgrace as the provincial Party Secretary
in Bashkiria (only to be reprieved as soon as the liquidation of Beria and
his faction removed the need for further camouflage and provided the
new Party leadership with an abundant supply of scapegoats). However,
not even once during the whole early period of de-Stalinization (the so-

[1] From *The Secret Speech*, introduced by Z.A. and R.A. Medvedev (Spokesman Books, 1976).
[2] However, it follows as closely as possible the facts as known at that time. Indeed, the quotations
were taken practically *verbatim* from the stenographic records of the trial of Bukharin in 1938,
the Slansky trial in 1952, and from contemporary comments and articles in the Soviet press.

called 'thaw') were the anti-Semitic roots of the 'Doctors' plot' alluded to. Indeed, Khrushchev pointedly omitted any reference to the whole issue in his 'Secret Speech' and in his subsequent pronouncements. To quote once more from his 'Secret Speech':

Let us also recall the 'affair of the doctor-plotters'. (Animation in the hall.) Actually there was no 'affair' apart from the declaration of the woman doctor Timashuk, who was probably influenced or ordered by someone (after all, she was an unofficial collaborator of the organs of state security) to write Stalin a letter in which she declared that doctors were applying supposedly improper methods of medical treatment.

Such a letter was sufficient for Stalin to reach an immediate conclusion that there are doctor-plotters in the Soviet Union. He issued orders to arrest a group of eminent Soviet medical specialists. He personally issued advice on the conduct of the investigation and the method of interrogation of the arrested persons. He said that the academician Vinogradov should be put in chains, another one should be beaten. Present at this Congress as a delegate is the former Minister of State Security, Comrade Ignatev. Stalin told him curtly, 'If you do not obtain confessions from the doctors we will shorten you by a head.' (Tumult in the hall.)

Stalin personally called the investigative judge, gave him instructions, advised him on which investigative methods should be used: these methods were simple – beat, beat, and once again beat.

Shortly after the doctors were arrested, we members of the Political Bureau received protocols with the doctors' confessions of guilt. After distributing these protocols, Stalin told us, 'You are blind like young kittens; what will happen without me? The country will perish because you do not know how to recognize enemies.'

The case was so presented that no one could verify the facts on which the investigation was based. There was no possibility of trying to verify facts by contacting those who had made the confessions of guilt.

We felt, however, that the case of the arrested doctors was questionable. We knew some of the people personally because they had once treated us. When we examined this 'case' after Stalin's death, we found it to be fabricated from beginning to end.

This ignominious 'case' was set up by Stalin; he did not, however, have the time in which to bring it to an end (as he conceived that end), and for this reason the doctors are still alive. Now all have been rehabilitated; they are working at the same places they were before; they treat top individuals, not excluding members of the Government; they have our full confidence; and they execute their duties honestly, as they did before.

It was under Khrushchev's rule (and that of his successors) that political anti-Semitism 'progressed' from a faint-hearted concession to the deeply rooted bias of backward Russian and Ukrainian peasants and peasants' sons, and from a semi-spontaneous discrimination against 'pushy' Jews, to an integral part of contemporary Communist doctrine and practice, both internally and externally. This aspect of the question therefore requires closer scrutiny if we are to understand how it happened that the Soviet Union has become the shrine of modern anti-Semitism, and its source of inspiration throughout the sphere of her direct and indirect political influence. To shrug it off as merely a vestige of the remote past, or even as a Stalinist perversion of socialism, will simply no longer do.

Although a specific strain of anti-Semitism is discernible at the very beginning of the socialist movement – the young Marx, after all, regarded the Jews as particularly obnoxious exponents of capitalism – generally speaking, socialism as an ideology of human liberation consistently rejected all forms of racial, national or religious discrimination. Equally, the workers' movement fought consistently against anti-Semitism, condemning it as a diversion calculated to distract the toiling masses from the class struggle and their revolutionary tasks. The Bolshevik Revolution, by removing at one fell swoop all the legal restrictions imposed by the *ancien régime* on the world's largest Jewish community, not only paved the way for an unprecedented eruption of new talent in fields hitherto closed to the Jews, but by the same token won for its cause large numbers of Jews in Eastern Europe, and many of their fellow-Jews throughout the world. The honeymoon proved, however, to be of very short duration, though the rise of Nazism, with its racial doctrines and implacable opposition to Communism, helped to delay the inevitable break.

In point of fact, it was as early as the 1920s, and especially in the 1930s, that the Soviet government, under the leadership of Stalin, discovered the advantages of political anti-Semitism. Having jettisoned the lofty ideals of the founding fathers and begun to consolidate their sway over the enormous Russian land mass ('socialism in one country'), they immediately inherited the goals and methods of their Tsarist predecessors. Nationalism proved a far more effective means of commanding people's obedience than the somewhat vague ideals of socialism and the international brotherhood of the toiling and exploited masses, and in backward and traditionally expansionist Russia, socialism emerged in the form of xenophobic chauvinism combined with a drive to subjugate the neighbouring nationalities. Within the heritage of Asian despotism, Greek-Orthodox bigotry, Great-Russian chauvinism, and Tsarist autocracy and imperialism – by then engraved on pseudo-Marxist tablets – there was ample scope for political anti-Semitism, along with, *inter alia*, the revival of the traditional hatred and distrust of Russian and Ukrainian peasants for the

Polish *pans* (landed gentry). Whether such sentiments conformed to the Marxist writings, or reflected the genuine anti-Jewish, or for that matter anti-Polish, bias of their originators, is totally irrelevant. They were used or discarded solely in accordance with political expediency. Though it has been pointed out that whereas all totalitarian régimes require the notion of a potential 'enemy' as an object of hatred and persecution, the choice of that enemy may never be entirely arbitrary: it must, at the least, appear plausible. In this respect, the Jews fitted the bill better than most.

Political anti-Semitism in the Soviet Union, already sporadically though sparingly exploited in connection with Stalin's struggle against the inner-party opposition in the 1920s and the Great Purges of the 1930s, assumed massive proportions in the immediate post-war years in the guise of an all-out campaign against 'rootless cosmopolitanism'. It is often mistakenly assumed that the anti-cosmopolitan campaign was the direct outcome of the creation of the State of Israel, or, more specifically, of the sudden outburst of enthusiasm with which Soviet Jews welcomed the first Israeli envoys to Moscow. This fallacy can easily be refuted by a simple reference to the chronology of events. While the Soviet press was already raging against Jewish intellectuals, and playing to the gallery by 'exposing' their Jewish-sounding patronymics, Soviet diplomats in the United Nations supported the establishment of a Jewish state in Palestine, Czech arms were delivered to the Hagana, and Golda Meir presented her credentials at the Kremlin. From at least 1947 onwards Stalin was firmly convinced that an armed confrontation with the United States was not only inevitable but imminent, and his preparations for that war included strengthening the totalitarian nature of the Soviet régime. The Jewish 'potential enemy' had by then become an 'objective enemy', not only because of the deeply rooted layers of anti-Jewish prejudice ('folk anti-Semitism') among a part of the Russian, Ukrainian and other East European peoples Sovietized during and after the war, but also because of the Jews' actual or alleged family ties with the influential American-Jewish community. The 'Kremlin doctors' plot' thus can be seen as concomitant with the anti-cosmopolitan campaign – even if the nomenclature was slightly altered (with 'Zionists' replacing 'cosmopolitans'): thus the Jewish denigrators of Russian culture were finally unmasked as spies, terrorists and agents of American imperialism.

The overtly anti-Semitic edge of the *Zhdanovshchina* (as the anti-cosmopolitan campaign was later known) and of the case of the 'murderers in white gowns' should not, however, conceal the true purpose of each exercise: the Jews were the intended victims, but not the ultimate goal. In the first instance what was involved was the overall strengthening of the ideological, political and police controls that had been relaxed by the war and the widespread hopes it had aroused – the restoration in full of the totalitarian character of the Soviet régime and its establishment over the newly-acquired empire. Secondly – or so at least it may be supposed, for Stalin's death put paid to the next stage before it could come into the open – a further round of purges was to be introduced at the highest level of the Soviet hierarchy, of a scope to equal or even exceed the Great Terror of 1936–8. It is, therefore, futile to speculate on the measure of guilt or innocence of the Jews themselves: whatever they might have done or not done is entirely immaterial. Whether Communist or Zionist, religious or atheist, assimilated or nationally conscious, 'pushy' or reticent, shock-workers and eminent scientists or social parasites and black-marketeers – they were equally guilty as the 'corporate Jew', the Enemy Number One of Socialism and Holy Russia.

If Stalin's death averted a disaster, the reforms introduced by Khrushchev (and partly revoked by his successors) did not substantially improve the Jews' lot. Political anti-Semitism remained, as it had under Stalin, an integral and seemingly legitimate part of Communist doctrine and practice. While Khrushchev denied vehemently that anti-Semitism of any shape or form was compatible with Communism, he was nonetheless sufficiently outspoken, both in his public pronouncements and in his memoirs, to admit that, in common with quite a large number of the Russian and Ukrainian peasants, he shared all the ancient anti-Jewish prejudices. He insisted, for example, on referring to the Jews as 'they', as opposed to 'us' (i.e. the rest of the population). He told a visiting parliamentary delegation of French socialists in 1957 that

Antisemitic sentiments still exist in the USSR. They are remnants of a reactionary past. This is a complicated problem because of the position of the Jews and their relations with the other peoples. At the outset of the Revolution, we had many Jews in the Party and State leadership. They were more educated, maybe more revolutionary than the average Russian. In due course we created new cadres....

In keeping with this conviction, Khrushchev imposed a virtual *numerus clausus* for Jews, not only in various 'sensitive' occupations and activities (the armed forces and security forces, Party, Komsomol, trade union apparatus, diplomatic service, foreign trade, etc.), but also in the sphere of higher education: the alleged disproportion between 'our' (i.e. native) and 'their' (i.e. alien) cadres was thus bound to disappear.

Racial discrimination, however obnoxious or contrary to socialist ideas, must not be identified with political anti-Semitism.[3] The roots may

---

[3] Political anti-Semitism is promoted by the Soviet authorities rather than by the populace, who, like the general public in other countries, are basically peaceloving.

be the same, but the purpose is quite different. Khrushchev did not shrink from using anti-Semitism as a political weapon, particularly in the early 1960s, when it became evident that his boastful promise of 'overtaking' America would remain unfulfilled, and a scapegoat was thus urgently required for inadequate economic development and recurrent shortage of consumer goods. The 1961–4 campaign against economic crimes (for which the death penalty was reintroduced) bore an unmistakably anti-Semitic character. It is difficult to believe that the disproportionate percentage of Jews among the 'economic offenders' executed or sentenced to heavy terms of imprisonment (more than one half throughout the USSR generally, and 80 per cent in the Ukraine) faithfully reflected their share of the blame; but even if that had been the case, there was no justification for the insidious anti-Semitic propaganda in the mass media. If the individuals' names (often maliciously distorted) supplied no clear clue as to the national origin of the profiteers and black-marketeers allegedly responsible for all conceivable economic and social ills, the writers were under an obligation, in order to dispel all possible doubt, to mention their links with 'the synagogue' or with relatives abroad. To avoid possible misunderstanding: the question of actual individual guilt does not enter into our considerations. Even assuming for a moment that Captain Dreyfus was indeed in the service of the German military intelligence, this would by no means have justified the accusation of treason levelled against all French Jews at the turn of the century. The notion of 'collective guilt', or 'guilt by association', which substitutes the 'corporate Jew' for individual Jews, whether guilty or innocent of the deeds ascribed to them, has always been, and remains, at the roots of political anti-Semitism.

Khrushchev was also the first to realize the advantages that could be gained from anti-Semitism in Soviet foreign policy, in particular in the Middle East. Zionist ideology had always been opposed by Communists who, while they admitted the existence of a specific 'Jewish question', saw its ultimate solution in total assimilation. The struggle against Zionism was, however, usually left to Jewish Communists, just as Polish Communists were to combat Polish nationalism or Moslem Communists in Transcaucasia to defeat the Musawatists. Anti-Zionism, therefore, should not automatically be equated with anti-Semitism as long as it is considered an internal affair of the Jews, even if these conceptions are sometimes hardly distinguishable. But Soviet Communists recognized early enough the practical value of anti-Zionism as a cover for Jew-baiting: in the last years of Stalin's rule the terms 'Zionism' and 'cosmopolitanism' were interchangeable, each serving as a cover for political anti-Semitism.

Stalin never demonstrated much interest in the power game in the

Middle East: his primary concern was the consolidation of the Soviet empire. His successors, both Khrushchev and Brezhnev, attempted in pursuit of their global strategy to win over Arab nationalists and gain a foothold in the Mediterranean, in the Middle East and in North Africa. Then, and only then, did anti-Zionism and anti-Semitism become synonymous, serving simultaneously the interests of an expansionist Soviet foreign policy and the consolidation of totalitarian power within the USSR.

Political anti-Semitism, or more precisely the cynical exploitation of popular dislike and distrust of Jews, was a Soviet export even at an earlier stage. Possibly this was the result of Stalin's appreciation of the successes that Nazi anti-Jewish policies had scored both in Germany and in the occupied countries. Communist rule, imposed on Eastern and Central Europe by the Red Army, was presented from the very beginning under a 'patriotic' and sometimes rabidly nationalistic label. Although it chiefly bore an anti-German edge, it contained under the surface an anti-Jewish streak too, and its influence grew as the small local Communist clandestine organizations expanded into mass parties and painlessly absorbed millions of newly recruited members, who were either politically inexperienced or had for many years been subjected to chauvinistic and anti-Semitic indoctrination. The new rulers, acting on Moscow's orders, made no attempt to eradicate this heritage of hatred: ostensibly in order to avoid antagonizing the masses, but in fact because by that time the potential value of anti-Semitism was already fully understood by the Kremlin bosses.

Hannah Arendt wrote in 1951 of 'the sudden entirely unprecedented emergence of governmental anti-Semitism in the Soviet Union, which may be calculated to win sympathies for the Soviet Union in the European satellite countries'. She thus drew the conclusion that Stalin's anti-Semitism was but a concession to popular moods prevalent among the conquered peoples. In fact, Moscow did not always seek accommodation with the local 'folk anti-Semitism' but sometimes imposed its own brand whenever and wherever it suited its purpose. The most eloquent example may be found in Czechoslovakia: among all the people of Eastern and Central Europe the Czechs (though not the Slovaks) were the least infected with 'traditional' anti-Semitism. Despite this, it was in Prague that the Soviet-inspired anti-Jewish frenzy reached its peak in the infamous faked trial of 1952 against Rudolf Slansky and other leading members of the Communist Party, most of whom were of Jewish origin. In no other socialist country did anti-Jewish hysteria at that time assume such disgraceful proportions. Thanks to a commission of inquiry set up in 1968, during the short-lived Dubcek régime, to investigate the circumstances of the Slansky trial, we now have irrefutable documentary evidence that not only the trial itself but also its anti-Semitic overtones were carefully stage-managed by Soviet secret police 'advisers' who received their directives from, and submitted their reports to, Moscow. Police and intelligence services throughout the satellite countries were in any case the very first to be subjected to a Soviet-style *Gleichschaltung*. It is thus no coincidence that in the case of any outbursts of official anti-Semitism the trail led directly to the local security apparatus, itself heavily staffed with Soviet officers, experts and advisers.

The question, why anti-Semitic policies were introduced in some socialist countries but omitted or soft-pedalled in others, or why they were pushed to the fore in some periods only (by no means at the same time in different countries), cannot be answered by referring solely to the local circumstances, e.g. the size and social composition of the native Jewish community, or the national history and tradition of popular anti-Semitism. In each case one would find evidence pointing to some powerful political forces – the Soviet overseers, the local Party leadership, or a faction aspiring to power – which became convinced that to fan anti-Jewish sentiments would best serve their particular interests.

This is best illustrated in the case of Poland, both because of the common fate it shares with other countries under Communist rule, and because of the peculiar features which distinguish it from its companions in distress. In the late 1960s, Poland emerged as the scene of a most violent anti-Semitic campaign inspired by the Communist Party, supported by the powerful apparatus of the totalitarian state, and directed against a handful of citizens of Jewish origin – amounting to barely one per thousand of the total population. By no stretch of the imagination could this handful of Jewish citizens be regarded as a menace to the state and society, not even as a national or ethnic minority, differing from, or alien to, the remainder of their fellow-countrymen. Whereas the ideological rationale of this wave of persecution was tacitly rejected by most Poles, the indifference and helplessness of the atomized society enabled the rulers to come within an inch of achieving two ultimate aims. Firstly, the *ostensible* aim was the expulsion of the great majority of the 30,000 surviving Polish Jews or Poles of Jewish extraction, thus putting an end once and for all to the thousand-year-old existence of Jews in Poland. However, the *real* aim was the strengthening of totalitarian controls over a nation predominantly opposed to a régime considered alien to its tradition and imposed forcibly by a despised but powerful neighbour.

This book explains what actually happened in Poland in 1967–8. It could have happened in other Communist-ruled countries also. It can happen again should the circumstances be propitious and the powers-that-be determined to attempt to solve their difficulties at the expense of some minority, possibly the Jews. For this reason alone, the story has lost none of its value, even though a decade has passed since these events took place.

2. The Power Game

THREE and a half million Jews, comprising one-tenth of the total population of thirty-five million, lived in Poland in 1939. More than three million of them perished in the Holocaust. Of the survivors, the majority probably lived at one time or another in 'People's Poland', but in the mid 1960s, according to the most generous estimates, no more than some thirty thousand still lived amongst a Polish population that approached the pre-war total.

Many reasons account for the reluctance of the overwhelming majority of the survivors to rebuild their lives in a country where they were born and bred, and which their ancestors had inhabited for over a millennium. Some of these reasons were ideological in origin: the rejection of Communism as a way of life (this was especially marked among those who had passed the war years in enforced exile in the Soviet Union), or the hope of fulfilling the dream of a Jewish state in the Holy Land. Others, rather more pragmatic, believed that the West offered them greater security and prosperity. There were also emotional reasons: many felt revulsion at the prospect of living in a country which had become a vast graveyard for their kith and kin, and a profound distrust towards part of their Gentile fellow-countrymen who, even before the war, had been sympathetic to anti-Semitic propaganda, and under the Nazi occupation were to some extent indifferent to the unprecedented slaughter of those whom they considered 'aliens'. This question will be dealt with in greater detail in a later chapter.

Post-war Poland is a Communist country not because this was the will of the majority of her population, or even of a sizable part of the working class. The Communist régime was imposed on her by the victorious Red Army and consolidated by the Soviet authorities who came in its wake, with the full connivance of the Western powers. Poland was, and remains, of supreme importance for the Soviet strategic grand design, both on account of its geographical position at the approaches to the Russian heartland and because its area and population make it the most important among the European Soviet satellite states. Poland is at the same time perhaps the toughest nut to crack, being a nation bound to the West by its entire history and tradition and deeply attached to the ideals of national independence and freedom. According to a deep-rooted stereotype the Russians have traditionally been, and are still believed to be, hostile to Polish national life. The Roman Catholic Church in Poland has successfully retained a degree of independence and influence over the masses which is quite inconceivable in any other totalitarian state. The Polish peasants successfully withstood all attempts at enforced collectivization. Such a nation inevitably poses the most difficult problems to the Soviet rulers and their allies.

The subject of this book is the persecution and expulsion of post-war Poland's tiny Jewish minority. It is neither a critical assessment of that country's social and political system nor a history of the struggle against the régime. It should be stressed once again that, apart from some elderly people who had nowhere to go when escape was possible, the majority of the Jews stayed in post-war Poland of their own free will. Their attitudes and behaviour were neither better nor worse than those of their Gentile neighbours; they in no way represented, nor could they represent, a danger to the national interests of Poland or her Communist government.

Nevertheless, through no fault of their own, they fell victim to arbitrary persecution, and were slandered in a manner seemingly unthinkable after the horrors of the Nazi period, and were finally driven out of their country. This book is, therefore, concerned with the mechanisms of a totalitarian state which in its quest for scapegoats does not shrink from exploiting the vilest means at its disposal. At another level, it is concerned with a problem that civilization has so far been unable to solve or has solved only in part: the question of tolerance towards, and integration of, groups which, because of their minority status or lack of adequate defensive power, require the understanding and protection of the majority and of the government.

In fact, majorities and establishments seldom spontaneously hate, oppress or persecute minorities or the under-privileged. Before a state of co-existence – even one which may not be based on mutual friendship – is transformed into an aggressive conflict, there is always a propaganda campaign. This campaign may be conducted by a medicine-man or a chieftain who incites people's passions against an adjacent tribe which is singled out for attack, or by politicians who act in a similar manner against those who are different in their national, linguistic, religious or any other traits. Such a hate campaign is successful whenever there is a sufficiently large group of people who see in it a chance of increasing their own political or economic power, however slight or insignificant that increase may be.

This is an age-old game; civilization has only given it more sophisticated forms whilst retaining its basic pattern. Hitler described the most important rule of the game in *Mein Kampf*:

In general the art of all truly great national leaders at times consists among other things primarily in not dividing the attention of a people, but in concentrating it upon a single foe. The more unified the application of a people's will to fight, the greater will be the magnetic attraction of a movement and the mightier will be the impetus of the thrust. It belongs to the genius of a great leader to make even adversaries far removed from one another seem to belong to a single category, because in weak and uncertain characters the knowledge of having different enemies can only too readily lead to the beginning of doubt in their own right.

Once the wavering mass sees itself in a struggle against too many enemies, objectivity will put in an appearance, throwing open the question whether all others are really wrong and only their own people or their own movement are in the right.

And this brings about the first paralysis of their own power. Hence a multiplicity of different adversaries must always be combined so that in the eyes of the masses of one's own supporters the struggle is directed against only one enemy. This strengthens their faith in their own right and enhances their bitterness against those who attack it.[1]

Hitler's arguments have, unfortunately, a historical logic of their own, though obviously they pass over in silence the dreadful consequences that such concentration of passion against a single adversary has always had. But the phrase 'all truly great national leaders' suggests at least the real motive for starting the game again and again; the question always concerns winning power, or securing and defending power once achieved.

Defamation of those who are different or think differently is often but the first step towards winning power: that is how sympathizers and volunteers can most easily be rallied. The second step consists in paralysing institutional barriers against the abuse of power. The third is to take control of those institutions which confer power over the people as a whole: an individual can then no longer invoke any neutral authority, and the settling of accounts can begin in earnest. Once such authority is rendered harmless, the leader's power is strengthened and the people may start believing that the victims of his persecution had been justly attacked.

The fervour with which Hitler denigrated the democratic machine of the Weimar Republic is well known. Having seized power he maintained the division of power as a façade only, but in fact he created an instrument for exercising a power of his own. While this process continued, no organized power remained able to challenge the war he had declared

[1] Adolf Hitler, *Mein Kampf*, tr. Ralph Mannheim (Hutchinson, 1969), pp. 108–9.

against world Jewry. Without interference Hitler was able to build up anti-Semitism as one of the mainstays of his rule in the Third Reich; nothing was better calculated to overcome the differences of opinion than the image of the enemy, built up with demagogic skill.

Marxism-Leninism demands the liberation of the underprivileged and of minority groups from their ghetto existence. Consequent upon the emergence of this doctrine there appeared a political force which saw through this game of seizing and retaining power at the expense of the defenceless or those less able to defend themselves, and declared war against it. Leaders of Communist states claim that they are faithfully following the Marxist-Leninist doctrine and plead allegiance to its humanitarian aspects. The East European Communist states, even more than the Western democracies, are anxious to keep alive the memory of the crimes committed there under Nazi rule – in particular against their Jewish subjects. But in spite of all this, anti-Semitism in the Soviet-bloc countries is especially venomous today. How could it have happened in our times that, in spite of so many impeding factors, hatred towards a minority was fomented for so long, that it finally produced effects which are the subject-matter of this account?

Once more, it is power that provides the answer; once more, a minority has been abused in order to seize power, to maintain power, or to consolidate it. The lust for power ruthlessly brushes aside the constitution and laws of the state; it even allows for a total and clear break with the basic tenets of the very same doctrine on which Communist states have allegedly been constructed. Violence defeats ethical principles, man becomes defenceless. All this had nothing to do with socialism – even if this label was used. It had to do with the politics of power which managed to evade popular control.

For centuries and under the most divergent social circumstances, there have been in various countries anti-Jewish pogroms and discrimination against Jews. In Tsarist Russia anti-Semitism had a long tradition; more often than not, Tsarist police took the part of *agent-provocateur*. It would be nice to believe that the experience of Hitler's mass slaughter of Jews, Gypsies and dissenters had brought about a salutary shock. But anti-Semitism, rampant for a time in People's Poland, was nonetheless stage-managed by power-hungry people, and finally organized and encouraged on a governmental level. One of the reasons was provided by the politico-strategic interests of the Soviet Union in the Middle East, where it conducted a policy favourable to the Arabs and therefore detrimental to the Jews; another motive was to steer popular dissatisfaction away from those really responsible for the country's economic ills. This latter method had been successfully tried out under Hitler's rule with *Der Stür-*

mer's slogan – 'The Jews are our misfortune' – in order to turn the people's discontent against an unpopular minority group.

There were, as this book will attempt to show, many other reasons also. All of them can be explained away, but that would not make them any the more justifiable: they are all immoral if only because of their consequent effects. In a democratic society, state-inspired immorality would encounter resistance and lead to a change of government. This, however, was not the case in Poland, nor in Stalin's Russia. There can be no doubt that the less efficient is parliamentary control over government, the more are demagogues free to start their work; they will never be short of followers, provided they are skilful enough to hide their lust for power behind a façade of objectives that are both popular and praiseworthy.

The Soviet-bloc countries provide a doubly favourable climate for this kind of activity. The instruments of democratic control have, to a great degree, been done away with, and this has been compounded by the futility of Soviet-style planning of the national economy, by the weakening of the economic system to serve an inflated bureaucracy, and by inordinately high spending on armaments. In consequence, both blue-collar and white-collar workers are forced to work much harder than their Western counterparts, and at the same time make do with a much lower standard of living. This in turn gives rise to widespread and permanent dissatisfaction which is pent up and erupts in troubles and disturbances whenever bottlenecks in supply occur or civil liberties are curtailed with more than usual severity. In every case the reaction to such disturbances is dictated by the current interests of the bureaucrats in power or of those who aspire to power: it may involve the use of police or military force, plots and a bloodless change of personnel, or the condemnation of alleged culprits.

None of these measures is new: each of them can be used in spite of the laws in force or declarations of intent, even if such laws or declarations were originally proclaimed with the express aim of preventing certain abuses of power. In Poland, where the Jewish population had been almost totally exterminated by the Nazis, adequate legislation was introduced after the country's liberation from German occupation to prevent the defamation and persecution of minorities, of people of different religious beliefs, and even of dissenters. As early as 22 July 1944 the Polish Committee of National Liberation in Chelm issued the so-called July Manifesto which contained the following passage concerning the restoration of democratic liberties:

The Polish Committee of National Liberation ... solemnly proclaims the restoration of all the democratic liberties: equalities of rights for all citizens, irrespective of their racial origin, religious belief, or nationality; freedom of political and trade union organizations; freedom of the press and conscience. The Jews, brutally oppressed by the [Nazi] occupiers, will be assured of recon- struction of their means of existence, as well as of legal and actual equality of rights.

The July Manifesto was tantamount to a political programme. It was proclaimed as soon as the Red Army, and the accompanying units of the Polish Army formed on Soviet territory, set foot on Polish soil. The Manifesto claimed to be the political platform of all the Polish left-wing parties: it was presented to the Polish people by a group of Moscow-supported party leaders and army officers who had formed a provisional government called the 'Lublin Committee'. July 22, the day the Manifesto was proclaimed, still remains a national holiday in the Polish People's Republic. On its eighth anniversary, 22 July 1952, the *Sejm*, the legislative assembly in Warsaw, adopted a constitution of the People's Republic, whose main provisions, in spite of recently introduced amendments, have never been abrogated.

The July Manifesto, which in present-day Poland is virtually inacces- sible in its original, unabridged form, was therefore by no means only a provisional declaration. Its ideas and conceptions were embodied in the constitution as well, which in Article 69, paragraph 1, proclaims:

Citizens of the Polish People's Republic, irrespective of nationality, race or religion, enjoy equal rights in all fields of public, political, economic, social and cultural life. Infringement of this principle by any direct or indirect granting of privileges or restriction of rights on account of nationality, race or religion, is subject to punishment.

The constitution further bans discrimination on religious or racial grounds, any display of hatred or contempt, as well as any actions likely to stir up quarrels or strife for the above reasons. It guarantees to all citizens freedom of expression and of the press, expressly confirms the right to freedom of assembly, demonstrations and speeches. Article 71, para. 1, proclaims the inviolability of homes and secrecy of correspon- dence, and permits house searches only in clearly defined cases (Article 74).

Appropriate safeguards have also been built into the so-called 'Little Penal Code' (MKK). It provides, in Article 31, for imprisonment or deten- tion of up to five years for 'whoever defames, derides, or degrades a group of the population or individual people on account of their national, reli- gious or race affiliation'. This provision was included in the new penal code introduced in the 1970s.

According to Article 30, all those who publicly instigate or approve of national or racial conflicts are liable to imprisonment of up to five years. Such unambiguous legal provisions would presumably not have been enacted, had the authors of such concepts collectively and from the very outset been prepared to expose certain groups of the population to renewed prosecution. As this nonetheless happened only a few years later, it cannot but confirm and justify the fundamental mistrust with which the identification of verbal claims with actual intent in such solemn declarations should always be treated. This by itself does not prove that immediately after the Second World War there was no intention at all of protecting the survivors of Jewish and other minorities. Indeed, Boleslaw Bierut, then President of the Republic, proclaiming the Polish constitution of 22 July 1952, stated in the *Sejm*:

Unlike the bourgeois constitution, the basic law of a people's state should be no mere verbal declaration of civic and democratic liberties, but a guarantee of their protection.

Five years later, in April 1957, at the end of a short period of de-Stalinization and of attempts at democratization of public life in Poland, when disturbing symptoms of a discreetly stage-managed anti-Semitism, fanned by opponents of the democratic revival, started to appear all over the country, the Warsaw Secretariat of the Central Committee of the PUWP[2] issued a confidential circular letter to all the provincial, city, district and local party committees, part of which follows:

Discerning in occurrences of chauvinism, anti-Semitism, and racism a serious danger threatening the vital interests of our country and our party, the Central

[2] Polish United Workers' Party, established following the enforced merger of PPS (Polish Socialist Party, from 1892 a party on social-democratic lines) and PPR (Polish Workers' Party, founded in 1942 as a continuation of the Communist Party of Poland, KPP, dissolved by Stalin in 1938). Apart from the Party congress, convened in principle every four years, the most important bodies of the PUWP are:

1) The Central Committee, whose plenary sessions constitute something resembling a Party legislative assembly. Plenary sessions are usually held several times a year, and adopt decisions considered to be binding guidelines for the party and government. Plenary sessions are held between congresses and are marked with consecutive numbers, starting anew after each congress. 'The 7th Plenary Session of the Central Committee' together with the date (year) denotes the seventh session since the last party congress.

2) The Politbureau, whose members are formally elected by the party congress. In fact, it is a self-perpetuating body, rejuvenated by co-option. All members of the Politbureau are members of the Central Committee. The Politbureau might be defined as the Central Committee's presidium.

3) The Secretariat of the Central Committee, too, is supposed to be elected by the party congress. It meets very frequently and decides all current issues. Its main source of strength derives from its tight hold on the whole Party apparatus and its control over personnel policy not only in the party but in state administration as well. The First Secretary (or Secretary-General) of the Central Committee is the Party's supreme leader and has the decisive voice in the Party and in the state. As a rule, in all Soviet-bloc countries the Chairman of the Council of State (President of the Republic) and the Prime Minister follow the Secretary-General.

Committee appeals to the entire party, and calls for a determined struggle against such occurrences. We emphasize once more with the utmost determination the internationalist character of our party. There is and can be no place in it for people propagating nationalistic, chauvinistic, and racist views.... Particularly stringent demands in this respect must be put to comrades holding responsible party or state positions....

We grant to all national minorities equality of national rights – the right of all minorities to schools in their native language and to full respect for and development of their national culture, the right to establish cultural associations, to publish newspapers in their native language, etc. We reaffirm the principle that every citizen has the right to national self-determination....[3]

The Party regards the tendency of the Jewish population to emigrate from Poland as the result of insufficient counteraction by the Party to anti-Semitism. We consider it to be one of the most urgent tasks of the party to wage war against it. At the same time we must persuade the Jewish population to stay in our country. This duty devolves in particular upon party committees in those localities where there is a considerable concentration of the Jewish population. Jewish party members in particular should be more active in their work in Jewish communities, and should take a determined stand against verbal and written propaganda and against an unjustified atmosphere of panic, fanned by Jewish nationalistic elements.

To this end the Central Committee considers it necessary to convene a national conference of activists of the Social and Cultural Association of Jews in Poland, to be attended by representatives of those *voivodship*[4] committees where there are Jewish communities. All party committees should discuss the Central Committee's letter at their meetings and draw appropriate conclusions for their activity in the fight against the nationalistic atmosphere.

This appeal is proof that there was indeed at that time a considerable intensification of anti-Semitism. But whereas in 1957 the Secretariat of

[3] In English, as in most West European languages, 'nationality' is synonymous with state citizenship; in Eastern and Central Europe in the past, and in the Soviet bloc at present, there is a distinction which readers should keep in mind. When official forms, for example, ask a citizen for his 'nationality' they usually refer to his ethnic origin or affiliation. The criteria are vague, often arbitrary, sometimes different in various countries. In the Soviet Union, for example, a citizen is not always allowed to define his 'nationality' at will, especially if he is of mixed parentage, unless he prefers to consider himself Russian (or rather Great-Russian), but even this does not apply to Jews who are described as such in all official documents and identity cards whether they want it or not. In post-war Poland most Jews put down their 'nationality' as Polish, unless they were Yiddish-speaking and regarded themselves as members of a national minority. No questions concerning religious belief or affiliation to a church or a religious community or denomination are officially allowed in Communist countries.

[4] A higher-level administrative division, province. Until 1975 there were 17 *voivodships* in Poland, now there are 49, as the medium level (equivalent to district or county) has been abolished in an attempt to restrict the power base of the provincial Party bosses, sometimes compared to feudal barons.

the Central Committee of the PUWP at least attempted to react against anti-Semitism, even if mainly for economic reasons, in subsequent years the situation changed radically: anti-Semitism once more became an important lever in the exercise of power within the Party and the state.

The Polish population as a whole realized that from the 1960s on anti-Semitism was instigated by the authorities themselves. This was reflected in the joke then current in Poland, concerning the difference between pre-war anti-Semitism and the present one: 'Before the war it was not compulsory.'

Unfortunately, the 'compulsory' anti-Semitism in Poland found a propitious breeding ground among those who for many years had been obliged to conceal their true opinions, and were now only too eager to give vent to their prejudices. Of even more serious consequence among the population was the skilful propagandistic exploitation of the major role played by some Jews among the Communist cadres during the first post-war years in Poland. They included a relatively insignificant number of Jewish Communists who in 1939 escaped to the Soviet Union and in 1944 returned to their native country in the wake of the Red Army. Most of them sincerely believed the Communist doctrine and the Communist social order would provide a solution for the future of their economically under-developed country, plagued by crises and unemployment.

In Stalin's lifetime factional struggles in the top Party leadership in all the people's democracies were deliberately misrepresented as a conflict between people who during the war had stayed in their native country, and the 'Muscovites' who returned from the Soviet Union with the Red Army. In Poland this alleged conflict was rekindled anew in the 1960s, in connection with the anti-Zionist campaign; it was even more demagogically distorted and, with utter disregard for historical truth, presented as a confrontation between Jews (Muscovites) and non-Jews (patriotic Poles). This was, of course, false, and a list of members of the party and state leadership in Poland easily shows that among those arbitrarily labelled as 'Muscovites' were many more non-Jews than Jews. The equation Muscovite = Jew was, however, in spite of its patent falsity, a handy demagogic weapon. Because of the alleged Muscovites' Stalinist past, it was suggested that the Jews who were said to have dominated the Stalinist Muscovite faction were solely responsible for all past errors. In fact, by 1964, actual or alleged Stalinists had long been purged from all major posts, and among the few survivors there were considerably more 'Aryans' than Jews: apart from Zenon Nowak, Kazimierz Witaszewski, Wladyslaw Kruczek, many more leaders could be named who in the twelve years 1945–56 bore at least equal responsibility for Polish politics as the relatively few of their comrades who were subsequently denounced as Jewish. It was, therefore, an obvious falsification when the 1968 events were justified as the settling of accounts with 'Jewish-Muscovites', the survivors of the Stalinist era – all the more so as from 1965 onwards an obviously neo-Stalinist development was accompanied by an openly anti-Semitic propaganda. The lie nonetheless worked, partly because among the majority of the Polish people, indifferent and resigned as it was to political issues, there was a latent tendency to oppose whatever had originated in Moscow; and partly because such propaganda was apt to find support among the well-developed network of Party functionaries all over the country who, unlike the earlier idealists in the Communist movement, were not particularly concerned with humanity or justice and were primarily interested in maintaining and consolidating their newly won privileges of power.

Around 1937, when Stalin murdered or sent to forced labour camps millions of people, including leading Soviet Communists, he initiated perhaps unwittingly a process – probably unavoidable in a dictatorship following a revolution – of removing old cadres to make room for new ones, of replacing revolutionaries by bureaucrats, *apparatchiks*, yes-men. Some observers of the Soviet scene explain this process by pointing to the necessity of replacing idealists lacking professional qualifications with technocrats who have no ideals at all or who treat them with disdain. An additional consideration is the negative selection under totalitarian rule, which emerges after the seizure of power as soon as the system deviates from its initially humanist ideals. Whatever the truth of this theory there is no denying that in such a dictatorship former revolutionaries are as harmful as independent-minded, critical citizens. People of blind obedience, easy to corrupt, are in demand because they are primarily interested in their own position of power and in their own professional career.

This process, carried out by Stalin by means of wholesale slaughter, was achieved in Poland virtually without bloodshed. Gomulka in the last years of his rule managed to carry through an almost complete replacement of cadres at all levels. In 1964 and in 1968, when Party congresses appointed members of the Central Committee, the number of former genuine Communists or Socialists who at least in their youth acted out of sincere idealism shrank to a bare minimum. Gomulka made room for his stalwarts who had long been impatiently waiting in the wings for a change of guard and were ready to support any conceivable policy, provided it speeded up their own promotion.

Still, it is just possible that had Gomulka been the only one to wield power, there might have been none of those almost incredible events which are depicted in this book. In fact anti-Semitism re-emerged in

Poland mainly as a result of a struggle for power, waged with no holds barred, against a background of economic and socio-political misery in the country as a whole. The Jews were but 'munition' in that struggle: originally, the in-fighting had nothing to do with race, nationality, or religious differences. But for the Jews it had the worst possible consequences, and reactivated anti-Semitism in a generation which had apparently just overcome this madness.

Leading political figures in People's Poland appear here in a most unfavourable light. They are squarely denounced – not because they were Communists (so were many of their victims), but because, having brought under their control all the levers of the state apparatus, they misused the legislative, executive and judicial branches of government and turned them into instruments of their own lust for power, ruling without the slightest consideration for the constitution or the laws, or their fellow-countrymen.

In totalitarian countries only a few exceptionally brave people dare revolt against the persecution of dissidents or minorities. Their appeals to world public opinion testify to the suppression of freedom, arbitrariness and oppression, are nothing but a call of protest. They are usually unable to rally effective support for individuals who have fallen victim to political power.

That is precisely what this book attempts to explain, in an effort to keep alive the watchfulness of the ordinary citizen in those countries where democratic institutions still continue to assure him the possibility of controlling and exerting influence upon those who wield power or strive for power.

3. The Police Faction

EVERY society has its share of opportunists ready to offer their services, mostly for purely selfish reasons, to leaders eager for power, irrespective of their image. In the countries of Eastern Europe the consolidation of dictatorial power was further facilitated by a large group of idealistically minded people.

In the wake of the terrible sufferings of their countrymen during the Second World War, many of them were convinced that the doctrines of Marx and Lenin offered hope for a peaceful existence, free of conflict: they gave their support to a political leadership which had proclaimed humane ideals of peace, freedom, brotherhood, equality and friendship among nations. They realized too late that many ideas had gradually undergone a process of erosion, often assuming a meaning contrary to their original content.

The frequent use of terms which have in fact acquired quite contrary meanings is by no means unusual in political life, and is not restricted to totalitarian states alone. Certain doctrinaire fanatics employ the word 'democratization' to describe the enforced imposition of their own doctrine; 'normalization' in a most devious way describes abnormal circumstances. States where the very idea of socialism has been suppressed by the omnipotent bureaucracy enjoying a virtual monopoly of power call themselves, and are often called by the rest of the world, 'socialist', although the prevailing system has partly or even totally suppressed all the political, economic and social rights of the working people to which socialism aspires.

In countries with unrestricted freedom of the press and of expression, individuals remain able to judge for themselves the agreement between theory and practice; this ability to form one's own judgement is, however, severely curtailed or even totally eliminated in a system of censored communication. A 'prescribed phraseology' creates deception throughout the process of transformation of the meaning of a term, and by perpetual repetition brings about, first, an impairment and finally a distortion, accepted in everyday usage, of the true meaning of words. This is a major device for controlling people, and since the Second World War the totalitarian states have undoubtedly demonstrated an uncanny skill in endowing once unambiguous concepts with ambiguous, or even quite different, meanings.

Disruption and deception, joined to the threat of physical violence against dissidents, have left people with virtually no option. The consequences followed quickly: submission, accommodation, even collaboration in the inevitably implied moral corruption.

In a society moulded in such a way, conditions are right for police informers, the secret police, and for slander, as well as for the cant and hypocrisy of a dictatorship. To Kuznetsov 'the horrors caused by the suppression of dissidents surpass even genocide which destroys human life. The extermination of dissent destroys the soul, the true essence of life.'

In post-war Poland public dissent, freedom of expression in the press and broadcasting, were abolished at an early stage or rather had no opportunity to blossom at all, as the 'dictatorship of the proletariat' only permits a Communist-controlled press to operate. States with a muzzled press resemble companies which, aiming at the successful marketing of their products, centrally control their information policy and allow publication of only such news as enhances the image of the company and its products. Money is spent exclusively on information liable to bring in profits.

It is true that pressure groups all over the world, big business, unions, parties, administrations and governments, act according to a similar principle, but the dangers inherent in it remain largely irrelevant as long as the company continues to be but one among many competitors and its statements can freely be compared with the statements of its competitors, or when a group of interests must submit to public criticism and control, and virtually all information is subject to scrutiny.

In countries enjoying freedom of speech and of the press people are exposed to a bewildering amount of often contradictory news and comment. While a fully objective judgement of an issue is possible only in exceptional cases, people do not live and act free from doubt concerning the surrounding reality, because of the multiplicity and diversity of opinion and information.

Leaders of totalitarian states have to restrict such doubts and to eliminate them altogether whenever possible. Their rule would be inconceivable if they allowed the independent checking role of a free press. They are quite right to fear freedom of opinion and of the press, and like a company without competitors, i.e. like a monopoly, they use all the media to serve aims favourable to their own interests. Since the principle 'Good news is no news' retains its validity among free journalists, it follows as an absolutely natural consequence that an incomparably greater proportion of derogatory news in circulation concerns democratic states and their societies than totalitarian regimes and their population. And from that follows another logical consequence: free peoples who have all the communication media at their disposal are liable to gain the impression that law and order, the social systems and humane living conditions are better served elsewhere as they seldom hear or read anything positive about the circumstances in their own country, or in other countries with a similar social order.

Such dangerous illusions favour those who suppress free opinion in totalitarian states not only in respect of foreign policy: weak or totally absent protests by public opinion abroad paralyse opposition forces inside the country, and strengthen the trend toward accommodation and submission.

All this should be borne in mind by people who wonder why the Poles have remained more or less passive witnesses while some of their fellow-countrymen were slandered and expelled. Had a pressure group in a democratic country made an attempt to unleash an anti-Semitic campaign, it would most probably have been exposed and frustrated. But in a state which has a monopoly of all forms of military, political, economic and propaganda power, and is itself part of a community of states ruled under similar circumstances, the mass media, the economic levers of command, as well as the physical power of control over the population can all be engaged in a concentrated drive to achieve political aims. That state is not only free from any kind of check on the part of supervisory organs which intact democratic societies have at their disposal – i.e. newspapers, radio, television, political parties, parliaments, etc. – but is even supported in its campaign by all these instruments taken over and abused by the state itself. If, even in a democratic state, an individual is often too weak to secure a hearing, how much more must this apply to a state in which anyone who dares to criticize exposes himself to physical danger?

The Polish People's Republic is one of those states where the Party and the government have under their control the entire range of information media. No newspaper or periodical editorial board, no radio or television broadcaster, no writer, can publish or circulate opinions directed against the official policy line and escape punishment. More than that: even in areas apparently free of politics no person can act outside the limits set and tolerated by the authorities. Certain failure awaits the person who tries to swim against the stream – quite apart from possible personal reprisals – if only because all the facilities for the dissemination of information, e.g. the distribution of newspapers and periodicals, the news agencies, radio and television transmitters, are totally under state control. The state, therefore, in most cases does not even need to use its means of suppression: an administrative order not to put newsprint at somebody's disposal is sufficient to ban unwelcome information. When in the

spring of 1973 the Party leader Edward Gierek lifted preventive censorship of the Party daily *Trybuna Ludu* and weekly *Polityka*, presumably
because their editors-in-chief, Jozef Barecki and Mieczyslaw F. Rakowski
respectively, had often complained about the censor's interference, harmful to every form of journalistic practice, even of the most loyal kind,
the West German news magazine *Der Spiegel* wrote about Polish censorship:

Whenever a Polish businessman, any Mr Kowalski, wants to print fifty new
visiting cards, he has to submit the proposed text at the Mice Street in Warsaw,
as it is there, at *ulica Mysia*, that the 'Main Office for the Control of the Press,
of Publications, and Performances', i.e. the central office of Polish censorship
over every kind of printed matter, is located.

Just as in other socialist countries, a host of fussy officials rigorously scru-
tinize every word even before publication to ensure that whatever the Poles
get to read or view does not contradict the will of the state: newspapers,
periodicals, publicity pamphlets, books, stamps, labels for drink bottles, cinema
tickets, sweet wrappers, as well as films, theatre productions, radio plays, tape
recordings, and records, are subject to censorship all over the socialist world.

The lifting of preventive censorship on those two papers did not, of
course, bring about a licence to broaden the range of opinion: the censor's
task was simply transferred to the desks of the two editors-in-chief, both
of them, by the way, loyal Gierek followers. (Incidentally, the experiment
failed and censorship was reintroduced.)

Current political and propaganda guidelines for the entire information
apparatus all over the country are given at briefings for the Party activists,
held in the Party's Central Committee building. Among those invited to
such briefings are senior editors and selected commentators of opinion-
forming newspapers and periodicals, of radio and television services.
There is no need to remind those attending of the prohibitions and restrictions, well known throughout the country, thanks to the official
memoranda which serve as directives for all the employees of the
apparatus of censorship.

In order properly to assess the facts recorded in this book one should
therefore bear in mind that in 1967–70 no press item or pamphlet could
appear, no radio talk could be broadcast, no theatre or cabaret performance could be produced without the formal permission of the censorship
officials.

The practical result of the omnipresence of Party guidelines and of censorship has been that whatever is published can be considered to be the
opinion of the entire power élite, or at least of its more influential part.
There is therefore no need to treat the contents of press reports or

commentaries as personalutternaces or the independent opinionsof their authors. The writers are to a large extent free only to shape the form, while the content is inspired by the Party and the state, or at least tolerated by them.

The anti-Semitic campaign in Poland therefore came not as a result of coincidental accord among editors and commentators. Whatever was published in newspapers, periodicals and books, or broadcast by radio and television, was done so by remote control from the party and the authorities. The anti-Semitic campaign in Poland offered an opportunity to monitor the entire control mechanism of the political régime. The most vulgar role was assigned to *Kurier Polski*, an evening paper published by the puppet Democratic Party. Its editor-in-chief, Henryk Tycner, appealed chiefly to the followers of this party – the small tradesmen, artisans, middle-level white-collar workers. A part of this social stratum in Poland had quite strong anti-Semitic traditions. An ideologically leading role was assumed by the press of Pax, an organization headed by Boleslaw Piasecki.[1] An article signed by him inaugurated the aggressive Jew-baiting campaign. Piasecki's readers are to be found chiefly in Catholic circles disavowed by the official Church hierarchy, but his call was immediately echoed by all the mass media, including the central and local Party press.

The theme was then taken up by the newspapers *Zolnierz Wolnosci*, organ of the Polish army's Main Political Directorate, *Prawo i Zycie*, organ of the Association of Polish Lawyers (edited by Kazimierz Kakol, one of General Moczar's henchmen),[2] *Walka Mlodych*, a weekly of the

[1] Before the war Boleslaw Piasecki created the *Falanga*, a Catholic fascist organization whose members, imitating the Nazi SA Brownshirts, wore green shirts as a sort of uniform. As Leader of the *Falanga* Piasecki advocated the expulsion of the Jews as a precondition for a revival of Polish Roman Catholicism, nationalization of industry, and the maintenance of a private economy structure in agriculture and handicrafts. In 1937 he publicly demanded the 'systematic and radical elimination of Jews from Poland'. He survived the war although he had been temporarily detained first by the Gestapo and then by the NKVD. He was released from Gestapo detention presumably thanks to the intervention of Benito Mussolini. After the war he founded, with the assistance of the Communist Party, his Pax movement, aimed at creating a split among the followers of the Roman Catholic Church. Pax grew into a powerful concern, with a chain of stores, numerous factories turning out consumer goods, and a publishing enterprise of its own, including six dailies and periodicals. On 22 June 1971 Piasecki was appointed member of the Council of State of the Polish People's Republic, the supreme state authority. He was presumed to entertain close relations with the Soviet secret service; in Polish internal politics he invariably sided with the most oppressive, Stalinist forces in the ruling party.

[2] Mieczyslaw Moczar, a Ukrainian by birth, for many years head of the security service, and leader of the so-called 'police faction'. Born Nicolai Demko in 1913, at the age of twenty-four he is said to have joined the Communist Party. In 1938 he was sentenced and imprisoned for subversion. During the Second World War he organized Communist guerrilla detachments in the provinces of Lublin and Kielce. After the war he was head of the *Bezpieka*, the dreaded secret police, in Lodz. He was later promoted to Deputy Minister of Public Security. Dismissed from this post during the purge of Gomulka-ite 'right-wing nationalist deviationists' in 1948–9, he nevertheless

Union of Socialist Youth (ZMS), some provincial dailies, especially those brought out in cities like Lodz where somewhat larger Jewish communities still existed, and in addition, of course, by radio and television. Central Party organs, like *Trybuna Ludu*, *Nowe Drogi* and *Zycie Partii*, were assigned a somewhat more moderate role: *Der Stürmer*-like slogans were hardly suited to papers read abroad as well as at home.

Long before it became obvious that a state-controlled campaign against an ethnic minority had in fact begun, Poland turned into an even more closely knit police state, and the Polish people lost every opportunity to resist effectively such an authoritatively propagated anti-Semitism. The people were being corrupted by a small stratum of power-holders trying to convince the population that it was expedient to behave in a non-conformist way and above all to take heed and to escape unhurt; the propensity to anti-Semitism, traditionally latent in some backward groups of the population, gave the rulers the additional certainty that they would find eager followers for their anti-Jewish policy even though Nazi atrocities were still fresh in people's minds.

All this happened despite the fact that post-war Poland had a fleeting moment for reflection on the essence of Communism: the so-called 'Polish October' of 1956.

A lot of depravity, injustice, and painful disillusion has piled up during the previous years. The ideals of socialism, connected with the spirit of the freedom of man and respect for civil rights, have suffered ... gross violation.... I am deeply convinced that those years are now over and will never return.

It was on 24 October 1956 that Vladyslav Gomulka expressed this conviction in front of 300,000 listeners and thereby gave new hope to millions of people. He had just been rehabilitated and returned to the PUWP Central Committee from which he had been excluded in 1949, charged with right-wing nationalist deviation.

This time Gomulka did not spare promises: his programme of reforms included workers' self-management in industrial plants, support for

retained his membership of the party's Central Committee and was a *voivode* (province chief) in various parts of the country. A few months after Gomulka's return to power in October 1956 he was appointed head of the security apparatus and then Deputy Minister of Internal Affairs. For a long time Gomulka treated Moczar with full confidence, although the police chief obviously attempted to usurp total power in the state. When Moczar was promoted to Minister of Internal Affairs in 1964 he already controlled a well-organized and highly efficient power structure of his own, a widespread network of agents and informers, and a card-index with dossiers concerning all the significant personalities in Poland. His decisive voice in the field of personnel policy enabled him to put his followers, the self-styled 'Partisans', in key positions. He projected himself as a Polish patriot and presided over the 300,000-strong Union of ex-servicemen, ZBOWID (Union of Fighters for Freedom and Democracy); in this way Moczar hoped to shed the hated image of a policeman and become a political personality in public life. The March 1968 events and their preliminaries were closely linked to Moczar, his 'police faction' and their drive for power.

housing and the consumers' industries, freeing the peasants from enforced collectivization. The *Sejm* (parliament) was to receive more responsibility, local government more power; relations with the Church were to be normalized. Cardinal Vyshynsky, in detention since 1953, was soon allowed to return to Warsaw; Soviet Marshal Rokossowski had to give up his post as Polish Minister of National Defence.

All these developments were the result of the deep dissatisfaction of the Polish people with the political and economic situation. On 28 June 1956 the Poznan workers struck and marched in protest against raised work norms and the high cost of living. Industrial action developed into an open revolt of broad strata of the population, ultimately suppressed by the use of troops.

Although on the face of it the change in the state and Party leadership was accomplished successfully, the fight for freedom was nevertheless only seemingly won. Gomulka, enthusiastically hailed in 1956 by almost the entire Polish population, showed his true nature in subsequent years, agreeing to become a docile tool of his former political opponents who had managed totally to isolate him from the feelings of the country. The achievements of the Polish 'Springtime in October', won in fact prior to Gomulka's return to power, were gradually eroded following consolidation of his rule. In 1967, as discontent all over Poland once more assumed dangerous proportions, the Party found a lightning conductor, pointing a finger at intellectuals – and at Jews in particular. Just as during the Russian revolution embittered workers had been incited by a slogan originally coined by the Tsarist *Okhrana* (secret police), and propagated by the arch-reactionary 'Black Hundreds', the instigators of bloody anti-Jewish pogroms, *Daloy gramotniye* ('Down with the literates') – so the wire-pullers of the new anti-intellectual campaign in Poland exploited the complexes of the proletariat in order to prevent a workers' revolt, and at the same time to get rid of a stratum which because of its thinking and critical abilities had become inconvenient for the technocrats of power. The hour of the so-called 'Partisans' – more accurately dubbed by public opinion 'the police faction' – had struck.

Skilfully exploiting Soviet anti-Israeli policy subsequent to the 1967 Six-Day War in the Middle East, a group inside the PUWP, then already well organized under the leadership of the Minister of Internal Affairs, General Mieczyslaw Moczar, and firmly entrenched in the secret police, in the military counter-intelligence service, and in the army's political directorate, as well as in the middle-level Party apparatus, set off a witch-hunt which ultimately led to a frosty political and cultural climate in Poland, while the economic crisis was only delayed, not solved.

In December 1970 workers in Poland's Baltic ports revolted once more in protest against the Central Committee's decision drastically to raise prices, primarily of staple foodstuffs. Gomulka was toppled and replaced by Gierek. The police faction, in spite of the major role it had played in the overthrow of Gomulka's rule, did not manage to achieve its aim and to seize the highest posts of command in the state.

Paradoxically, the group which had tried to enforce its ascendancy through an internal political coup and achieve an enormous increase in power, thereby further reducing the already very limited scope of civil liberties in Poland, failed because of a foreign policy event, the Czechoslovak tragedy. The masters in the Kremlin who had for years been happy to encourage Moczar's unbridled personal ambition and to support the pseudo-patriotic demagogy of this 'police faction' – provided the nationalistic resentments of the Poles remained channelled in the safe direction of anti-Semitism and an anti (West)-German bias – when confronted with the upheavals of the 'Prague Spring' suddenly changed their tune. They realized that Polish nationalism, once unleashed, must find its natural direction – against Russia, Poland's traditional rival. Gomulka, who for reasons of his own not only supported Soviet plans for an armed intervention in Czechoslovakia but egged the Kremlin on to act more resolutely, was by then considered a much more trustworthy ally than the untested, unreliable Moczar with his nationalistic slogans. Soviet army divisions, crossing into Czechoslovakia, preferred to have in their rear a Poland efficiently pacified by Gomulka, rather than a country torn by interfactional struggles where most people, rejecting a naked police dictatorship tainted with subservience to Moscow, were apt to come out in support of the Prague reformers.

Moczar had no choice but to bide his time. In effect he definitely missed his chance. When after two and a half years he made another attempt at seizing power, this time in collusion with Edward Gierek, who was more popular in Poland and more acceptable to Moscow, the new pretender welcomed the support of the police faction, only to cut them down to size a few months later. Moczar disappeared from the political scene apparently for good – today he is virtually forgotten.

Only his victims are not likely to forget him as easily as that: it was they who, through no fault of their own, had to meet the bill for this power-struggle in which only the role of victim was reserved for them.

4. The Scapegoats

LONG before the outbreak of the Second World War and the occupation of Poland by German and Soviet troops, certain groups in the Polish population had already been affected to a greater or lesser extent by anti-Semitic propaganda. Anti-Semitism was accepted even by the ruling OZON (Camp of National Unity), and long before that was a major element in the political platform of the right-wing opposition, the National-Democratic Party (*Endecja*) and its fascist offshoots, the ONR (National Radicals) and *Falanga*, under the leadership of Boleslaw Piasecki. Leading politicians of all these parties publicly advocated anti-Jewish policies. General Skwarczynski, head of the ruling OZON, said that 'the solution of this problem [of national minorities in Poland] involves a radical reduction in the number of Jews in Poland'. Prime Minister General Slawoj-Skladkowski proclaimed the slogan: 'Physical terror – no; economic boycott – certainly', propounding an ostensibly liberal alternative to pogroms instigated by the extremist groups. Such a seemingly moderate policy was at best of course a slightly modified form of anti-Semitism. A little later the Prime Minister, trying to outbid his openly Jew-baiting right-wing adversaries, replied to a parliamentary question in the *Sejm*, submitted by General Skwarczynski and 116 other OZON deputies:

The Government of the Republic is in full accord with the questioners that one of the most important measures in the solution of the Jewish question is a major reduction in the number of Jews by way of emigration.

Even some isolated groups in the Polish Socialist Party (PPS), the official left-wing opposition in Poland, were convinced of the need 'to solve the Jewish question' in Poland. M. Borski, member of the PPS, published an article in *Robotnik* (*The Worker*) in which he declared in a mixture of regret, resignation and approval:

In spite of all this, a considerable proportion of Jews is bound to emigrate.... The idea of emigration has indeed struck roots and nothing better can be devised....

Finally, the programme of the People's (Peasants') Party, adopted in December 1935, also postulated the solution of the Jewish question through emigration. Part of the Polish middle classes, living in fear of a revolutionary spark from the neighbouring Soviet Union, and fascinated by Adolf Hitler's national-socialist policy, moved steadily to the right. An essential component of their policies contained prescriptions for the solution of 'the Jewish question'.

National-Radical leagues were not content with the officially approved economic boycott; they tried to drive the Jews out of Poland by staging bloody pogroms in the countryside and instigating and organizing riots at the universities. They publicly demanded a *numerus nullus* for Jewish students who, in many universities, especially in the faculties of medicine, had in any case long been the victims of discrimination. Whenever, for lack of sufficient facilities, a *numerus clausus* was imposed, the quotas provided that the proportion of Jews among the students admitted was not to exceed 10 per cent – and in consequence the number of applicants rejected was much larger among Jews than among Gentiles.

In some universities so-called 'ghetto-benches' were imposed – Jewish students were forced to take isolated seats. During riots and brawls the police, under the excuse of complying with the extra-territorial rights of academic bodies, often refused to restore order and to protect the minority. Artur Sandauer, a well-known Polish author of Jewish origin, in his *Book of Reminiscences 1919–1939* (Warsaw, 1960), writes as follows:

The University of Lwow in 1932–6, as I experienced it, resembled to a certain degree a jungle. We used to walk around with eyes wide open and ears strained: an attack might come any moment, from any corner. From time to time during seminars students would raise their heads from above the textbooks: a stampede, a scuffle and cries would come from the corridors.

Some professional associations of engineers, lawyers and physicians amended their rules by introducing an 'Aryan clause', while an association of Christian tradesmen propagated such slogans as 'Don't buy from Jews' or 'Support your kith and kin'; special posters were put out to distinguish between 'Christian' and Jewish shops. In the *Sejm* Deputy Benedykt Kiencia introduced a bill to deprive Jews of their right to vote and stand for election, of their right to military service, to employment in the civil service and in certain state establishments and enterprises, of their right to work as teachers in schools and universities or even to study there. The bill was also intended to ban Jews from contributing to the radio, the film industry or the press, from holding responsible positions in banks, from purchasing real estate, as well as establishing new industrial enterprises or trade, transport and handicraft companies, etc. Kiencia, who submitted his bill at the beginning of 1939, obviously tried to have enacted in Poland the same kind of discriminatory laws which, albeit in a much more drastic form, were already in force in Nazi Germany.

The anti-Jewish campaigners often made use of the slogan 'Down with the Jewish–Communist Conspiracy', thus leading them to string together anti-Semitism with anti-Bolshevism, and by way of a vulgar over-simplification to denounce the entire Jewish minority in Poland – regardless of its own class divisions or differences of political opinion – as not only Communist-minded but as a political network in the service of the Soviet Union.

In those years all the anti-Semitic tendencies had one feature in common: they aimed to overcome the country's social and economic troubles by expelling the Jews. Poland was incapable of introducing reasonable reforms in agriculture; there were not enough incentives to invest in industrial development. In this respect the conditions prevailing on the eve of the Second World War were somewhat similar to those in Gomulka's Poland: in both cases anti-Semitism was considered a safety-valve for all the economic and social troubles the rulers were unable to prevent, or were incapable of dealing with adequately.

When the Germans invaded Poland, there were people, especially among the backward sections of the middle classes, who were at first rather sympathetic to the anti-Jewish policy of the Nazis. Even as the horror of the Holocaust drew nearer, some of them would not bother to conceal their satisfaction that 'the Jewish question in Poland will be solved by German hands', and that 'at least in this respect the Germans are going to do us a favour'. Economic sanctions against Jews in the first years of the war, and even their confinement in ghettoes and forced-labour camps, were tacitly welcomed by those too short-sighted to realize that it was not only a prelude to the 'Final Solution', but a dress-rehearsal for a very similar treatment of the Polish 'sub-humans'. Although the Polish government-in-exile and its civilian and military agencies in the underground inside Poland continued to protest against the genocide, their capacity to oppose it and to give the persecuted Jews active support was in any case very limited. The Jews, aware of the hopelessness of their situation, could not expect much from these quarters.

It was therefore natural, indeed unavoidable, that both those doomed to perish in the ghettoes and camps and those who dared to seek refuge among their Gentile fellow-countrymen or to take to the woods set their hopes on a speedy victory of the Soviet armies. Meanwhile they looked for support on the left: there, it seemed, was an ally, certainly not without blame and reproach, but at least it paid lip-service to ideals which promised the persecuted a ray of hope. Even people who for social and ideological reasons felt no affinity with Communism had no other choice left: their physical survival depended on the assistance offered by those who before the war consistently opposed national discrimination and anti-Semitism, and now called for a determined struggle against the common enemy.

Polish Jews who had been deported to Russia or found their way there as refugees became active in the pro-Soviet 'Union of Polish Patriots' and volunteered for service in the Polish army units formed in the USSR. Those under Nazi rule tried to make contact with the left-wing underground movement, widely thought to be free from anti-Semitic tendencies (and therefore to offer them a chance to resist the Nazis without losing their identity) and ready to accept all those eager to fight. The reality, however, proved to be far from an idyll. First, in early 1942, when emissaries of the Comintern (including a considerable proportion of Jewish Communists) were parachuted into occupied Poland and began to unite loose groups of left-wingers into the nucleus of the Polish Workers' Party (PPR), a parallel development in the Warsaw Ghetto was already much more advanced. There were more organized Communists active there in the underground resistance movement than in the rest of the country. The first 'Aryan' Communist cells in Warsaw benefited from financial and technical assistance (printing presses, distribution network, etc.) rendered by the Jewish comrades behind the Ghetto walls. Secondly, Communist guerrilla detachments were reluctant to accept Jewish volunteers unless they were able to bring arms and money with them, as the Party was careful not to mar its recently acquired and widely disbelieved veneer of patriotism and allegiance to 'the national cause' by admitting too many Jews. The support allegedly given by the Communist underground to persecuted Jews was by no means as general as official propaganda subsequently claimed.

In spite of all this, once the country was liberated by the Soviet army and a Communist régime imposed, many Jewish survivors rallied with enthusiasm to the great task of post-war reconstruction. Often over-zealous like all neophytes, they not only took up responsible jobs but, within the Party, sometimes became masters of the doctrine and the liturgy. Dedicated to the ideals of internationalism but at the same time proud of the part they had played in the armed struggle against the Nazi invaders, they often considered themselves more patriotic than their non-Jewish fellow-countrymen. Their contribution can easily be proved by recalling the names of the many Jewish guerrilla leaders and groups, though this is distorted, or even suppressed, by present-day Polish historians. There is, nonetheless, no denying the fact that the active resistance of the Jewish left-wing groups had also inspired their non-Jewish fellow-countrymen in their will to fight. General Jerzy Kirchmayer, one of the best-known Polish writers on military history, confirmed this in his work on the military significance of the April 1943 uprising in the Warsaw Ghetto:

The defenders of the Warsaw Ghetto fell, but the idea of armed struggle ... crossed the Ghetto walls, survived and lived to see victory. It was propagated by those who having escaped from the Ghetto reinforced various guerrilla detachments. In fact, following the April [1943] uprising, Jews were to be found in virtually all the forest detachments. The military significance of the uprising in the Warsaw Ghetto consists chiefly in the response it found among the Polish population.

On the other hand it would be unjust to overlook the fact that many Jews were helped by their Gentile Polish neighbours. While bearing in mind the despicable attitude of some Poles, homage must be paid to the bravery and courage of those who defied the danger to their own lives and that of their families, and undertook the most courageous relief actions. In all Nazi-occupied Europe Poland was almost a case on its own in this respect – to offer shelter to persecuted Jews or to give them help of any kind meant risking certain death. The graves of many thousands of Poles testify to the fact that they did not shrink from the greatest danger in order to help other human beings in dire need of assistance.

Such individual acts of courage were, unfortunately, counterbalanced by individual acts of betrayal – with disastrous consequences for their victims. It goes without saying that Poles, much more easily than Germans, were able to pick out a Jew. A different pronunciation, of which Germans would probably be unaware, the use of words, external appearance – all this made it relatively easy for a Pole to recognize a Jew in a crowd, in the street or in a public building. Such identification could often be fatal unless the victim had the means to buy off his blackmailer. Polish post-war propaganda usually overlooked all this, or even denounced such reports as a hostile anti-Polish campaign. In fact, however, such bloodhounds were among the worst misfortunes, as they deterred the Jews from leaving the ghettoes. Bernard Goldstein noted this in his book *Martyrs and Fighters* (New York, 1954):

I have already mentioned the activities of such blackmailers and persecutors, called '*szmalcowniki*'. The word is derived from the Polish *szmalec*, which means lard or fat. The scoundrels approached their victims demanding: 'Give up your fat!' For the Jews hidden on the 'Aryan' side it was a dreadful plague. Students identified their colleagues, erstwhile neighbours recognized Jews who used to live in the same street or in the same house, while shopkeepers and pedlars recognized their erstwhile clients or competitors, policemen denounced those who used to live in their precinct. Many *szmalcowniki* often operated in gangs. They established a widespread organization, dividing the city into quarters. Each group kept watch for victims in its own quarter, checking every non-resident in the street, every stranger in a streetcar or on a train, tailing him everywhere and making hell for everybody suspected of being a source of easy money. Once they had spotted their man, the *szmalcowniki* had a simple method of checking his origin: they pushed him to a house entrance or to an alley, and unbuttoned his fly to find the fatal trace of circumcision.

The Polish police, employed by the Germans and acting under their orders, generally did nothing to put an end to such outrages; on the contrary, they often collaborated with the Nazis – as they collaborated with them against the Polish underground movement.

When Goldstein and other eyewitnesses testify that some Poles behaved with indifference or even malice towards their Jewish countrymen, one is inclined to think that such behaviour was typical of the entire Polish population. Other accounts are often very contradictory. But if in one case or another accusations against the few prevail over gratitude to the many, that is simply because of the unavoidably subjective nature of all personal accounts. Nobody should regard it as an attempt to accuse the Polish nation as a whole of anything resembling collective guilt.

One example, among many, will illustrate the point: in the suburbs of Tarnow, in Southern Poland, east of Cracow, a Polish peasant family concealed a Jewish family of four in one of their two rooms behind a wall specially built to form a cubicle 32" × 112". In this confined space, equipped with two wooden cots placed one above the other, four people spent over two years as if buried alive – and were thus spared certain death. What is most instructive in this case, however, is the condition of the peasant family, which also consisted of four people, the parents and their two children: all of them, though probably not to the same extent, realized that should the hidden Jews be discovered they themselves could expect nothing but death. For over two years they had to live with that threat, especially since the disaster might be brought about either by a search ordered by the German authorities or by involuntary negligence on the part of one of the hidden Jews. It must be borne in mind that at the time the Jewish family went into hiding the younger child, a boy, was but two years old, while the girl was some four years older: the baby's whimper was quite enough to reveal the family's presence, with all its dire consequences. To make matters worse, the boy while in hiding fell victim to typhoid fever accompanied by a very high temperature which caused him to lose control over his reflexes, including the impulse to weep or cry. This was all the more dangerous as the hiding-place adjoined a part of the hut occupied by the house owner's mother-in-law and sister-in-law, neither of whom must have any idea of the hidden Jewish family, not because they were suspected of bad faith but because their knowledge would create an additional source of danger for all of them, as any indiscretion, any sign of hysteria caused by fear, could precipitate disaster. On top of it all, in the immediate vicinity of the hut a German anti-aircraft unit was billeted and the soldiers used to visit the room adjacent to the hide-out in order to take a bath, to clean their equipment, or just to relax near a fire. All this increased the nervous tension, and after a time the peasant woman could stand it no longer: she began to beg her husband repeatedly to find another hiding-place for the Jewish family. Unfortunately no such place could be found, as the peasant and his wife were well aware. Nevertheless she kept pleading, imploring him to have mercy if not upon themselves, then at least upon their children, who were certain to die if the Germans ever detected the hidden Jewish family. The danger of discovery came nearer each day as the German military and police authorities in their pursuit of the guerrillas started to search all the households in turn. Still, the Jewish family was not turned out, and they managed to survive and see the country's liberation.

On the other hand, Leon Brandt, in his 'Reminiscences on the 30th Anniversary of the Uprising in the Warsaw Ghetto', published in *Die Welt* in 1973, not only confirmed the indifference of some Poles and the existence of the *szmalcowniki*, but by adding details about the attitude of world public opinion, of the London-based Polish government-in-exile, and of the British authorities, he also showed that readiness to come to the aid of Jews in distress was exceptionally weak – by no means among Poles alone:

With their 'armaments' consisting of only one rifle the Jewish youth organizations in the Ghetto merged on 18 July 1942 and formed the 'Jewish Fighting Organization' (ZOB). Chief of staff of the ZOB was 24-year-old Mordechai Anielewicz and his deputy 'Antek' Cukierman. Paying incredibly high prices, the ZOB managed to buy from the Polish underground movement their first small arms, and subsequently to make use of them.... All over the Ghetto pill-boxes were built with feverish haste, underground lines of communication were established, cellars adapted for survival. Each house was transformed into a fortress. The first major supply of arms obtained from the Polish underground movement consisted of 50 pistols, 50 hand-grenades, and eight pounds of explosives. We had to pay 10–15 thousand zlotys for a pistol. With the help of messengers of the Polish underground movement, the first situation reports on the Warsaw Ghetto were sent to the Polish government-in-exile in London – but to no avail. A clandestine transmitter of the ZOB broadcast to the world emotional appeals – without eliciting any response. In the Parliamentary Assembly supporting the Polish government-in-exile under Wladyslaw Raczkiewicz, one of the deputies was Mr Shmuel M. Zygelboim, a prominent leader of the Jewish Socialist party in Poland, *Bund*. Zygelboim constantly put pressure on the government-in-exile to help the Warsaw Ghetto, and appealed to the world's conscience, equally to no avail. In that fateful hour of danger the attitude of the British Foreign Secretary, Anthony Eden, was particularly disastrous. The Polish ambassador in London, Count Edward Raczynski, was the first to submit to the British government the Ghetto reports from Poland, asking for help. Eden – according to Count Raczynski's memoirs – dismissed the reports as unreliable, and took a negative attitude.

It is difficult to say, even today, to what extent Count Raczynski's account is true. In any case the Warsaw Ghetto remained forsaken, forgotten, and abandoned by the world. Crushed by his impotence, Shmuel M. Zygelboim committed suicide on 12 May 1943, to protest against the passive attitude of the London government-in-exile and of the Allies.

Acting on orders from *SS-Reichsführer* Heinrich Himmler, General of the SS Jürgen Stroop arrived in Warsaw on 17 April 1943 to command a military operation against the Ghetto.... But Stroop's tactical plans for a *Blitz*-action proved unsuccessful, and his aim of presenting a 'city purged of Jews' as a birthday gift to Hitler on 20th April was based on a miscalculation of the Jews' power of resistance. Only some 600 Jews took an active part in the fighting, there were not even enough self-made arms for more fighters.... Every street was fought over ferociously. Having suffered heavy casualties the SS had to use armoured units. Whole blocks of flats were blown up, cellars were burnt out with flame-throwers, underground passages flooded with water. In one house after another life was extinguished.

Let me repeat once more: an account concerning an event as complex as the uprising in the Ghetto is bound to be of a subjective nature. The report just quoted underlines the partly criminal, partly indifferent attitude of some Poles towards the Jews. In a book which is intended to be objective it would be a mistake to omit such opinions, just as it would be wrong to claim that the behaviour of some individuals could serve as an extenuating circumstance for the SS or to accuse, by way of an inadmissible generalization, all or the majority of Poles of complicity.

However, in the context of subsequent events it was not entirely without significance that even the inhuman SS terror failed to move some to reflection or a change of heart – nor even to horror which the discovery at the end of the war of the atrocities committed in the extermination camps caused all over the world. It was this considerable group of the unrepentant and the unconvinced among the Poles who later provided Moczar and his police faction with the 'crack élite troops' for the revival of anti-Semitism. The security minister could not, obviously, rely solely on them. Equally necessary was the propaganda campaign which blamed the Jews for all the post-war deficiencies. But then the police faction never lacked adroitness: in 1967–8 Poland had 32 million inhabitants and some 30,000 of them, not even one per thousand, were Jewish, mostly fully assimilated, speaking Polish fluently and flawlessly, steeped in Polish culture and tradition. Like all other Poles, they took an active part in the reconstruction of the economic and political life of the country after the Second World War.

The anti-Semitic campaign against this tiny group of people, which finally led to their exodus, had two distinct peaks: the first, following the Six-Day War in the Middle East, was initiated by the speech delivered by Vladyslav Gomulka, then Secretary-General of the PUWP, on 19 June 1967; the other followed the so-called 'March 1968 events', a wave of student protests and demonstrations at all the major universities. Both actions had been prepared long in advance by the Moczarite police faction, which regarded anti-Semitism as the most efficient weapon in their efforts to rid themselves of their rivals inside the Communist establishment and seize power in the country. Once set in motion at all levels of the party apparatus and state administration, with the full use of the mass media, the anti-Jewish campaign was accompanied by economic terror as well, the state having a virtual monopoly of employment and professional facilities.

To accuse their opponents of 'revisionism'[1] alone would hardly have

[1] A pejorative term used by orthodox Communists to describe attempts to revise the thought of Karl Marx and to bring it up to date. The spiritual father of revisionism was Eduard Bernstein (1850–1932), who at the turn of the century in a book *The Pre-Conditions of Socialism and the Tasks of Social-Democracy* claimed that some of Marx's theses (e.g. concerning the impoverishment of the working class and the concentration of capital) were not, or no longer, valid. Bernstein appealed to social-democrats to give up waiting for a revolution and to seek political and social development by parliamentary means. In 1933 revisionism, opposed by Karl Kautsky, Rosa Luxemburg and (temporarily) August Bebel, was officially condemned by the congress of the German Social-Democratic Party (SPD) held in Dresden, but in subsequent years it had an ever-growing influence on the policies pursued by the SPD and by most European socialist parties. In the Soviet bloc, revisionism is considered a dangerous deviation from orthodoxy, hostile to the policy of the CPSU. The *Dictionary of the Current German Language*, published in East Berlin by the Academy of Sciences of the German Democratic Republic, gives the following definition of revisionism which can be regarded as authoritative for all the Soviet-bloc countries: 'Opportunistic tendencies within the international workers' movement, directed against Marxism-Leninism, proclaiming basic Marxist-Leninist teachings on revolutionary struggle as outdated and in need of revision, and attempting to replace them with bourgeois economic, philosophic, political, and other theories.'

served the Moczarites' purpose: it was an abstract, hollow-sounding notion, unlikely to stir deeper emotions among the party bureaucrats, not to mention wider strata of the population. The great purge, considered a prerequisite for the planned *coup d'état*, already carried out in all the civilian and military branches of the security services and well advanced in the army officers' corps, was to be extended to scholars, writers, journalists, film directors, students and other intellectual groups, and was ultimately to include economic managers, civil servants and Party functionaries as well. This could best be accomplished by using Jews as scapegoats.

For tactical reasons – to make full use of the Soviet anti-Israeli, pro-Arab policies in the Middle East, and to avoid possible censure from public opinion abroad, including the Western Communist parties – anti-Semitism was disguised as a fight against Zionism.[2] This camouflage served a double purpose: for appearance's sake Jews were purged, slandered and persecuted not *qua* Jews but because of their alleged Zionist, pro-Israeli inclinations or, in some cases, as 'revisionists' deviating from true Marxist-Leninist orthodoxy, while Polish public opinion, especially its more backward elements, was sure to get the message that in fact Jews were the target. The true aims of the wire-pullers were thus doubly concealed: whereas most educated people could easily discern the anti-Semitic reality behind the almost transparent facade of 'the fight against Zionism', only few people realized that this was but another diversion calculated to disguise the real goal of seizing power. Unless this Machiavellian design is constantly kept in mind, many events of those memorable years 1967–8 become incomprehensible.

Immediately after the Six-Day War, the anti-Zionist campaign was fed with innumerable stories, gossip and rumours of alleged drinking bouts arranged to celebrate Israel's victory over the Arab states. Such accusations, as a rule patently false, were quite sufficient to secure the dismissal from their jobs or expulsion from the Party of those suspected of having taken part, or even of not having condemned them out of hand and denounced them to the authorities. But the first batch of victims of this purge, carried out with special zeal in the armed forces, consisted not only of citizens 'of Jewish origin' as it was called by officialdom, but of

---

[2] Originally a purely religious yearning for Jerusalem, the name Zionism derives from Mount Zion in Jerusalem. At the end of the nineteenth century Zionism emerged, largely thanks to Theodor Herzl, as a political ideology and movement. It acquired political significance at the first Zionist Congress in Basel in 1897 which formulated the demand for a Jewish national home in Palestine, guaranteed by public law. The Balfour Declaration of 2 November 1917, the end of the British mandate in Palestine on 14 May 1948, and the proclamation of the State of Israel with Chaim Weizmann as its President (on the same day) were the major milestones on the way to the fulfilment of the Zionist idea.

at least equally numerous pure-blood 'Aryans', deemed for various reasons undesirable by the ringleaders of the 'police faction'. When Vladyslav Gomulka had recourse to 'anti-Zionist' arguments in his public accusation, presenting Polish Jews as a potential treacherous 'Fifth Column', as people having 'two fatherlands' and a 'double allegiance', who therefore could not be fully trusted, this, too, served as a rationale for purging not only Jews. As a result of a thousand years of coexistence, many Polish urban middle-class families, from which a considerable part of the intelligentsia originated, had some kind of relationship with the Jews – and, therefore, if the need arose, could be denounced as 'pro-Zionist' or 'crypto-Jewish'.

There was no improvisation about it. Long before 1967 the Ministry of Internal Affairs had begun to compile special files on Poland's Jewish citizens. In the ministry headed by General Mieczyslaw Moczar, the Department of Nationalities under Colonel Tadeusz Walichnowski[3] was responsible for this operation.

This was unlawful, as Polish legislation allows administrative authorities to classify citizens only according to criteria included in official questionnaires required for the issue of identity cards. As a result of the separation of state and Church in Poland since the Second World War,[4] it was forbidden to include in such questionnaires questions relating to religion. Unlike the situation in Poland between the two world wars, there was now no legal possibility of officially ascertaining the Jewish or non-Jewish origin of a citizen. Questions concerning national affiliation, nationality or language were as a rule answered by Jews with the word 'Polish'.

The officials in the Department of Nationalities in the Ministry of Internal Affairs could fulfil their task of registration of Jews only by means of genealogical research of their own, or by having recourse to informers. The saying attributed to Göring, 'I determine who's Jewish'[5], was happily, if rather gruesomely, revived when the description 'of Jewish origin' was introduced; whoever was undesirable would thus become a Zionist or a revisionist, as the case may be. 'Jewish affiliation' turned

---

[3] From 1966 onwards the Ministry of Internal Affairs had a 'Jewish section' headed by Colonel Tadeusz Walichnowski; its staff of over two hundred was kept busy compiling 'genealogical charts' of the Jewish population, listing – as far as possible – parents, grandparents and sometimes even great-grandparents. Walichnowski wrote several anti-Semitic articles, as well as an anti-Zionist book *Israel and the Federal Republic of Germany*, published in Warsaw in 1967 in a popular edition.

[4] Before the Second World War religious bodies had exclusive rights to register births, marriages and deaths in most of Poland. Since 1945 state registry offices alone keep population records, regardless of whether the person was baptized or not, legitimate or not.

[5] Before Göring a similar phrase was used by Karl Lueger, a pre-1914 leader of the Christian-Social Party in Austria and mayor of Vienna, regarded as the spiritual father of pre-Nazi 'folk' anti-Semitism.

into a political notion, not necessarily connected with national, religious or racial criteria.

In the Polish state re-established by the Versailles Peace Treaty over 30 per cent of the population belonged to national minority groups: Ukrainians, Byelorussians, Germans, Gypsies and Jews. The Jewish minority of nearly three and a half million people was clearly distinguishable by its religion, language and folklore, often by its physical appearance, attire and economic role as well. The 1967 population knew this ethnic group from reading, pictures or hearsay only as victims of Nazi gas chambers and crematoria: by then over one half of the Polish population consisted of people born since the war.

Before the racist witch-hunt was unleashed, the young generation at least did not associate any negative image with the notion of Jewry. The majority of them had only a very vague idea as to who was in fact Jewish and as to how this one per thousand of the population was different from the other Poles. In the light of the experience of Polish Jews in the first post-war years, this was fully understandable.

The great majority of the Jewish survivors of the Nazi 'Final Solution' emigrated directly after the end of hostilities. They had suffered in Poland too much to be able to accept the country as their place under the sun. Their families had been exterminated by the Germans, they mistrusted the new rulers, justly so as it later turned out, or believed they would be able to find more comfortable living conditions in the West. There were other reasons for emigration, amongst which one of considerable signficance was the Zionists' hope of establishing a Jewish state in Palestine, which, in fact, materialized in 1948. By then, however, the Polish authorities, following Soviet directives, put an end to Jewish emigration and prohibited it until 1956 when the second exodus took place.

In 1971 a book was published in Warsaw by Stanislaw Wronski, then Minister of Culture and the Arts, and Maria Zwolakowa; it was entitled *Poles and Jews 1939–45* and was designed to provide documentary proof of the assistance rendered by Poles to their persecuted brethren during the years of the German occupation. The authors put the number of Polish Jews who managed to survive the Nazi rule at 500,000. This is probably an exaggerated figure, unless it includes all those who had been deported to Russia – only part of whom managed to return to Poland. All in all, probably between 250–300,000 Jews lived in post-war People's Poland at one time or another, but even this figure is a rough estimate.

In any case, this is by no means an academic issue of demographic statistics. Wronski, who during the war served with a Soviet guerrilla detachment in Eastern Poland, was later considered to be a liaison man between the Soviet authorities and the 'police faction' in Poland. Even after Moczar's disgrace he managed to keep his ministerial post, and though later dismissed for non-political reasons, he is still a member of the party's Central Committee. But when he gave the inflated figure of Jewish survivors of the Holocaust, he was presumably not aware of the implications of his exaggeration: even if we reduce his estimate, the number of survivors would still run into six figures. This means that some 90 per cent of them chose the path of emigration, as in 1967 there were only 30,000 Jews still living in Poland. The Polish authorities, unlike the Soviet, did not as a rule try to prevent those wishing to leave (the years 1949–55 were an exception), and at times even actively encouraged emigration. And yet the overwhelming majority left the country of their ancestors in several waves of mass emigration, while most of those who chose to stay considered themselves Poles and Polish patriots.

Most of those relatively few Jewish Poles who did not follow the general emigration drive, when they were once again free to leave the country after 1956, consciously opted for People's Poland as their home, or, being fully assimilated, did not even consider the alternative. Neither religious nor any other ties bound these people into a distinctive minority group. To them apply the words written by the great Polish poet, Julian Tuwim, himself Jewish:

There is the blood which flows in the veins; I do not believe in such a blood community. But there is the blood let out of the veins: in such a blood community I do believe.

The older generation of these survivors included many Communists, Socialists, left-wingers. Only a few had ever been members of the Communist Party of Poland. Some merely entertained vague sympathies for its policies, expecting Communism to solve all national problems. On the other hand, the young people brought up in People's Poland grew up in an internationalist atmosphere. They treated anti-Semitism as a prejudice long overcome, at most a stupidity, but by no means a menace. Most of them lived as Poles among Poles, having dropped all the distinguishing marks which had once set their parents and ancestors apart from the rest of the population.

In consequence, the re-emerged anti-Semitic campaign hit no clearly defined targets. No wonder that many Polish nationals were accused or discriminated against because, for example, of their physical appearance, of their German-sounding names or of a police denunciation. Some of them were able to prove their 'pure' origin by pointing to their grandparents' grave in a Catholic graveyard, to their parents' certificates of baptism or even to their fathers' police service under the *Sanacja*[6] rule or during the Nazi occupation.[7] In such cases, provided they were not active opponents of the police faction, all troubles in their place of work or among their neighbours were usually settled, and they regained their right to promotion, to a pay bonus or to a travel permit. Sometimes the authorities would even admit their mistakes. For Polish Jews, however, regardless of their politics, there was no escape from economic and social discrimination. To set them apart as scapegoats, the authorities gradually cut them off from any possibility of earning a living, and by means of an aggressive propaganda campaign isolated them from their fellow-countrymen.

For them it was an unmitigated disaster to find themselves suddenly surrounded by an artificially incited anti-Semitism. By then to be Jewish had come to be considered evil and sinful – not only by a handful of incorrigibles, but by the mass media and in official pronouncements as well. The speed with which old prejudices had re-emerged could well have caused a shock. It took only a short time before there appeared in current everyday usage the description, later repeated in official police investigation records: 'At first she claimed to be Polish, but finally admitted being Jewish' (from the record of interrogation of an 18-year-old student in March 1968).

Many Western observers were under the false impression that the anti-Semitic witch-hunt actually began only after the 1967 Arab–Israeli war. That is not so: there had been an upsurge of anti-Semitism since 1956, though the pressure was in fact enormously increased following the Six-Day War, and in particular during the March 1968 events in Poland.

An incredibly large number of human problems resulted from the revived conflicts of identification. This question will be discussed in a later chapter, but here are some examples, though, having regard for the people involved or their families who are still living in Poland, generally names will not be mentioned.

A high-ranking army officer, whose wife was of Jewish extraction, was repeatedly interrogated about his wife's alleged contacts with Israel.

---

[6] After Marshal Pilsudski's *coup d'état* ('march on Warsaw') in May 1926, parliamentary democracy in Poland was severely restricted. Pilsudski, originally leader of the nationalist wing of the Polish Socialist Party (PPS), came to an arrangement with Polish industrialists and big landowners and established (using slogans of 'moral sanitation' – hence the name *Sanacja*) an authoritarian conservative régime, a semi-dictatorship which did not exclude non-Communist opposition either of the left or of the right. On his death in 1935 he was succeeded by the so-called 'Colonels' who claimed to be continuing and consolidating his policy, but in fact moved far to the right, borrowing a large part of the programme of their *Endecja* rivals, including anti-Semitism.

[7] In the pre-war 'Blue Police' (*granatowa policja*), which voluntarily collaborated with the Nazis under the German occupation, there were virtually no Jewish functionaries.

When he was eventually told he had to divorce her if he wanted to remain on active duty, the officer committed suicide.

In a town in the Wroclaw *voivodship* the Party committee forced an elderly Jew to found a local branch of the Social and Cultural Association of Jews in Poland, because in neighbouring towns branches of the Association had just carried motions condemning Israeli aggression, while 'here, in our town, there is nobody capable of adopting such a resolution'. Bowing to Party pressure the man, himself a veteran Communist, finally managed to recruit two other Jews and to persuade them to sign such a declaration. His wife, however, was so incensed by this that she left him, while the Party functionaries blamed him because the declaration was 'not consistent enough', and threatened that unless he wanted to lose his special old-age pension he must draft another, more condemnatory, declaration. He obliged once more, but in spite of that he was summoned shortly afterwards to the Party Control Commission and accused of having had contacts with Israel. As a matter of fact, he had a relative living in Israel, who once, many years before, had sent him a parcel of *matzos* for Passover. His accusers charged him now with 'not having been honest with the Party', expelled him and deprived him of his Party pension.[8] His 'deceitful attitude' was denounced by the local Party press.

Nina Karsow, secretary of the blind writer, Szymon Szechter, was arrested and accused of having prepared manuscripts for publication abroad. It was only during the interrogation that she was told she was the child of Jewish parents: Mrs Karsow, whom she had considered hitherto to be her own mother, had in fact hidden and adopted Nina during the Nazi occupation. In October 1967 Nina Karsow was sentenced to three years' imprisonment; as Amnesty International proclaimed her 'Prisoner of the Year' she was released after a year in prison and was allowed to leave the country together with Szechter.

In the second half of 1967 a controversy arose between the local Party cell in the power-station of Turoszow and the PUWP *voivodship* committee in Wroclaw. The controversy lasted for a full year: the *voivodship* committee wanted to have their candidate appointed as Secretary of the Turoszow cell, which however remained adamant and elected its own candidate, a Jewish welder, presumably trusted by his fellow-workers. The *voivodship* committee refused several times to approve his election;

---

[8] Old-age pensions in Poland, part of the earnings-linked social security system of which Socialist countries are so proud, are as a rule inadequate to ensure even the bare subsistence minimum. The Party pension given *ex gratia* to veterans of the revolutionary movement and to Party stalwarts is usually much higher than the ordinary old-age pension; in consequence such pensioners cannot escape total subservience to the Party whose line they have been obliged to toe blindly throughout their adult lives.

it argued, pleaded and finally employed open threats. The candidate himself was quite ready to give up the appointment, but the workers would
not have it. The *voivodship* committee treated the workers' attitude as
a hostile demonstration, instigated, moreover, by a Jew. Only when they
saw his livelihood to be endangered did the workers agree to release him
from his task and accepted a secretary brought, as the saying goes in
Poland, 'in a brief-case' from Wroclaw, i.e. imposed from above upon
people who had never even heard of him.

A Warsaw journalist spent his holidays in the Journalists' Rest Home
in Kazimierz on the Vistula. The night the Arab–Israeli war broke out
he was sitting in the bar, as he used to do every night of his holidays.
When he returned home he was dismissed from the editorial board,
because he had allegedly organized a drinking bout to celebrate Israel's
military victory.

The Party committee in the army's General Staff in Warsaw convened
a meeting during which a colonel was denounced as a concealed Zionist;
a motion was put forward to expel him from the Party and from military
service. The Colonel had dark, curly hair, a long crooked nose and spoke
with a slight lisp, but he was not Jewish. As a veteran Communist, who
had spent many years in pre-war Polish prisons, he thought at first that
it would be undignified to defend himself and to plead he was neither
Jew nor Zionist. Eventually, however, he had no choice but to produce
at the next meeting his certificate of baptism, signed by a Roman Catholic
parish priest. By then it was too late: he was expelled from the Party
and dismissed from the armed forces for his 'passive attitude during the
Israeli aggression'.

At a Party meeting in a Warsaw institution a Jewish official was accused
of having brought up his children in a Jewish religious atmosphere. During a lengthy debate one speaker after another denounced his hypocrisy,
and the motion to expel him from the Party was carried unanimously.
After the vote was taken the victimized official rose to speak and
explained that he had no children at all. The Party committee, discon-
certed, interrupted the meeting and went into conference. After some
twenty minutes they came back and announced that the official had been
expelled because of his provocative silence during the debate on his
case.

A rather funny story shows that most people were, in fact, quite ignorant of the real aims of the witch-hunt. After a general meeting in a provincial factory, the workers went out with a banner proclaiming: 'Zionists, go to Siam!' The same night the slogan astounded many television
viewers (television used to broadcast such mass rallies with particular
relish), but the puzzle was not difficult to solve; the workers had been

told to put out a slogan against Zionists, but as they had no clear idea what Zionism was all about, and the word in its Polish spelling seemed to them like a derivative of Siam – *syjonisci, Syjam* – they responded with that categorical demand.

All these instances, particularly the last two, have something grotesque about them, and in the West they might be considered satire. But to those affected every such arbitrary decision spelt economic ruin, sometimes even outright starvation. The authorities were quite happy to attack their victims and self-righteously continued their propaganda against the tiny minority of Jewish citizens. They were given a degree of publicity which was ominously out of all proportion to their numerical strength and significance.

Amid that hostile propaganda and the mass hysteria provoked by it, the handful of Jews was virtually defenceless. The state and Party apparatus, and also the people at large, were in such dire need of scapegoats for the years of mismanagement that the Jews had to submit to the stereotyped accusation that they were agents of an international Zionist conspiracy and bad Poles – by having to leave their country for ever and thereby also losing much of their property. As explained in a later chapter, the authorities facilitated the emigration procedure, but also demanded in every individual case a written declaration that the witch-hunt unleashed by the state and Party leadership had in fact concerned not Poles, but enemies of the people and, in any case, aliens – that is to say, Zionists.

Every prospective emigrant was handed a form with a printed request to the Council of State, asking for release from Polish citizenship. Only after having signed this document, which was supposed to provide evidence of a lack of affinity with the Polish nation, could he get his exit permit, that is to say a chance to reconstruct abroad his life shattered in his native country.

Subsequently, around mid-1969, somebody presumably realized that a signature on a printed form would not be enough to provide the authorities with a sufficient excuse for Polish and foreign public opinion, and that it was quite invalid under international law. From then on prospective emigrants were instructed to submit a handwritten application; they were warned in advance that the only reason for a favourable decision concerning their application for leaving the country was a declaration stating that the petitioner considered himself attached to the state of Israel rather than to Poland. Whether the emigrant had indeed any intention to settle in Israel, or elsewhere, was quite irrelevant. The signed declaration was considered sufficient evidence that the emigrant was in fact a Zionist. His travel documents consequently named Israel as the country of his destination. The propaganda claim alleging that most Jews were Zionists and revisionists, people with a double allegiance, enemies of Poland, of the Arabs and of socialism, had thus transformed pure fiction into an apparently documented reality. The new policy of affirming 'national allegiance' – as the smear campaign was officially described – apparently hit the guilty men, people who according to their own signed statements did not wish to remain Polish. It did not matter in the least that such crass falsification closely resembled a Kafkaesque surrealist world; Polish politicians were quite happy to pretend before the world and Polish public opinion, and not without success, that they were acting in a just and proper way.

5. The Enemy Image

IN every totalitarian régime the police are at first an auxiliary force subordinated to the political power; later, however, the relationship reverses, the police try to restrict the politicians' room for manœuvre by putting physical and psychological pressure on them, and what has begun as a Party dictatorship ('dictatorship of the proletariat') soon turns into a Party apparatus and a police dictatorship pure and simple. That is how the Soviet régime gradually degenerated under Stalin's rule, and the same pattern was closely followed in all the satellite countries, including Poland. The 1955–6 'democratization' was an attempt to reverse the process, but after Gomulka's return to power, that process began once more, albeit in a slightly modified form, and by 1966 was already well advanced. The so-called 'revisionists', or reform-Communists, proved incapable of reversing the trend or of offering effective resistance to the gradual transformation of Gomulka's régime, which under the growing pressure of the power-hungry Moczarite 'police faction' assumed an increasingly neo-Stalinist character. The steady growth of police power continued virtually unchecked for at least a decade: under the pretence of keeping up with the times 'organizational changes', sometimes apparently harmless, were introduced, more liberal laws were annulled as remnants of an outdated political system, patterns of social life were destroyed whenever they clashed with newly imposed authoritarian methods of government. Perhaps the most important and far-reaching change was achieved by means of a skilful personnel policy: 'unreliable' people who would not adapt themselves easily were removed from their posts and gradually replaced by faithful followers and obedient tools of the 'police faction'.

The *modus operandi* was (and still remains) basically the same: some event of internal or foreign policy was magnified out of all proportion and presented as an imminent threat to the nation, its state and its frontiers, to the social system, to socialism. If no such event occurred, one could always be faked and, in the circumstances of total control over the mass media and sources of information, presented and interpreted to resemble a real menace. Once the alert is sounded, it provides justification for a purge and for intensified coercion. In conditions resembling a state of emergency, physical and psychological terror could be counted on to stifle any kind of resistance, protest, or even doubt.

It was in such an atmosphere of grave national crisis and under the guise of an emergency that the 'police faction' in Poland was able to stage in 1967–8 a mass purge hardly imaginable in a more relaxed climate, with some vestiges of democracy and the rule of law still in force. The preparations for this operation, which had been going on for quite a long time, as well as its mechanism and the methods used, closely resembled the events of the 1930s and of 1948–9 in the Soviet Union, as well as the show trials and mass purges imposed on the East European countries during the first post-war decade.

Without attempting to trace in detail the political developments in Poland after the war, it should be pointed out that the roots of the events dealt with in this study go a long way back. Poland embarked on the road to a totalitarian police dictatorship – and its prerequisite, a state of political lethargy and surrender of the nation as a whole – when the victorious Red Army in 1944 brought with it a puppet administration, hand-picked and trained by the Soviet authorities. Due to the acquiescence of the Western powers its rule was imposed on a reluctant nation. Poland's loss of sovereignty received some semblance of legal sanction, when the provisional Polish government, which had emerged out of the 'Polish Committee of National Liberation' (the Lublin Committee), signed (on 21 April 1945) a treaty of friendship and mutual assistance with the Soviet Union.

As the Lublin Committee was no more than a group of Communist activists formed for the purpose of taking power, it was at first denied recognition by the Western powers. The refusal of recognition was, of course, vigorously condemned at the time by Communists and pro-Soviet apologists, but a quarter of a century later Khrushchev himself admitted:

In fact ... the composition of the Committee was approved by our leadership – namely, by Stalin – because it was formed on our territory, supported at our expense, and would have been impotent without our help. It was in our interest to create a Polish leadership consisting of worthy people, allies who shared our goals and would be faithful to us later on.

As soon as the Lublin Committee, having moved to Warsaw, broadened its base by co-opting to the cabinet (on 28 June 1945) some members of the London government-in-exile, the Western powers recognized it (on 5 July 1945) as a legitimate government, presumably not realizing that the cabinet, comprising an overwhelming Communist majority, would assign to members of other political groups no more than nominal roles. The Communist Party, originally quite insignificant in numbers, had a disproportionate influence within the government, and having got control over the armed forces and the security services, occupied all the key positions in the economic and political life of the country. The Peasants'

Party under Stanislaw Mikolajczyk,[1] at first numerically much stronger, was forced into opposition and subsequently reduced to the status of an insignificant organization which had to accommodate itself to the new circumstances, and whose role, both inside the country and abroad, consisted mainly in appearing to prove by its very existence that Poland had a democratic, multi-party political system.

The agrarian reform, proclaimed on 6 September 1944, divided large and medium-sized estates without adequately meeting the peasants' hunger for land. The process of nationalization of industrial plants began in 1946. In 1948 the Socialist and Communist Parties were forcibly merged into the Polish United Workers' Party (PUWP). The London-based government-in-exile continued its shadowy existence, protesting in vain against the Sovietization of Poland, while inside Poland relations between the state and the Church became more and more tense. In 1949 the Council for Mutual Economic Aid (CMEA or Comecon) was established in order to bind together the national economies of the countries of Eastern Europe; in 1950 public administration was reformed according to the Soviet model. In the same year the Six-Year Plan 1950–5 set targets for Poland's industrial development, to be assisted by Soviet credits worth 2.2 billion rubles. Its character, which was originally in general reasonable, with well-conceived objectives, was later completely revised: following the outbreak of the Korean War Soviet pressure toward a speedy build-up of the armaments industry (and heavy industry in general) was stepped up and was unopposed by the Polish government, by then reduced to blind obedience to Stalin's orders. In 1952 Poland's adjustment to Soviet patterns finally culminated in the adoption of a constitution closely following the Soviet model. All resistance to complete integration in and subordination to the Soviet empire was brutally suppressed. Vladyslav Gomulka, reputed to have opposed this trend (though he was in fact only mildly critical of the pace and methods of enforced Sovietization), was expelled from the Party and put in jail on trumped-up charges of Titoism or national-communist deviation.

In 1953 Stalin died, and in 1955 the Soviet Union imposed the Warsaw Treaty on the so-called People's Democracies. According to Soviet interpretation (strongly contradicted by the political and military leaders of

---

[1] On General Sikorski's death in an air crash in Gibraltar in 1943, Stanislaw Mikolajczyk became Prime Minister of the Polish government-in-exile in London. Invited by Stalin to Moscow in 1944, he negotiated with the Lublin Committee on Poland's future government. He lost the support of the Western powers and resigned his exile post, but in 1945 decided to join the 'Government of National Unity' in Warsaw as a Deputy Prime Minister. After the January 1947 parliamentary elections, considered by the USA and Great Britain to have been rigged, he became leader of the opposition, but in November 1947 he fled to the West, and shortly after he was deprived of his Polish citizenship.

Czechoslovakia in 1968), the treaty gave the USSR the legal right to intervene militarily in those countries (the claim was made public only in connection with the so-called Brezhnev doctrine).

Encouraged by the successful defiance of Stalin's orders by Tito's Yugoslavia[2] and strengthened by Moscow's seemingly more liberal course after Stalin's death, the critics of the evident shortcomings of the dictatorial system, even within the Polish Communist establishment, gained new courage. The censuring of Stalin at the Twentieth Congress of the CPSU in February 1956 raised new hopes for more freedom at a time when popular anger against economic poverty and oppressive work norms reached its climax. In late June 1956 a spontaneous uprising broke out in Poznan, sparked off by the protests of workers in a local engineering plant, and in the autumn of that year, after a few months of soul-searching among the Polish Communists and of an intense interfactional struggle, Vladyslav Gomulka again assumed the post of Secretary-General of the PUWP. His programme of structural reforms was at the time acclaimed in wide strata of the population: Poland's independence and equality of rights *vis-à-vis* the Soviet Union, moderation in relations with the Catholic Church, workers' self-management, maintenance of private farming, respect for Poland's cultural heritage: in short a specifically 'Polish road to socialism'. The whiff of freedom which came with 'the thaw' was enthusiastically welcomed by the people, who groundlessly and carelessly took it for granted that Gomulka's aims were identical with their own.

The profound economic crisis revealed after a decade of Communist rule was explained away by 'errors and distortions' for which the former Party leadership, and in particular the security police, were solely blamed. The fundamental policies were defended as basically right: only 'errors and distortions' had prevented the establishment of a just, socialist mode of life in Poland. An ill-considered, blind imitation of Soviet patterns and the arbitrary rule of Soviet advisers, it was alleged, had provoked the uprising of the Poznan workers, and had been responsible for the unfavourable economic and social record of the first decade, 1945–56.

At closed Party meetings and conferences of Party activists it was hinted for the first time that the Soviet Union in its Stalinist period exploited its weaker partners in Comecon. Poland, for example, had been forced

[2] After the war Yugoslavia willingly followed Soviet political and economic patterns with disappointing results, but she opposed direct Soviet domination in her internal affairs, in particular close control over her security forces, UDBA. This led to disagreement with Stalin, and in 1948, when Tito began to insist on a 'national' form of Communism as more appropriate for his country, the Communist Party of Yugoslavia was expelled from the Cominform. A witch-hunt directed against alleged 'Titoists' in all socialist countries culminated in spectacular show trials and the judicial murder of many leading Communists.

to supply the Soviet Union with coal at prices considerably below those paid in the world market, especially at a time of coal scarcity and a price boom. The collectivization of agriculture, too, had been enforced by Soviet advisers: it had been a false and damaging policy, but was now to be replaced by a voluntary association of peasants in agricultural co-operatives.

Poland's own road to socialism was presented as a cure for all the deficiencies. Gomulka, the alleged national-communist persecuted by Stalin, was supposed to be its personification. He was hailed as a legendary hero and a true patriot not only by his own countrymen: European and American mass media lavishly praised him in advance without bothering to check his credentials, or even to listen to what he was saying in public. They even associated him with Cardinal Vyshynsky, just released from detention in the Komancza cloister, regarding them as two Polish patriots of different persuasions, but equally dedicated to their country's well-being.

Gomulka did not in fact initiate the 1956 reform programme: he only rode the tide – and soon tried to stem it – when the entire nation, as a result of a genuine revulsion against Stalinism, was engaged in a passionate debate concerning its past, present and future. But as a victim of Stalin's arbitrariness, Gomulka was considered by many the right man to submit and to carry out a socialist counter-programme which then seemed possible, for political terror had been stopped, collectivization of agriculture halted, and outright confrontation with the Church avoided.

The limits of political democratization in Poland were drawn at a point where the power interests of the Soviet bloc seemed threatened. The debates going on in Poland were considered too far-reaching by other conservative Communist régimes, especially in Czechoslovakia and East Germany. The Soviet Union, too, clearly indicated by its 1956 armed intervention in Hungary that the Poles had better not push democratiza-tion and aspirations for national independence too far. Besides, Gomulka, who was as eager as Khrushchev himself not to allow the dis-mantling of the Communist rule in Poland, by no means approved of all the reform plans. From the very outset a considerable part of his prom-ises had no more than rhetorical significance, but they allowed the new Secretary-General to gain popularity, power and time. First of all he had to satisfy popular sentiments, and only then could he proceed with the consolidation of the slightly modified régime.

Shortly after Gomulka's return to power the first signs became apparent of a partial retreat from the ideals propounded in the first half of 1956, and wrongly identified with the so-called 'October achievements'.

Gomulka won over the Party apparatus, consisting chiefly of hard-liners opposed to any relaxation of controls. He banned the weekly *Po Prostu* which had been influential in intellectual circles, and provided for the renewed build-up of the police apparatus which had been discredited by its crimes and at first drastically reduced. His vociferous campaign against alleged 'revisionists' within the Party gradually made it abundantly clear that he included in this category all advocates of the misnamed October programme of democratization. Such 'revisionists' were now removed from responsible Party posts and from the state administration; the economic reforms introduced in 1956 were also abandoned. Step by step Poland was returning to old conceptions and methods discredited under Stalin's rule.

The decisive retreat took place in 1959. Once more there were shortages of goods and in their wake popular dissatisfaction increased. When a prominent official in military intelligence, Colonel Pawel Monat, a former military attaché at the Polish Embassy in the USA, defected to the West, Gomulka reacted in a tough manner, replacing politicians suspected of 'liberalist' inclinations with reliable hard-core Stalinists. General Moczar was thus able to improve his position considerably: the hour of the police faction, the self-styled 'Partisans', had struck.

Patriotism has always been a strong political driving force in Poland. Moczar and his 'Partisans' realized that nationalist, or rather chauvinist, demagogy, thinly disguised as a patriotic programme, might well succeed even under Communist rule: they revived the slogan of national-communism, well aware that Gomulka had been toppled in 1948 because he was blamed for overemphasizing Poland's national peculiarities, and that if the need arose the USSR would prevent a politically independent Polish solution with the same brutality it had used in Imre Nagy's Hungary in 1956.

For obvious reasons Russia and Germany, traditionally regarded as Poland's enemies, were excluded as potential targets in hate-mongering propaganda and in consequence neither anti-Soviet nor generally anti-German (i.e. including the German Democratic Republic) sentiments would have any place in Moczar's pseudo-patriotism, at least in public. But in any case the 'police faction' was not in the least concerned with Poland's external political sovereignty: they aimed at seizing power inside the country and therefore saw no immediate need to direct their chauvinistic campaign against neighbouring powers. It was enough to turn on internal enemies, who could at the same time be accused of being hostile to the Soviet Union. Such a policy was irreproachable in its foreign aspects, and could become most popular inside the country as the mere vocabulary of 'patriotism' raised hopes of at least some measure of liberation from dependence on the Soviet Union, even though such expectations could never be voiced publicly in so many words.

Both the 'revisionists' and the 'Zionists' could well serve as appropriate internal enemies. In order to slander political opponents or merely undesirable citizens, one had only to accuse them of revisionism or Zionism – no more precise charges were needed. Both labels were opportune not only because of their virtually universal application; whoever accused others of thinking and acting in a revisionist or Zionist way automatically presented himself in the role of a true and loyal Communist, zealously and vigilantly defending the orthodox doctrine according to the general line set by the CPSU, which set the course for all fraternal parties in the Soviet empire.

The Soviet comrades, therefore, had to treat the accusers as reliable and model pupils, particularly in view of the fact that Moscow's anti-Israeli policy had made anti-Zionism especially fashionable. All this meant that the direction of attack had been appropriately chosen. Moreover, both those targets were well suited to revive old anti-Semitic prejudices, still latent in certain strata of the Polish population ever since pre-war times. Anti-Semitism, coupled with xenophobia and an anti-intellectual bias, would appeal to people who by then constituted a not inconsiderable part of the nation: born and raised in the countryside, in a relatively parochial and partially backward atmosphere, only superficially did they change their way of thinking after having moved to the cities in the wake of the intensive industrialization and the emergence of the ruling 'New Class'. Such people, motivated both by class jealousy and by a strong drive for social advancement, could be counted upon to resent the preponderance of a relatively influential group of the old intelligentsia in the Party apparatus, the civil service, the universities, the press, in radio and TV, in the professions, even in the managerial classes – particularly so, since the proportion of Poles of Jewish extraction among them, though insignificant in numerical terms, was naturally much higher than among farmers, manual workers, or even white-collar workers who had their roots in the countryside. The others, the 'pure-blood Aryans', if not ready to toe the line, could always be presented as 'concealed Jews' or simply as 'Jewish flunkeys'. Removing them from their posts, even under such flimsy pretexts as 'alienation' or 'parasitism', would allow the police faction to promote their obedient followers and thus seize the commanding heights of power, hitherto beyond their reach.

For this chauvinistic anti-Semitism Moczar, therefore, partly found support both among the old-style petty bourgeoisie and the growing new petty bourgeoisie, i.e. the Party and state officials, and in particular in the police apparatus which he had expanded on Gomulka's instructions. The police had consistently enrolled people of implicit submissiveness, though they were often incapable of competent administrative performance. An apparatus designed for a rule of terror and oppression binds its members by common immorality and guilt, and unites them in opposition to any kind of democratic revival, because in their case it would mean demotion and the loss of their position of power. 'Illiterates can but dictate' runs an inspired aphorism by the Polish-Jewish writer, Stanislaw Jerzy Lec.

It is quite irrelevant whether the key figure in this struggle for power, the Minister of Internal Affairs General Mieczyslaw Moczar, was, or was not, a convinced anti-Semite. It was quite sufficient that this exceptionally vain and ambitious politician deliberately made use of anti-Semitism to promote his own interests. Moczar dreamt of playing the part of a national hero, of a saviour of Poland chosen by Providence. Like the Austrian Hitler who was more German than the Germans themselves, the Ukrainian Moczar tried to assume the image of a Polish patriot. His smear and hate campaign against the Jews was presumably a coolly calculated means in his struggle for power. Gomulka, despite the fact that he had not carried out most of his promises as Secretary-General of the PUWP, still enjoyed considerable popularity all over the country. General Moczar had therefore only one hope of getting round Gomulka, by trying to convince the population that there was indeed an emergency which only a tough policy executed by a proven patriot could overcome.

Since 1959 his 'Partisans' had managed with increased efficiency to infiltrate all sectors of public life. Moczar, who even then was almost certainly closely connected with the Soviet secret service, organized his faction as a kind of Mafia to seize control over all major bodies and institutions. Vladyslav Bienkowski,[3] Gomulka's former intimate

---

[3] Vladyslav Bienkowski belonged to a handful of Polish intellectuals who joined the underground Communist movement during the Nazi occupation, motivated mainly by anti-fascism and patriotism: his friendship with Gomulka dated from the wartime resistance. When Gomulka was ousted in 1948 Bienkowski, then head of the Education Department in the Party's Central Committee, was expelled as well, victim of a purge ostensibly aimed at the Titoist heresy. Stalin distrusted all 'native' Communists without pre-war Comintern experience, in particular those who had joined clandestine parties during the war to fight the Nazis; he considered them susceptible to 'nationalist' deviations, and therefore preferred to replace them with tested party members who had spent the war in the USSR (the 'Muscovites'). In Poland, however, the dichotomy 'natives' *vs*. 'Muscovites' was largely meaningless, because as a result of the annihilation of most leading activists of the KPP (Polish Communist Party) during the great purges in the late 1930s, almost all the survivors (Gomulka included) spent at least part of the war years either in Russia or in Soviet-occupied Eastern Poland; Bienkowski was among the few exceptions.

In 1956, on his return to power, Gomulka appointed Bienkowski Minister of Education, but the erstwhile comrades evolved in opposite directions: Gomulka gradually turned into a narrow-minded dogmatist, while Bienkowski continued to support more liberal policies. In 1959 their ways finally parted: Bienkowski was dismissed and in 1968 expelled from the PUWP for public opposition to the party's 'anti-Zionist' and anti-intellectual line. He tried to defend his views in letters

collaborator, described one instance of this activity at the time when he served as Minister of Education after Gomulka's return to power:

Just a few days after the [October 1956] Eighth Plenary Session [of the PUWP Central Committee] the elements hostile to October [reform] founded an organization to fight against the newly introduced school and education policy. That is how the Association of Undenominational Schools came into being: its founders [this was known to only a few initiated people] were almost exclusively former members of the security organs and the party apparatus, dismissed from their posts in October [1956]. Only later did some teachers and other people connected with educational work join the Association which gradually developed into a parallel 'Party' Ministry of Education, supported by local Party committees against the school administration, and thanks to this support it was able to arrange for various diversionary actions. I betray no secret in revealing that the chief goal pursued by these conservative and sectarian elements was to undermine the confidence of the masses of the Party leadership headed by Gomulka.

The police faction gradually won considerable influence in the Party apparatus, in the armed forces, in the Ministries of Foreign Trade and Foreign Affairs, and later in the mass media as well. Although public opinion did not realize until 1967–8 how purposeful their drive had been, they had in fact already asserted themselves at the Third Party Congress in 1959. The motions then carried were tantamount to a final rejection of the 1956 programme of socio-economic reforms. A propaganda pretext for such retreat had been provided by the allegedly grave menace of 'revisionism', whose advocates were said to have prepared the ground for a 'second stage of the restoration of capitalism'.

The pace and extent of this revival of Stalinist practices were remarkable. At the end of 1962 there were many more UB (police security service) informers than in the worst years of Stalin's rule. The network of agents was particularly well developed inside the Party apparatus, among students, in the propaganda services, in radio and television, and in the press. It became clear that the Party leadership was determined to avoid at all costs any repetition of the 1956 thaw.

The Party leadership was not particularly careful in its use of means and instruments. It relied not only on the Pax organization under Boleslaw Piasecki's leadership, but on a greatly extended censorship as well: the spiritual and cultural life of the country became more and more constricted. The many different publications banned by the censors included even the resolutions carried at the 1956 Eighth Plenary Session of the

addressed to Gomulka, to Party newspapers and to the Central Committee, but his writings only appeared abroad, in the *émigré* monthly *Kultura* in Paris.

PUWP Central Committee, and Gomulka's report delivered there. The censorship was so effective that up to the time of Gomulka's disgrace in 1970 not a single word might appear in print likely to question what was going on in Poland, or to reveal the true political economic situation of the country.

The re-Stalinization was obviously accompanied by appropriate personnel changes in various offices and institutions. Influential officials suspected of liberalism were consistently dismissed, and they at once became the whipping boys for the undeniable abuses of power. Thus the Party and state leadership could range themselves on the side of the dissatisfied critics, provided it managed to shift the blame, and consequently popular anger, on to others who would fit the hostile image so skilfully presented.

From the very beginning in 1944 the Communist régime in Poland had always had recourse to such scapegoats in its attempts to overcome internal difficulties. The enemy target was periodically revised according to current needs. At first, former soldiers of the Home Army[4] were slandered as 'spit-soiled dwarfs of reaction'; then came 'kulak-exploiters' opposing the abolition of the oligarchy of grand landowners; next came 'profiteers', as representatives of capitalism; the 'farmer of Marszalkowska Street' (Warsaw's main thoroughfare) served as a bogeyman to warn off followers of Mikolajczyk's Peasants' Party. Once the 'traitorous Tito clique' had been denounced as an instrument of the Americans, US imperialism was being built up as a major menace, whose Fifth Column allegedly included the Church hierarchy headed by Cardinal Vyshynsky. The most durable of all enemies remained West German militarism and revisionism, presented as Hitler's 'posthumous offspring'.

Gomulka, himself a target of a similar 'enemy image' in 1948–56, built up in the form of 'Gomulkaism' and denounced as a 'right-wing nationalist deviationist', was now in turn in need of an enemy image of his own, to justify re-Stalinization as a necessary defence against internal and foreign enemies. Himself once slandered as a revisionist and class enemy, he now discovered 'neo-revisionists' – as his 1956 promises had been gradually exposed as hollow verbiage.

In fact, under Gomulka's rule Poland not only failed to make good its centuries-old backwardness compared with the industrial countries

[4] Armia Krajowa (AK) was under the Nazi occupation an underground organization of Polish resistance; at the peak of its strength it had some 300–350,000 sworn-in members, though only a small part engaged in direct armed resistance. The Home Army was responsible for the 1944 Warsaw uprising which continued for sixty-three days, but was crushed by the Germans because the Russians had halted their offensive at the gates of Warsaw and refused help to the insurgents. The Home Army owed allegiance to the London-based government-in-exile and was anti-Communist, especially in its higher-level commands staffed mostly by pre-war regular army officers. After Communist take-over many of the former AK members were persecuted; their rehabilitation was one of the few lasting effects of the 1956 upheaval.

of Western Europe; it was outdistanced even in what was traditionally its strongest sector – agricultural production – to say nothing of its industries, paralysed for over a decade as a result of an inflexible investment policy. Economic targets were laid down not on the basis of a comprehensive analysis of objective factors, but according to the subjective preferences and prejudices of a dictator who paid less attention to the experts than to the acclaim of a clique of Party stalwarts. The Polish experiment of 'socialism with a human face and skilful hands' was therefore doomed to bankruptcy even before the first modest attempts at reform could prove their worth. Competent people were at their wits' end, confronted as they were by a wall of stupidity, pettiness and stubbornness. They retreated or were pushed aside and vilified, and found themselves among the first victims of the anti-intelligentsia campaign which had accompanied the all-out drive against 'revisionism' and 'Zionism'. However, as there were relatively many Jews among the critical intellectuals, it did not take long for the new enemy image of 'revisionism' and 'Zionism' to become sufficiently and vividly established to give free rein to anti-Semitism pure and simple.

Gomulka, who had developed an increasing tendency to isolate himself after his 1956 return to power and to listen to only those advisers who agreed with him, found himself ultimately surrounded by a network of reliable Moczarites, who never missed a chance to frighten him with 'liberals' wanting to bring about a new revisionist development in Poland. The Party and state leader thus became more and more a spiritual prisoner of his security chief, the only man who seemed capable of safeguarding internal stability in Poland by means of his 'iron hand'. The fact that Moczar's platform of nationalist 'revival' rallied round him many discontented people must have seemed to Gomulka an acceptable risk. Both he and his followers approved of Moczar's anti-Semitic slogans without undue reservations, even while condemning some later excesses, and Gomulka did not hesitate to take the wind out of Moczar's sails to thwart his drive for power. He did not want to appear less 'patriotic' than the 'Partisans', and for this purpose he could find no better means than to jump on the anti-Semitic bandwagon. It would, therefore, be wrong to make Moczar and his followers solely responsible for the culmination of post-war anti-Semitism in Poland. Gomulka made use of the hate campaign with equal lack of compunction or scruple in order to prop up his dwindling power. The peculiar blend of Communism and rabid chauvinism (discussed in detail in the concluding chapter of this book) can justly claim Gomulka as its spiritual father. Moczar was only more efficient and ruthless in pushing the Gomulkaite doctrine to its logical conclusion – until it clashed with Soviet interests and had to be cut down to size.

6. Poland's Early Spring

THE elbow-room that Polish politicians enjoy is always forcibly restricted to an area tightly defined by the political tendencies prevailing at any one time in the USSR. Just as in 1948–9 and in 1955–6, so in the 1960s the signals for initiating an anti-Semitic campaign came from Moscow. At the 21st Congress of the CPSU (27 January–5 February 1959) Shelepin, the newly appointed head of the KGB (Committee for State Security), sounded the alarm because the Communist states were allegedly threatened by the Western secret services:

> In the American CIA, for example, over 20,000 people are now employed.... In West Germany alone 40 American secret service agencies are active. The American secret service engages in preparing terrorist attempts and political plots, and it instigates conspiracies in different countries, particularly in the Middle East. The enemy does not relax, he is always active, looking for the smallest cracks on our armour.

The stress laid by Shelepin on conspiracies, in particular in the Middle East, was not coincidental: with the 21st Congress a new chapter opens in the history of anti-Semitism – this time under the banner of a struggle against international Zionism and its incarnation, the state of Israel. Soviet propaganda, followed a little later by Polish echoes, took up the call for the hate campaign.

Shortly after the 21st Congress of the CPSU a book called *The State of Israel*, by K. Ivanov and Z. Sheynis, was published; it was translated a few months later into Polish and appeared in the bookshops in 1960. The title of the book is misleading because the authors were not at all concerned with the Jewish state proclaimed in 1948. They dealt just with the Jews, and depicted their history in the most sinister colours. Such an overtly anti-Semitic, cynical 'historical' compilation could not have appeared even under Stalin. It maintained and purported to demonstrate that Jews had always and everywhere been flunkeys of reactionary powers. To avoid the charge of anti-Semitism the authors used a simple enough gimmick: when dealing with periods preceding the foundation of the Zionist movement, they divided Jews into 'good' ones and 'bad' ones. The good ones were simple, poor people, the others represented a cunning, perfidious oligarchy which imposed its will and policy on the remainder. In dealing with the period after the emergence of Zionism

1. Cover of a French edition of *The Protocols of the Elders of Zion*, 1934.

2. 'The Israeli extremists' appetite' is the caption given in *Sovetskaya Moldavia*, 4 June 1968. The Israeli soldier is shown grasping the Arab states.

the authors attempted to make their readers believe that they were only critical of the Zionist movement, but time and again they unwittingly or wilfully identified Jewry with Zionism. Neither in the Soviet Union nor in Poland did this remain the only book of its kind: it was followed by many others of an equally anti-Semitic nature.

Around 1960–1 the range of problems allowed for public debate in Poland was again restricted. The scope of information diminished, while attacks against an alleged revisionist menace became more and more frequent. There was as yet no official anti-Semitic campaign, but in an increasing number of cases Jews were being eased out of their jobs under the cover of a struggle against 'revisionism'.

By 1961 virtually all Jews had already been dismissed from the security apparatus, the police (*milicja*), and many branches of the armed forces. Police interference in the personnel policy of many institutions, initially the ministries of Foreign Affairs and Foreign Trade, and in the press, radio and television, became normal practice. At first the police were content to ban Jewish officials from business trips abroad, particularly to the West. Later they usually managed to use their agents in order to secure dismissals. In the Ministry of Foreign Affairs, however, the police met with resistance: when Minister Rapacki received a list of persons whose dismissal was recommended by the police, he ordered that it be filed without doing anything about it.

The reactionary struggle against the allegedly revisionist tendencies towards liberalization, prevailing ever since October 1956, had by then assumed an increasingly anti-Semitic character, if only because among the so-called liberals or people suspected of revisionism, there was a considerably larger proportion of Jews than would follow from their numerical strength in the population at large. The police faction was determined to deprive its opponents of any influence among the bureaucracy in research and education, in the economy and in politics, and was happy to be able to camouflage its objective by using the anti-Jewish cover. Vladyslav Bienkowski, no doubt one of the most perspicacious observers of Poland's political scene after the Second World War, described this development:

The process which was going on inside the party under the impact of total war against 'revisionism' brought in its wake the expulsion from this organization, or even the annihilation, of people with a propensity for independent thought, for initiative, for critical assessment, even just for honesty. This set off a mechanism of negative selection, because whenever appointments, promotion, or awards were granted, preference was given to people guaranteeing unconditional manageability and passive obedience. Great opportunities were opened to various shady characters, hypocrites, and careerists. Able and honest people could secure promotion only if they managed to conceal their true opinions.

This, however, was by no means evident to most onlookers, who sincerely believed the purge concerned Jews alone, and therefore was no business of theirs.

The network of agents and informers relied mainly on morally corrupt elements, often the scum of society – and they in turn influenced other circles. They obeyed orders from above, and owing to rapid promotions they came to occupy various positions, among others, in the field of 'education' in mass organizations.

At the turn of 1961 an event took place which alarmed the 'liberals'. Police functionaries searched the flat occupied by a well-known journalist and Party activist, Henryk Holland, previously arrested on 'suspicion of espionage', and interrogated him non-stop for twenty-four hours. According to the official account, Holland feigned nausea during the search, asked for permission to open the window and before anybody had time to intervene, climbed over the sill and jumped out of the fourth-floor window. There are still serious doubts whether this was the true version. The police have been suspected of having murdered Holland. Numerous facts strengthen such a suspicion. Those responsible obviously did everything to circumvent all the legal safeguards whose strict observance would have permitted the subsequent clarification of the case. A house search without independent witnesses was in itself a violation of the law in force. Strict rules concerning such searches provided, *inter alia*, that the suspect should never be out of sight (to prevent attempts at concealment or destruction of evidence, giving signals, or committing suicide). Even the opening of a window, as Holland had requested, was contrary to those rules. Besides, after 1956 a Party member could be arrested only with the prior consent of an appropriate Party committee – in Holland's case, of a high-level Party body. In fact, however, most members of the Politbureau knew nothing about the search in the journalist's flat – whether Gomulka had been consulted remains in doubt. Flagrant abuses of rights and laws by police functionaries were in any case never revealed.

Holland was Jewish. On 6 April 1956, at a conference of Party activists, he was the first to demand in public the revocation of the 1948 charges against Gomulka which subsequently led to his expulsion from the Party and to propose his return to its supreme decision-making body. It is possible that Holland had to die because in the light of his popularity his arraignment for alleged espionage and his denunciation as a Zionist would not have had the desired effect. Probably nothing definite will ever be known. In any case, his death was interpreted as a signal for a definite stop to any attempts at democratic reforms, as a starting-point for more severe police repression and interference in internal party politics. Gomulka presumably did not realize that he had unleashed forces which would fatally undermine the confidence he had hitherto continued to enjoy in the country.

It became obvious that Moczar was making use of Gomulka's popularity to build up his own power base behind the scenes, and to strengthen it on the quiet so as to be able one day to replace the Secretary-General without running undue risks. Although as security minister he could not become at all popular among the population at large, he well knew how to win as many followers as possible. He placed himself at the head of the ex-servicemen's organization ZBOWID, and built it up so that it became a virtual state within the state and to a certain extent a rival to the Communist Party itself. To attract former members of the Home Army (in previous years he had imprisoned and tortured hundreds of them) and of the Polish armed forces in the West, he gave the organization a distinctly nationalist profile. He succeeded so well that very often the notions of 'nation' and 'nationalism' were identified all over Poland with his own name. He was greatly assisted in his task by the fact that the staffing of the mass media, of the party apparatus and of the state bureaucracy, with people who had linked their personal expectations with Moczar's plans, had already been well advanced.

By expanding the police apparatus to an extent unknown even in Stalin's period, Moczar helped compliant officials to secure higher salaries and privileges so as to be able to corrupt them yet more. He had no compunction or scruples even in hushing up the criminal deeds of his subordinates; as a consequence, when the new Secretary-General, Edward Gierek, who had taken over power at the beginning of 1971, decided to put an end to his former ally's authority, he was able to dismantle his network by putting in jail a number of senior officials in the Ministry of Internal Affairs, guilty of corruption and smuggling deals. Among them was a Deputy Minister, Moczar's second-in-command. Although they were purged for purely political reasons, there was no need to trump up charges against them – only to put an end to their immunity.

In 1962 two literary weeklies, *Przeglad Kulturalny* and *Nowa Kultura*, were suspended. In their place a new weekly, *Kultura*,[1] appeared with an editorial board composed of people blindly obedient to the Party line.

---

[1] Not to be confused with the Polish *émigré* monthly *Kultura*, published in Paris, whose title was borrowed by the new weekly. In consequence, since the establishment of the Warsaw *Kultura* there have been two periodicals of the same name, totally different editorially and ideologically.

A year later, in July 1963, a plenary session of the Central Committee was convened ostensibly to deal with ideological issues, but actually it provided the hard-liners with an opportunity to launch a general offensive in all fields of spiritual and artistic life. Writers, sociologists, historians, film producers and theatre directors were strongly attacked, but the sharpest criticism was levelled against the publishing houses for their 'lack of fighting spirit in the struggle against revisionism'.

Simultaneously anti-Jewish propaganda in the Soviet Union was again being intensified. The magazine *Narody Azii i Afriki* carried in its fourth issue of 1963 an article by P.J.Potapovskii, entitled 'The Federal Republic of Germany and Israel', in which, by means of ingenious constructions and a blatant falsification or distortion of historical facts, Nazi Germany, Zionism, the Federal Republic of Germany and the State of Israel were tied together in some devious complicity of an obviously evil nature. Potapovskii claimed, for example, that during the Second World War international Zionist organizations had been guilty of 'collaboration with the German fascists', because in 1944–5, as payment for the release of Hungarian Jews, they allegedly offered the Nazis arms on condition that they be used only against the Red Army. The same article described Zionist organizations in the USSR as 'field agencies of Western secret services'. All this was faithfully echoed by Polish propaganda.

Of exemplary significance for the fight against 'revisionism', still camouflaged as a campaign primarily against Jewish intellectuals, was the attack on Adam Bromberg, a man of deservedly high repute who was for many years head of the Polish Scientific Publishers. Bromberg, a Jew and a veteran Communist, was considered one of the best Eastern European experts in the publishing industry. Not only had he built up his enterprise into the leading institution of its kind in Poland, but through a fruitful exchange of licences with a number of other European publishing houses he managed to ensure that Polish scientific works circulated in Western countries, and was also able to import similar books from all over the world.

By 1964 the muzzling of cultural life and the anti-Semitic campaign were already so advanced that even such understandable and business-like exchanges of licences, when combined with the fact that the successful and well-known director was Jewish, could be considered ground enough to start legal proceedings against Bromberg. These continued for the next five years. The indictment charged him with high treason on the grounds of 'propagating bourgeois ideology', 'revisionism', 'Zionist plots', and embezzlement of money. By 1969, when Bromberg was finally found not guilty, the trial records filled many volumes. The press has extensively reported the court proceedings, but the acquittal was not even mentioned by the mass media. Public opinion thus continued to believe that the man once held in the highest esteem and respect was in fact a Jewish swindler who for his own personal gain had criminally misused the means of production put at his disposal by the Party and the state. Adam Bromberg was a ruined man and his life's work to a large extent destroyed.

Some intellectuals made various modest, and therefore unsuccessful, attempts to protest against the repression that was gradually growing and turning into a regular campaign of terror. One of these attempts in 1964 took the form of an open letter addressed to the Prime Minister by thirty-four eminent intellectuals and writers, asking for a relaxation of censorship and for a greater allocation of paper to publishing houses. This most prudently and tactfully formulated appeal was received by the Party leadership with extreme annoyance. The authorities claimed the letter had been written solely for the purpose of finding an echo in hostile centres abroad. While the signatories were being slandered and accused of high treason, attempts were made to force all the remaining writers to sign a declaration criticizing the letter. Those refusing to sign were threatened with reprisals, which in many cases were in fact shortly afterwards put into effect. Such official counter-pressure presented an opportunity to make use of slander and repressive measures for the intimidation and silencing of intellectuals, including Jewish intellectuals. This later became regular practice.

It was in such a climate that the Fourth Party Congress was convened in June 1964. It turned into an open show of hostility towards the intelligentsia. Shortly afterwards a speech delivered by Zenon Kliszko[2] at a scientific conference in Cracow evoked perplexity and even shock in intellectual circles: Kliszko openly praised Roman Dmowski's views.[3] A prominent Communist took a leaf out of his nationalist and reactionary predecessor's book. Presumably Kliszko intended to demonstrate the allegedly 'patriotic' policy of the Party, as the notions of 'patriotism' and

---

[2] Zenon Kliszko, as the Party 'ideologist', was second-in-command in Gomulka's régime from 1956 to 1970. Although he had studied law and dabbled in literature before the war, Polish writers used to call him in jest 'a one-quarter intellectual'. In 1948, as head of the Personnel Department of the Party's Central Committee, he was dismissed together with Gomulka; in 1970, as a close collaborator of the discredited Secretary-General, he fell victim to the changes at the top. In the field of ideology Kliszko frequently assumed nationalist positions with anti-Jewish overtones.

[3] Roman Dmowski (1864–1939), founder of the National-Democratic Party (*Endecja*), the main political opposition to Pilsudski and the *Sanacja* rule, advocated an alliance with Russia as the great Slav power, but preached hatred towards Germans and Jews. In his speech of 19 March 1968, Gomulka closely followed Dmowski's old differentiation between three categories of Jews: those with Zionist sympathies, nationally indifferent Jews, and Jews committed to the Polish national cause. *Endecja* originally waged a sacred war against Jews included in the first two categories; in the late 1930s its extreme right wing (e.g. Piasecki) gradually adopted Nazi racist ideology and sought accommodation with the ruling *Sanacja*.

'nationalism' were by then replacing the old internationalist slogans. With his Cracow speech, Gomulka's closest collaborator and ideologist joined the chauvinistic campaign in the course of which General Moczar not only inflated out of all proportion his alleged contribution to the armed struggle for Poland's liberation, but even hinted at some kind of affinity with the 'father of Polish independence', Marshal Jozef Pilsudski,[4] still reviled by orthodox Communist doctrine.

Moczar's followers did not hesitate to explain all shortcomings, for which they were themselves at least partly responsible, as the result of the machinations of plotters, enemies of the people. They argued that in order to defeat the plotters, Poland needed a strong man who, like Pilsudski in his time, would finally restore law and order in the country.

In 1965 some Polish newspapers attacked Israel because its government allegedly tolerated organizations of Jewish immigrants from Silesia, acting under the aegis of refugee associations in the Federal Republic of Germany. For many years Polish propaganda was naturally most hostile to German refugee organizations, who never ceased to present territorial claims to their former homeland that now formed part of the Polish state. In Israel there were many different associations grouping immigrants from various countries – Poland, Morocco, Iraq or Germany. Every such organization published newspapers and bulletins in the vernacular, but was mainly concerned with facilitating the integration of new immigrants. German-speaking societies in Israel had nothing in common with the refugee organizations in the Federal Republic. Besides, Israel was the very first country outside the Soviet bloc to extend official recognition to Poland's new western frontiers on the Oder and Neisse rivers. The Polish press passed over all this in silence. Its attacks against associations of Israelis of German extraction were calculated to impress upon its readers that these were public bodies of a distinctly anti-Polish character.

This impression was strengthened by the fortnightly *Prawo i Zycie* which in its issue of 21 November 1965 published an article by W. Zabrzeski entitled 'Alliance Between Victims and Executioners'. The author claimed, without giving a single shred of evidence, that the Israeli associations were financed by West German 'revisionist refugee organizations' and that their activities were inspired by the Embassy of the Federal

---

[4] Jozef Pilsudski (1867–1935), co-founder of the Polish Socialist Party (PPS) and leader of its nationalist wing, in 1918–22 was head of state of the Polish Republic and Commander-in-Chief of its armed forces; under his leadership 'the miracle of the Vistula' was performed in 1920, the Red Army driven back from the suburbs of Warsaw, and an independent Polish state, far exceeding its ethnic territories (the 'Curzon line'), was established and consolidated. Pilsudski resigned as head of state in 1922, but staged a successful *coup d'état* on 12 May 1926 and put an end to the parliamentary régime. Though nominally only Minister of War (for a time also Prime Minister) he ruled over Poland as a rather benevolent dictator up to his death.

Republic in Israel. In the same year an obscure journalist, Andrzej Zeromski, brought out a book called *West of the Jordan River*, alleging a similar threat on the part of Israeli chauvinists and international Zionist organizations which had 'fraternized with Poland's most rabid enemies'.

On 19 March 1965 the police rearrested Jacek Kuron and Karol Modzelewski, both of them lecturers at the Faculty of Arts of Warsaw University. Kuron, born in 1935, had been a leader in the Polish Boy Scouts' organization, and was the author of several books on education. At the time of his arrest he was working on his doctoral thesis. Modzelewski (born in 1937), step-son of Zygmunt Modzelewski, the late prominent Communist veteran and the second Minister of Foreign Affairs in post-war Poland, was also writing his doctoral thesis. Both had been politically active since their schooldays, and were members of the PUWP. In October 1956 they actively participated in the Polish youth movement: Kuron was a committee member of the University organization of the Union of Socialist Youth and chairman of the 'Political Debate Club' established under the aegis of the Union.

Both of them submitted for discussion in this Club a critical analysis setting forth their conviction that they were actually living not in a socialist society, but in a state ruled by a monopolistic and monolithic party. But their hope of bringing about reform inside the Party was doomed to be frustrated: on 14 November 1964, they were arrested and their typescript of 128 pages was seized. Although they were later released from detention, without being prosecuted or put on trial, both were expelled from the Party and from the Youth Union.

This only confirmed Kuron and Modzelewski in their views. They subsequently wrote an analysis of Poland's socio-economic régime and addressed it, as an 'Open Letter to the Party', to the organizations from which they had been expelled. The document, containing not only criticism but also constructive proposals for reforming the system in order to bring about a democratization of the Party and the state and the restoration of the rights of the working people, reached the West and was published both in Polish and in several foreign languages.[5]

After almost four months of detention the authors of the 'Open Letter' were sentenced by the Warsaw regional court, Kuron to three and Modzelewski to three and a half years' imprisonment. The sentences were based on article 23 of the Small Penal Code, which states in para. I:

Whoever circulates or composes, keeps or transmits for circulation printing matter or illustrations liable to incite to the commission of a crime, or to

[5] For an English translation of Kuron and Modzelewski's 'Open Letter to the Party' see George L. Weissman, ed., *Revolutionary Marxist Students in Poland Speak Out*, New York, 1968, pp. 15–90.

approve of a crime, or whose contents are designed to remain concealed from state authorities, or which contain false information liable to cause serious harm to the interests of the Polish state, or to disparage the dignity of its supreme organs, is liable to a penalty of imprisonment for not less than three years.

The judiciary had again shown that it could not withstand the pressure of the police and Party apparatus. Citizens could no longer count upon its protection, since the judges of the Warsaw regional court passed a manifestly political sentence. The 'Open Letter' of the two idealistically minded young men had neither incited to nor approved of a crime, it was not confidential nor did it contain false information or detract from the dignity of the supreme state organs. What had become punishable was whatever infringed upon the current interests of Poland's rulers. Kuron and Modzelewski lodged an appeal against the sentences. If they remained in force, they would put an end to any kind of discussion of social problems in Poland. And yet, on 19 October 1965, the Supreme Court dismissed the appeal and confirmed the sentences. Conditionally released nearly two years later for good conduct, Kuron and Modzelewski were again arrested in March 1968 in connection with the students' riots, and on 15 January 1969 again sentenced to three and a half years' imprisonment.

In 1966 there was a further deterioration in the economic and political situation of the country. This was the first year of the new Five-Year Plan which was criticized by several leading Polish economists, including Professors Kalecki and Brus, as a step towards failure. While the plan was in the course of preparation, Gomulka and the rest of the Party leadership invariably reacted with sneers and ridicule to all warnings and alternative proposals. They had already decided that Poland had to tighten its belt yet further in order to ensure the fulfilment of the plan. The 7th plenary session of the Party's Central Committee was convened to discuss 'guidelines for modifications in industrial management'. In fact, however, the reports submitted to the plenary session and the resolutions adopted did not deal with any modification of the management system, but with ways and means of making workers increase labour productivity without raising their wages. In private conversations many Party and state officials, in particular managers of industrial plants and associations, did not conceal their anxiety. Many of them did not believe the session's resolutions could be carried out, and were embittered by the steadily growing interference of the Party in industrial management, which was only aggravating the existing state of disarray.

The mounting dissatisfaction of the working class could be overlooked no longer and nobody could go to the workers with demands for in-creased productivity without provoking a flood of accusations blaming the Party and state leadership for the deplorable situation. The continued fanning of pseudo-patriotic zeal carried with it the serious risk of a nationalist movement directed against Russia. But the experience gained during the previous years apparently promised success, provided 'patriot-ism' was linked with a struggle against internal enemies only. The cam-paign against revisionism and Zionism was therefore entering a new, more acute stage.

A massive anti-Semitic campaign, this time in the open, was duly un-leashed in radio and television broadcasts, in the press and at Party meet-ings. A few examples taken at random will give an idea of the inventive capacity of the mass media in this respect. In *Prawo i Zycie* of 10 April 1966 the editor-in-chief, Kazimierz Kakol, a prominent follower of General Moczar, dealt with a number of books published in the West by Jewish writers who described their experiences in Poland during the German occupation. To all these authors Kakol imputed the opinion that the Jews could easily have come to an understanding with the Germans had the latter not been obliged to take into account the feelings and ten-dencies prevalent among the 'Polish barbarians'. Kakol overlooked with total unconcern the fact that in none of the books slandered by him was there the slightest trace of such a preposterous argument. The books themselves were in any case unavailable to readers of the Polish press.

On 19 April 1966 the daily *Zycie Warszawy* published an article entitled 'The Witch-hunters' Ethics', claiming that in the USA a retired general named Klein had played a prominent role as a political agent of the Federal Republic of Germany. He was also alleged to be a leading Zionist who had financed the American visits of anti-Polish German politicians and extended his personal protection to organizations of former ethnic Germans (*Volksdeutsche*) in the USA. The only grain of truth in this story consisted in the fact that, in the Adenauer era, Klein had been employed as an officially registered lobbyist and public relations agent of the Federal Republic in the USA, but he had never had anything to do with anti-Polish activities.

The 1961–5 Five-Year Plan was supposed to bring a 20 per cent rise in real wages. According to official statistics, only an 8 per cent increase was achieved. In 1966, at the very start of the next Five-Year Plan, con-siderable price rises increased the strain on household budgets: rents went up by nearly 90 per cent, prices of some essential goods and foodstuffs by 10, 20 or even 30 per cent. Some financial recompense was offered, but this could not offset the damage done to working-class families by the price rises.

As dissatisfaction among the population grew, propaganda became more and more vociferous. A method well tested in Stalin's time was now being used once more to suggest a state of emergency, to evoke a feeling of living in a besieged fortress, surrounded by enemies.

In the second half of May 1967, shortly before the outbreak of the Six-Day War in the Middle East, the eighth plenary session of the Central Committee of the PUWP was devoted almost entirely to counteracting the influence of 'hostile propaganda' on Polish public opinion. Press reports on the session were accompanied by rabid attacks against Israel with the use of arguments taken directly from Arab newspapers. With no excessive concern for logic, opinions that the days of Israel were numbered because of a massive deployment of Egyptian troops on its frontiers were found side by side with accusations against Israel of preparing 'aggression against Syria'. Although similar reports appeared in the press of other Communist countries, Polish propaganda was this time distinctly the noisiest. It became obvious that a massive smear campaign, a general 'anti-Zionist' offensive, was under way in Poland.

The war in the Middle East suited to perfection the long-term plans of the instigators of these attacks, although the foolish and uncritical credence that they gave to the false reports of Arab news agencies brought them into a highly ridiculous position. In the first days of the war readers of the Polish press could not help getting the distinct impression that the Arab states were winning one battle after another. Press, radio and television newsmen were constantly being fed with biased reports and presented with official interpretations of the Arabs' war aims. The minutes of a press conference in the Polish Ministry of Foreign Affairs contained, for example, the following passages:

The situation is clear, comrades. Israel has attacked Arab states. All peace-loving countries, including Poland, are supporting the Arab states. It is difficult to forecast how the situation is going to develop.... But there can be no doubt the Arab side is incomparably stronger. I would like to emphasize, comrades, that there can be no question of a 'holy war' against Israel, as Western propaganda suggests. The United Arab Republic demands only respect for its sovereign rights in the Gulf of Aqaba and on the Suez Canal.

A newsman: Comrade Director, but there are official declarations by Arab statesmen that the war can end only with the annihilation of the State of Israel....

Reply: Comrades, a distinction must be drawn between statements of Arab politicians destined for abroad, and those for internal use only.... One must realize, comrades, that such slogans are only meant to rally public opinion in the

Arab countries. We have been assured by other sources – there is no need, however, to make them public – that such indeed is the case.

When it became obvious that Israel had defeated the Arab armies and the news of triumphant successes by Arab forces as previously reported in Poland was shown to be false, a wave of malicious joy swept over the Polish public. The Poles, who had been forced for many years to contribute to Arab rearmament – Polish ships, for example, carried Soviet and Czechoslovak war material to Egypt free of charge – were evidently overjoyed that the Soviet Union had indirectly suffered a political and military defeat in the Middle East.

Apart from the satisfaction caused by the Israeli successes, which was also based on general anti-Soviet sentiments, there were, anti-Jewish propaganda notwithstanding, manifestations of genuine friendliness towards the Jews as the underdogs. On 6 June Mass was celebrated by Cardinal Stefan Vyshynsky in Warsaw's St Anne's Church to commemorate Pope Paul's encyclical *Populorum progressio*. The sermon of the Primate of Poland expressed sympathy with that small country and 'the right of a people, so many times condemned to death, to its independent statehood'. The Cardinal's words were in no time repeated all over Warsaw. But the Party and state leadership would have looked ridiculous had they not made full use of the assiduously sharpened weapon of anti-Zionism. With increased vigour they at once began to denounce Israel as a military aggressor, and to condemn the Jews living in Poland for showing friendliness to a criminal régime. The anti-Jewish campaign unleashed by the mass media in connection with the Six-Day War surpassed the worst slanders of the past. Gruesome reports about alleged atrocities committed by Israeli troops in occupied Arab territories culminated in the accusation by Kazimierz Rusinek[6] that Nazi criminals, 'according to my estimate, over one thousand of them', were acting as advisers in the Israeli Army. Simon Wiesenthal, head of the Jewish Documentation Centre in Vienna, challenged the minister to give at least a few names, but received no answer whatsoever.

Vladyslav Bienkowski wrote of the reaction of Jews and Gentiles alike to the conflict in the Middle East: 'It is understandable that in view of

[6] Kazimierz Rusinek was Deputy Minister of Culture and Art and Moczar's deputy in the leadership of the ZBOWID organization. Like Simon Wiesenthal, he had been in the Nazi concentration camp in Mauthausen, but after the war he was accused of torturing his fellow-prisoners. In postwar Poland he advocated a particular form of anti-Semitism, unflaggingly putting forward the thesis that during the Second World War Poles had, whenever possible, unselfishly saved their Jewish fellow-countrymen, only to be repaid with ingratitude. He slandered in a most vicious manner Jewish (and Polish) historians, essayists and publishers who truthfully recorded both Polish assistance and cases of collaboration with the German authorities. Adam Bromberg, the former director of the State Scientific Publishing House, was one of his victims.

the events that have taken place in the Middle East, Jews should show their friendliness towards Israel'. He added that such an attitude was, at least initially, common to an overwhelming majority of the Polish population, quite irrespective of their personal attitude to the Jews. This was quite understandable, as Polish press reports on the eve of the conflict had made it clear that the Arabs aimed at the total annihilation of Israel, and that Israel acted in self-defence. According to Bienkowski, even traditional anti-Semites were not interested in the annihilation of the Jewish state, as they themselves had always propagated the slogan: 'Jews, go to Palestine!'

To counteract pro-Israeli sympathies, Polish newsmen competed in inventing and circulating slanders and insinuations. The tune was now called by an ostensibly non-Party Warsaw daily, *Slowo Powszechne*, the mouthpiece of Boleslaw Piasecki's Pax movement. On 7 July 1967 the paper reported that the document proclaiming the incorporation of the entire city of Jerusalem in the state of Israel allegedly contained wording literally borrowed from the Nazi laws by means of which the Germans attempted to legalize their annexation of Austria in 1938.

Boleslaw Piasecki found like-minded followers in Kazimierz Kakol, editor-in-chief of the fortnightly *Prawo i Zycie*, several journalists on the editorial board of *Zolnierz Wolnosci*,[7] organ of the Ministry of National Defence, among members of the pre-war fascist parties such as Edmund Meclewski and many others, and in the people whom the security organs and the military intelligence had much earlier infiltrated into radio and television as well as into various Party and state bodies. Many of them had hitherto betrayed their anti-Semitic attitudes only under cover of the fight against 'revisionism' and 'Zionism', but now they were free to come out in the open and propagate their hatred for the Jews. At the same time anonymous rumours of all sorts of shady activities for which Jews were allegedly responsible were circulated. It was said, for instance, that the price rises had been brought about by 'disguised Zionists' in key positions in the state administration, or that state secrets were being betrayed by Jews to Israel. The 'Jewish' origin of unpopular politicians and officials was readily revealed, even when it did not conform to the truth. This by itself was usually sufficient to muzzle real or alleged opponents and to reduce them to silence.

The case of a radio journalist, Artur Fiszer, revealed shortly after the 1967 Middle East war the extent to which such a climate of overheated

[7] *Zolnierz Wolnosci (The Freedom Fighter)*, a daily paper published by the Polish Army's Main Political Directorate, should be regarded more than any other paper as an outspoken mouthpiece of Soviet interests. Almost totally subservient to the Soviet Army Command, the Polish Army reflects Soviet power interest to an even greater degree than other governmental agencies.

political propaganda in a totalitarian state makes life intolerable for those employed in the mass media who refuse to follow blindly the guidelines given from above and who have the courage to come out in the open. Fiszer wrote a letter to Cardinal Vyshynsky to express his gratitude for the Primate's words of support for Israel, included in the above-mentioned sermon. He sent his letter to the Cardinal together with a bunch of flowers and signed it 'Artur Fiszer, a Polish Jew, former political prisoner for many years, soldier of the First [Kosciuszko] Division of the Polish Army'. A few days later he received the Cardinal's reply stating, *inter alia*, that 'Polish Catholics are in favour of the independence of the state of Israel. We continue to pray for it to our common Father in Heaven.'

A few days later Fiszer was expelled from the Party and lost his job, and a publishing house rejected the book it had previously accepted from him and prepared for publication.

Moczar, for whose efficient secret service the time was especially propitious, submitted to Gomulka daily reports of the allegedly pro-Israeli sentiments of the population, of the 'drinking bouts in honour of the Israeli aggressors', of flowers having been sent to the Israeli embassy and of young people who had tried to register at the embassy as 'volunteers for the Israeli armed forces'. An innocent birthday party in the editorial offices of a popular women's magazine, *Pryzyjaciolka*, was reported by a police informer as a celebration to honour Israel's victory – and this subsequently led to grotesque consequences: when the 'police faction' later decided to get rid of General Czeslaw Mankiewicz, head of Poland's air defences, there was, among other trumped-up accusations against the veteran of the wartime Communist underground resistance, the charge that his wife, an editor of that magazine, had taken part in the 'drinking bout'. There is no need to add that the charge against General Mankiewicz, who was in fact dismissed for having written a military analysis critical of Soviet anti-aircraft defence systems used during the Arab–Israeli war, was confirmed even after it was proved that his wife had been out of Warsaw on the day in question. Several months later, when the drinking-bout myth had long been exposed as a brazen lie, ten women editors of the magazine had nevertheless to quit their jobs as they were charged with 'liberalism' and 'revisionism'; five of them were Jewish.

In industrial plants and offices mass meetings were staged to carry 'unanimous' resolutions. Israeli 'aggression' was denounced in similar ways and this was accompanied by demands to break off diplomatic relations with Israel and to dismiss 'Zionists' from all responsible posts throughout Poland. Texts of such resolutions had been supplied in advance by the Propaganda Department of the Central Committee or of the Warsaw Committee of the PUWP, although they were sometimes submitted by a local Party Secretary on his own. In the Warsaw car factory Zeran, for example, the Party Secretary Pietrzak, whose brother was commander-in-chief of the police and a close collaborator of General Moczar in the ZBOWID organization, presided over a workers' rally and demanded 'exemplary punishment for Zionists and other enemies of People's Poland'. If the press, radio and television were to be believed, the flood of resolutions and motions passed at such mass rallies was a spontaneous and indignant reaction of the working class against Israel and Zionism.

When diplomatic relations with Israel were indeed broken off, about one hundred demonstrators, mostly secret policemen and Party stalwarts, gathered at the Okecie airport to jeer and molest the departing ambassador, Dov Sattath. A Western diplomat present at the airport helped the ambassador's family to carry their luggage to the aircraft as nobody else was prepared to do so. Even though millions of Poles could see this on their television screens, an official pamphlet on 'Israel's Aggression' published shortly afterwards asserted:

Radio Free Europe, the Israeli press and the Zionist-inspired Western press have published a false report claiming that Israeli diplomats before leaving Warsaw were harassed by numerous inhabitants of Warsaw who supposedly gathered that day at the airport in order to demonstrate their hostility towards Israel.

In June 1967 Gomulka, together with other satellite leaders, was hastily summoned to Moscow for a one-day briefing. The agenda included a common policy towards Israel, but internal anti-Jewish policies may also have been discussed. This was at least partly confirmed by the fact that immediately after his return the Secretary-General convened a meeting of the Secretaries of all the *voivodship* Party committees and instructed them to pursue energetically the fight against 'pro-Israeli' elements and against the 'increased menace of revisionism'.

On 19 June 1967 the Trade Union Congress met in Warsaw; originally it was supposed to deal mainly with economic issues. Gomulka took the opportunity to call the audience's attention to the Israeli problem and to 'the Zionist threat to Poland'. The supreme Party leader then sounded the alarm for an all-out attack against Israel and against the Jews:

In a letter dated 5 June, the day of the Israeli aggression, the Prime Minister of that state, Levi Eshkol, turned to the Prime Minister of our government, comrade Cyrankiewicz. There is no need to repeat here the shameless and cynical contents of this letter, in which Eshkol attempted to justify the Israeli aggression.

And pointing an accusing finger at his Jewish countrymen, Gomulka went on:

> The state authorities treat all citizens of People's Poland equally, regardless of their nationality. Every citizen of our country enjoys equal rights and has to discharge equal duties towards People's Poland. But we cannot remain indifferent towards people who, in face of a threat to world peace, that is to say also to the security of Poland and to the peaceful work of our nation, come out in favour of the aggressor, the wreckers of peace who uphold imperialism. Let those who feel these words are addressed to them, irrespective of their nationality, draw the proper conclusions. A Polish citizen should have but one fatherland – People's Poland. We do not want a Fifth Column in our country.

Even before that speech was delivered slogans already appeared during May Day celebrations in Wroclaw proclaiming 'Down with the Jewish Fifth Column!' In Polish usage, 'Fifth Column' is synonymous with the activities of Nazi agents in pre-war Poland. Gomulka's call for a revival of anti-Semitic passions resolved the quandary into which he had been put. By then he must have been aware that anti-Semitism was the trump card of the Moczarite faction in its drive for power. On the one hand, he would not and could not leave this card to his rival, if only because this diversion to draw popular attention away from economic misery, and the production of scapegoats, were considered the most effective means of retaining power. On the other hand, he had to take into account some of his close collaborators who, although not Jewish, were increasingly accused by Moczar of revisionism and Zionism. Gomulka himself was particularly vulnerable: married to a Jewish wife, he could well fall victim to his own propaganda. He oscillated therefore between threats and half-hearted mental reservations. But whether he intended it or not, the initiative for anti-Semitic activities, after the briefing for the secretaries of the Party *voivodship* committees, ceased to come from Moczar's faction alone, although it was the latter that had started the ball rolling and continued to profit most by it. But now Party committees, no less than the secret police, became centres of the anti-Jewish campaign. The First Secretary of the Warsaw Party Committee, Jozef Kepa, particularly excelled in it. His 'double accounting' – he reported to Gomulka on the one hand, and to Moczar on the other – was no secret in the capital.

The previously sporadic campaign had by this time become well organized and systematic. The Party ordered a general reissue of membership cards accompanied by the verification of the entire membership. This led to the expulsion of many members. Particular attention was paid to 'Zionist and revisionist elements'. Carefully selected commissions composed of Party worthies and secret agents interrogated every Party member in turn about his attitude to Israel, Zionism and revisionism. At that time it often happened that Party members, by no means Jews alone, renounced their cards as a protest against the racist policy. The Central Committee issued a special directive not to recognize voluntary withdrawals from the Party, but instead to expel those who resigned. As a result non-Party people were 'expelled' from the PUWP. This ridiculous procedure helped in doctoring Party statistics: the number of voluntary withdrawals was minimal, while the number of expulsions, because of various deviations, sharply increased – a tangible indication that the verification campaign had indeed been necessary and was successful. The exchange of Party membership cards proceeded therefore without a hitch according to a precisely prescribed ritual.

A few months later the PUWP Central Committee issued another directive, ordering the appointment of special commissions to deal with questions connected with Zionism and revisionism not only in the lower-level Party organizations, but in state institutions and major industrial plants as well. The campaign had thus become institutionalized throughout the country.

The Polish armed forces were also not spared, even though the anti-Jewish purge in the army had been accomplished long before the Six-Day War. But for some time there had been a certain feeling of dissatisfaction within the officer corps with the arms supplied by the USSR and with the principles that the Russians laid down for their tactical deployment. According to some Polish military experts, the Six-Day War had confirmed the unsatisfactory quality of the Soviet intelligence services and of Soviet tactics. Doubts were voiced about the efficacy of Soviet-made weapons. Three senior officers of the Polish air defences, General Czeslaw Mankiewicz, mentioned earlier, his deputy in charge of political affairs, General Tadeusz Dabrowski, and his chief of staff, General Jan Stamieszkin, prepared a memorandum containing a critical assessment of the quality of arms and of some details in the regulations. The fact that conclusions had been drawn from the Six-Day War was considered reason enough to charge the authors with a 'pro-Israeli' attitude: all three were summarily dismissed.

In mid-July 1967 the purge struck the Polish armed forces once more. It was rumoured that it was the Soviet intelligence service which had warned Gomulka, through Soviet ambassador Aristov, about alleged pro-Israeli and anti-Soviet sentiments in the army. According to other sources, Moczar was the instigator. In any case, virtually all the Jews still serving in the armed forces, most of them in auxiliary services or in subordinate positions, had to quit the service. The dismissals were, as a rule, revealed in public, usually at Party meetings where somebody read out the charges from notes previously compiled. Attempts at self-exoneration were immediately denounced as cynicism and hypocrisy, or as philo-Semitism and friendliness towards Zionism. Arguments did not matter in the least: the sole purpose was to get at a certain person and to subject him to a ruthless character assassination. A Jewish major, for example, was accused of having shown a pro-Israeli attitude; the charge was substantiated by the allegation that he had not contradicted some other officers who, while drinking in a restaurant, expressed their joy at the Israeli victory. When he asked why he alone was being singled out for arraignment, although he had not uttered a single word during the party, his accusers replied that he, as a Jew, had had a special moral obligation to protest against pro-Israeli declarations. The major was dismissed.

A malicious smear campaign was directed against the then Minister of National Defence, Marshal Spychalski, an architect by profession, who owed his high post to his wartime service with Gomulka. In any case, many jokes were going the rounds about his military merits and qualifications. Spychalski, a close friend of General Mankiewicz, also found himself in the firing line of Moczar's followers, who were hoping that one of their own men would replace him as commander-in-chief. Spychalski's dark hair and appearance offered an excuse to label him a Semite: to be Jewish was by then once more considered a crime in itself. Spychalski was not in fact Jewish, but it is not easy to refute anonymous charges, and moreover, even without betraying any 'liberal' sympathies one might draw the line at having to defend oneself against a charge of being Jewish. Besides, it should be borne in mind that the clear-cut anti-Semitic campaign was always accompanied by an ideological 'correction', designed to explain that Zionists and Poland's enemies, both inside the country and all over the world, were slandering the People's Republic by trying to accuse it of anti-Semitism. Thanks to such a mixture of faked, deceitful indignation and self-pity, even officials, over-zealous in their fight against the Jews and liberals, could now assume an appearance of philo-Semitism; they were not persecuting Jews *qua* Jews indiscriminately, but, on the contrary, they were fighting against revisionists and Zionists only, that is to say against people for whom no socialist or patriot could entertain friendly feelings. Against such a psychopathic background anyone who, denounced as Jewish, tried too emphatically to deny it, was likely to make an impression of being an anti-Semite himself. In Spychalski's case the rumour was not restricted to the allegation that he was Jewish; he was at the same time accused of maintaining secret contacts with Israel, as well as selling state secrets. His wife was allegedly connected with Dayan, had visited Israel before the outbreak of the Six-Day War and had returned back home on the last scheduled flight before the outbreak of hostilities. Officers were found who publicly demanded the dismissal of 'the Jew' from the supreme military command, and that the ministry and the armed forces be purged of 'alien' elements.

Spychalski lost his post as Minister of National Defence, but did not disappear from the political scene. Presumably it ultimately stood him in good stead that he was actually not Jewish, and that Gomulka continued to support him. But the purge started in June 1967 relieved the armed forces of many hundreds of officers; only a tiny part of the victims were actually Jews, but all had been accused of harbouring philo-Semitic, Zionist, anti-Soviet or liberal sentiments.

A similar smear and purge campaign was going on in the mass media. Meetings were convened in all the editorial offices and Jews compelled to condemn Israel in public. Generally speaking it was enough to raise one's hand when an appropriate resolution was put to the vote; Jews, however, were pressurized to make a personal declaration of their own. Many journalists attempted, under one pretext or another, to avoid attendance at such meetings, but usually to no avail: they were summoned to their local Party committee and then, in front of a specially selected commission, had to deliver the prescribed statement. Those refusing to submit to such a humiliating ordeal were dismissed and expelled from the Party. Virtually all public institutions were supplied with lists of names of Jews employed there – without having asked for them. There is not the slightest doubt that such lists were based upon the card-index compiled well in advance by a section of the Nationalities Department in the Ministry of Internal Affairs, headed by Tadeusz Walichnowski. As usual, a harmless-sounding name was used as camouflage to cover this racist activity, difficult to square with Communist doctrine. In many cases people heard for the first time that they were of Jewish extraction when they found their names on such a list. The war had scattered many families; thousands of Jewish orphans had survived thanks to the protection given to them by Polish families and were subsequently adopted by them, or else were hidden in Roman Catholic convents and brought up as Christians. Children who had forgotten their parents or had never even heard about them were often kept by their adoptive parents in total ignorance of their origin. But Walichnowski's officials, having all the archives at their disposal, screened them with scientific precision equalled only by the Nazi *Sippenforscher* (race researchers).

Walichnowski himself contributed to the anti-Semitic campaign by publishing, in the autumn of 1967, his doctoral thesis on 'Israel and the Federal Republic of Germany'. In the introduction he claimed he had written his book before the Six-Day War, but its outbreak and the course of hostilities were in fact dealt with on pages 139, 206, 210 ff. The book was published in an exceptionally large number of copies, an unprecedented event for a doctoral thesis. In December of that year a second edition appeared on the market. It undoubtedly had the backing of the most influential people, because Polish publishing houses needed, as a rule, at least a year to bring out a second edition. Many valuable manuscripts had to wait for years in publishers' files because paper was always in short supply and reprints were particularly subject to delays. But the political and propaganda purpose of this resolutely promoted book was fully evident from the fact that it had been compiled in a hurry and that many passages were taken almost word for word from a Soviet work by K. Ivanov and Z. Sheynis, *The State of Israel*, which had been in any case accessible in a Polish translation since at least 1960. Walichnowski's 'doctoral thesis' nevertheless received exceptionally favourable reviews, was recommended by education authorities for school libraries and prescribed at Party meetings as obligatory reading. For a better understanding of the many seemingly unbelievable accusations against Polish Jews, some lengthy quotations from this book are necessary. The fact that many thousands of people more or less blindly accepted such arguments shows the high degree of success achieved by propaganda in a totalitarian state. Obsessive repetition of the same basic theme in thousands of variations in the mass media, coupled with the virtually total exclusion of the public from other sources of information, cannot in the long run remain without effect. This observation is made to prepare the reader, before acquainting him with a book containing allegations so absurd that informed people would immediately see through the transparent falsification. Walichnowski's main claim concerned an alleged conspiracy between Zionism and revanchist circles in the Federal Republic of Germany:

The Federal Republic, burdened with the Nazi crimes, would have been unable to play such a prominent role in NATO and in the anti-Communist European policy of the USA, were it not for its full rehabilitation by Israel and by international Zionist organizations. In return for money received [from Bonn] leading Israeli statesmen and Zionists all over the world have endeavoured to acquit the Federal Republic of Germany of its guilt for Nazi crimes. In this way ... the influence of West German revanchist forces has increased in Europe ... their main target being Poland and the other Warsaw Pact countries. The smear campaign against the Polish nation was unleashed by Israel and by Zionist circles at the same time that their rescue operation on behalf of the Federal Republic of Germany was intensified.

Up to the time of the signature of the East European agreements by the Brandt government, the Federal Republic of Germany was treated by Polish propaganda as the direct heir and successor of the Nazi régime. Adenauer, in particular, was slandered as the leading revanchist, imperialist and Poland's arch-enemy. In his book Walichnowski added to all the usual accusations the charge that Adenauer had become Israel's best friend because of his hostility towards socialist Poland. The informed reader in the West might well deride such allegations. But the Polish reader, subjected daily to this kind of propaganda, cannot in the long run retain the conviction that all the information provided by the mass media is totally false or distorted. There is, they say, no smoke without fire. That is true in particular where youth is concerned. Even the most abstruse argument leaves some trace in the reader's mind. Walichnowski's express intention was to impose upon his readers the prejudicial conviction that there was no fundamental difference between Hitler and Adenauer. Adenauer, the argument ran, dreamt of regaining Poland's western territories, and when Adenauer's Germany agreed to pay reparations to the State of Israel, this, too, was alleged to serve some devilish anti-Polish purpose. In consequence, Israel and the Zionists were said to have turned into an instrument of German revanchist plans:

The payment of reparations to Jewish victims of Nazism and the establishment of friendly contacts with Israel inaugurated the process of rehabilitation of the Federal Republic of Germany. The reparations have been mutually beneficial to the Federal Republic and Israel: Israel has acquired enormous financial gains, the Federal Republic incalculable moral ones. As far as the supply of war material to the Israeli government is concerned, the Federal Republic of Germany has played alongside the USA a steadily increasing role. At the time when preparations for the Suez war were going ahead, the Federal Republic of Germany already took a prominent part in supplying its partner with major strategic weapons, as well as in training Israeli officers. According to reports published by the daily Die Welt, West German military academies trained at the time some fifty Israeli officers.

Walichnowski attributed to the Federal Republic a considerable role in the build-up of the Israeli Army, and claimed that Israel was to give evidence of its gratitude inter alia by playing down the impact made by the Eichmann trial:

An important subject of their [Adenauer's and Ben Gurion's] meeting concerned Eichmann's case. Adenauer asked for Ben Gurion's promise that the Federal Republic would not be blamed at Eichmann's trial. At this very meeting Adenauer undertook the obligation to supply Israel with arms ... to the total value of DM 320 million. Until 1964 the Federal Republic supplied Israel with war material worth DM 200 million, including 200 tanks, five torpedo boats, as well as a number of combat planes, armoured vehicles, munitions, and various other most sophisticated weapons.

Only one Polish newspaper, the serious weekly *Polityka*[8], dared to express doubts concerning the obvious disparity between the weapons supplied and their alleged value.

In the concluding chapters of his book Walichnowski attempted to convince his readers that Jews and West Germans had co-operated in vilifying Poland:

Jewish nationalism which has reached its peak in Israel, fomented by the Zionist world movement in conjunction with the ever-growing German nationalism in the Federal Republic, has provided the breeding ground for wars and lawlessness. Nazi methods applied against the Arab population were simply appalling, but they received the moral and political support of former Nazi executioners enjoying impunity in the Federal Republic of Germany. The common aim of Israel and the Federal Republic, within the imperialist concept of the USA, has been to activate hotbeds of war, unite all forces hostile to peace and trample upon all the humanitarian achievements of modern civilization. One of the darkest spots in the Zionist movement has been the arch-reactionary role, contrary to the true interests of the Jewish masses, played by Zionist leaders in connection with the moral rehabilitation of the Federal Republic of Germany. In all the countries where Nazi rule had brought so much destruction, deep distrust of those elements which had taken power in the Federal Republic of Germany persisted for a long time after the Second World War. This distrust made German rearmament by the imperialist forces more difficult, and barred the way for the Federal Republic to emerge as a fully-fledged partner on the international scene. It is in these circumstances that the Zionists hastened to come to the assistance of the Federal Republic of Germany. In the press, radio and television ... Poles were presented as accomplices of Nazi Germany in the extermination of Jews. At the same time Germans were whitewashed, their crimes passed over in silence, the systematic character of these crimes and the mass participation of the Third Reich's

---

[8] *Polityka*, founded in 1957 as a Party press organ to counteract 'revisionist' tendencies, aimed at a reading public drawn mainly from the intelligentsia and the managerial classes; it tried therefore to avoid oversimplification and the crass vulgarity associated with most other Party newspapers. In consequence – and thanks to its editors and contributors of above-average intelligence and moral courage – it developed into Poland's most respected and serious periodical, usually quoted abroad as an authoritative mouthpiece of top Party and government opinion. Viciously attacked and slandered by the Moczarites as a hotbed of 'revisionism', *Polityka* managed nevertheless to steer the middle course and to avoid committing itself to the most distasteful anti-Semitic and anti-intellectual outbursts. It still tries to maintain its slightly tarnished 'liberalist' image, though it cannot in fact avoid giving its wholehearted support to the rulers and even their most unpopular measures. And yet it serves as a safety-valve of sorts.

population in the so-called Final Solution of the Jewish question overlooked. The purpose of the Zionist campaign has been to divert the attention of world public opinion away from the crimes committed by the Nazis, in order to make the Polish nation partly responsible for them.

In another passage the author wrote:

Anti-Communism and hatred for the Polish nation, the activities of pressure groups, and class interests – all this was interconnected in the campaign for the rehabilitation of the Federal Republic of Germany, to the detriment of world peace. Both the German revanchists, who would like to recover the 1937 and the 1914 frontiers, and the extreme right-wing Zionist groups influenced public opinion in the West in its attitude to Poland and the Poles. Both the former and the latter attempted to produce in the West an image of a barbarian Poland. The Federal Republic tied the interests of the Israeli government to its own interests. The power of Israel and of Zionism, skilfully exploited by the Bonn leaders, is a menace to world peace. The Second World War decimated and discredited the German 'Fifth Column'. The Federal Republic of Germany, linked with Israel by ties of anti-Communism, now pins its hopes on Zionism, as a dynamic, well-organized force.

However, the Third Reich and the Federal Republic were not the only subjects in Walichnowski's thesis for his doctorate:

In 1799 the wealthy Jewish aristocracy appealed to the Jewish people to support Napoleon's campaign against Syria and Egypt. Rabbi Aron Ben Levi ... called Napoleon a providential man. In the age of imperialism contacts between Zionists and the ruling classes of colonial powers became even closer.... In 1907, at the Eighth Zionist Congress, Zionist leaders swore allegiance to Abdul Hamid and expressed their feelings of respect for the Ottoman ruler. Herzl conferred with Kaiser Wilhelm II. He told him that Jewish settlements in Palestine would provide the best protection for German interests in that country, if only the Germans would support the Zionist plans.... In the summer of 1903 Herzl paid a visit in Petersburg to the Tsarist minister of internal affairs, Plehve. The minister was said to have assured him that 'the Tsarist government would be prepared to support Zionism and to use its influence in Constantinople if the Zionists' aim was the emigration of Jews from Russia'.

The reader was obviously supposed to infer that wherever imperialism and reaction were at work 'the Zionists' were involved. The fact that the French revolution brought emancipation to the Jews in France, that the Napoleonic Code introduced civil liberties and rights, and that for some time the Emperor was supported by progressive forces throughout Europe (and with particular enthusiasm by the Poles, who took part in

most of his campaigns) did not fit into the author's picture, and was therefore omitted.

When Walichnowski's book appeared, the first contacts between the
Federal Republic of Germany and Poland had already been established:
negotiations were under way concerning industrial co-production in
which, among others, Berthold Beitz, as general manager of the Krupp
concern, took part. This modest *rapprochement* between the two
countries was strongly opposed both by Ulbricht and by the neo-Stalinist
faction inside the Soviet leadership. At this juncture it should be
remembered that Moczar's faction, as well as Piasecki's Pax movement,
used their propaganda campaign against the Federal Republic in order
to defeat any attempts at *rapprochement*.

On 25 November 1967 the Central Committee of the PUWP met at
its tenth plenary session to discuss food shortages. Meat and meat products, butter and many other consumer goods were scarce, long queues
formed in front of the shops, housewives often had to start queuing in
the early hours of the morning in order to be served when the shops
opened. The Party's Central Committee reacted with a drastic rise in
prices: pork and veal, for example, went up by almost 25 per cent, some
varieties by as much as 45 per cent, poultry by 10 per cent, television
sets by 15 per cent, fish by an average of 9 per cent, coal by over 14 per
cent. These increases, on top of the massive price rises in the previous
year, provoked general dissatisfaction. It was, moreover, noted with ris-
ing anger that many price increases had been introduced surreptitiously,
without any previous public announcement. The public particularly
resented the new meat prices and the secret price rises of exercise books
and school textbooks, as these hit hardest at the most impoverished
groups of the population.

In order to counteract this resentment official propaganda simply
resorted to falsification of statistical data: it was claimed and 'proved'
by faked figures that meat consumption was steadily going up, and this
was used in turn to counterattack a population alleged to be indulging
hopes of immoderate consumption.

For fear of popular reaction, the authorities, two days before the price
increases were announced, proclaimed a virtual state of emergency
throughout the Party apparatus, police and security organs, as well as
in major industrial plants. In Party committee buildings special groups
were put on a twenty-four hour alert. Industrial plants submitted frequent
and regular reports on the workers' mood. Streets were guarded by ostentatiously strengthened police patrols. The population, however, maintained a sinister silence: there was no indication of demonstrations or
strikes.

At the end of 1967 an economic conference was convened in the building of the Council of Ministers, attended by heads of economic ministries, directors of industrial associations, managers of major plants, as well as senior Party and trade union officials. The debate, in which Prime Minister Cyrankiewicz, Party Secretary in charge of economic policy Boleslaw Jaszczuk and Deputy Prime Minister Franciszek Waniolka took part, was broadcast live by radio and television, and reported at length in the press. It was a massive attack on the working class, blamed chiefly for a steady decline in labour discipline. The speakers charged the national health service with providing too many exemptions from work. Workers were blamed for not making full use of normal working hours in order to get more overtime.

At the turn of 1967–8 censorship was tightened up in all domains of cultural and political life. News of internal and foreign policy was reduced to a bare minimum, as its obvious contradiction of the known facts became more and more flagrant. As a consequence there was even more interest in foreign radio broadcasts in Polish. The suppression of films, books and newspaper articles became as frequent as administrative orders banning cultural events. The situation became explosive when the Warsaw National Theatre included in its repertoire the great Polish national tragedy *Dziady – The Forefathers –* by Adam Mickiewicz, produced by its director, Kazimierz Dejmek. The play, considered the most important work of Polish early nineteenth-century romanticism, is a passionate call for liberty and independence, an appeal for resistance against Tsarist oppression. On 30 January 1968, after its thirteenth performance, the play was taken off the stage. This unprecedented ban had a shattering effect all over the country.

7. The March Events

I can well imagine you are expecting from me news on the Mickiewicz crisis. They say that November is 'the month of the Poles'. It starts with All-Saints' Day. In Warsaw it began in the National Theatre with Mickiewicz's *Forefathers*. It was the season's highlight, and Dejmek, undoubtedly a great director, confirmed his outstanding talent with this production. All over the world it is the public which determines how long a play runs – it is taken off when there is no more audience; as long as the house stays full, the play continues to runs. Here for every performance the public literally charged the box-office. When all seats were sold out, young people sat on the floor. No Polish theatre has ever had a success like this. But how did the theatre management react? Instead of nightly performances at first, it started to stage it once a week only. And finally the authorities took the play out of the repertoire. The last performance on 30 January turned into a big demonstration. From all over Poland directors and actors arrived to see Dejmek's *Forefathers* for themselves. Students laid a wreath at Mickiewicz's monument. The police forced their way into the theatre and arrested 35 students; eight of them were sentenced next morning in summary proceedings for 'rowdyism' and ordered to pay fines, totalling 15,000 zlotys. During a spontaneously organized collection for the benefit of the defendants, people were so eager to contribute that much more money was collected than the sum total of the fines imposed.

This passage from a letter written by a Pole to a fellow-countryman living in the West sheds some light on the importance attached to the performances and to the play itself, which, by the way, had been produced before in various cities and at various times – even in the worst period of Stalinist oppression – all over People's Poland without any obstacles from the authorities. After all, the Communists themselves in the early stages of their movement, and primarily Lenin himself, castigated the Tsarist oppression in no uncertain terms. Why then precisely in early 1968 could the play not be produced? The answer is to be found in the mysterious story of the ban. During the first performances the audience's reaction to passages referring to Tsarist despotism, to police methods, and to the dull-witted bureaucratic apparatus of Tsarist rule was particularly brisk and lively, and as these passages could be construed as hints and allusions to the then prevailing situation, the security authorities might well have decided to seize the opportunity and use provocation in order to bring the situation, which was in any case very tense, to boiling point. This by itself was nothing new. *Agents-provocateurs* had often been used by the Tsarist *Okhrana* (secret police) – for example the massacre of a workers' procession led by an Orthodox priest to the Tsar's Winter Palace in St Petersburg in January 1905. The same method was brought to perfection by Stalin's Cheka, GPU, NKVD and finally KGB.

In the case of *The Forefathers* there is, admittedly, no evidence of deliberate provocation on the part of the police or the Moczarite faction. But there are indications clearly pointing that way. The people at the box-office of the National Theatre could not help noticing that police officials booked an unusually large number of seats, particularly for the later performances, and that the uproarious applause which burst out whenever any utterance on the stage could be interpreted as having anti-Russian overtones came mostly from clearly identifiable groups in the audience. Weeks before the ban came into force it had been generally known that the performance on 30 January 1968 would be the last. That in itself was untypical of Polish censorship. As a rule a play was proscribed by the authorities before the first night; or a ban would be imposed immediately in the case of a play or – as used to happen more frequently – cabaret piece taken off after only a few performances. In this instance, however, for the first time the press announced in advance the banning of a play which was nevertheless to be performed twice more in as many weeks. Such an unusual censorship measure could only make sense if the police were interested in provoking a demonstration.

In these circumstances the last performance was bound to turn into a spectacular event. Vladyslav Bienkowski described the emotive attitude of the audience:

The authorities considered the behaviour of the audience as a *casus belli*, an attack against the interests of the state. The news of the order restricting the number of performances spread all over the town like wildfire. When the definite ban on the play was finally announced, the performance scheduled to be the last ended in a demonstration inside the theatre and at the nearby Mickiewicz monument. Although this had a rather symbolic character, the security 'organs' immediately went into action. As the small group of youthful theatre-goers started to disperse, they were seized in the street, interrogated, and some of them had heavy fines imposed on them by police magistrates. Anybody looking for a way to activate a rather passive and disintegrated student community could hardly find more effective means.

The provocation seems to have been planned to the smallest detail. For weeks preceding what was to be the last performance everybody in Warsaw, whether he wanted to know it or not, was told that there would be a demonstration at the entrance to the National Theatre. No wonder then that on the evening police vehicles appeared in force. As the performance drew to its end, and a small group of students started to protest against the ban, the police with unusual toughness went after some students, obviously singled out in advance, most of them Jewish. In flagrant violation of all the rules then in force, they were subsequently suspended from the university – an action which was bound to provoke the student community to resistance.

One other sign pointing to a provocation could have been the widespread rumour that the Soviet Embassy had been directly responsible for the censorship ban. Had such gossip given rise to anti-Soviet demonstrations by students or in literary circles, this would have provided an additional excuse for severe police measures. The rumour, however, was emphatically denied by counsellor Panfilov of the Soviet Embassy, who told the president of the Polish Writers' Union, Jaroslaw Iwaszkiewicz, that the Embassy had taken no part in the affair of *The Forefathers*, Panfilov himself having been painfully shocked by the ban. But the meticulously planned operation, presumably initiated by Moczar's faction, proved fully successful. On the day after the eight students had been fined, signatures were already being collected at several Warsaw institutions of higher learning for the following message to be addressed to the *Sejm* (Polish Parliament):

We, the student youth of Warsaw, protest against the decision banning the production of *Forefathers* by Adam Mickiewicz in the National Theatre. We protest against the policy of dissociation from the progressive traditions of the Polish nation.

The collection of signatures was hampered by all possible means: functionaries of the Security Office unlawfully entered Warsaw University campus and arrested three students. Plain-clothes policemen helped militants of the youth organizations, ZMS (Union of Socialist Youth) and ZSP (Union of Polish Students), to seize by force some lists of signatures. On 2 February the police started to summon students to the Mostowski Palace – the Warsaw police headquarters – and to interrogate them about the demonstration and the protest addressed to the *Sejm*. Next day a deputation of students appealed to the deputy rector of Warsaw University, Bazylow, to protect their colleagues, who had been sentenced to pay fines. He replied that he was unable to intervene as he had not been officially informed of the fines.

The collection of signatures continued on the following days despite the obstacles: student resentment was still growing. On 5 February, for example, a student fined for his part in the demonstration was deprived of his grant although he came from an extremely poor family. On 8 February eight students sentenced by police magistrates were summoned to appear before the University disciplinary committee. On 10 February the prosecutor arraigned a girl student, roughed up by plain-clothes police officials during the demonstration, and charged her with having beaten up and insulted police functionaries on duty.

On 16 February students submitted to the Marshal (Speaker) of the *Sejm* seventy-five lists with 3,145 signatures. In fact, many more students had signed the petition but the police and accomplices from the Party apparatus had seized many lists. At the same time the Union of Socialist Youth issued a communiqué admitting that a small group had managed to collect a certain number of signatures; this was attributed to the naïvety of some students whose action had been of a nationalist and anti-Russian character. To counteract this accusation, students of Warsaw University issued a leaflet setting forth the deeper causes of their demonstration and inviting the ZMS functionaries to discuss their point of view with the student body. A few days later, between 21 and 24 February, police officials distributed a leaflet with the following text, where all the names were those of students of Jewish origin:

Students,

Not for the first time the 'Commandos' [a nickname given to a group of dissident students] have attempted to disturb our peace. Michnik, Blumsztajn, Szlajfer, and company, try to incite disorder in our midst, to discredit the good name of the student community with the public. Making use of hypocritical and deceitful demagogy, they claim to represent the opinion of the whole student community. In fact, they represent the interests of their principals – the Zionists and Radio Free Europe. Let us not be deceived by them!

Michnik, Blumsztajn and Szlajfer cannot and will not teach us the patriotic traditions of our nation. That is duplicity and perfidy. They want to create confusion, uproar and seek recognition by Radio Free Europe. We will not allow riff-raff to run the show at our University!

We appeal to the University authorities . . . to free us from the 'Commandos'.

Those who do not traffic in their patriotism
but are proud of it:
STUDENTS OF WARSAW UNIVERSITY

The infuriated students replied forthwith:

With the obvious aim of counteracting the protests of the students against the banning of the *Forefathers*, the traditional weapons of the reactionaries have been used: anti-Semitism and provocation. A significant fascist leaflet has appeared at the University. . . . Its authors apparently do not like protests against the authorities' actions.... Their purpose is **provocation**. Will they not try to exploit the justified resentment against fascist excesses in order to introduce a **state of emergency** at the University?

The names of Michnik, Blumsztajn and Szlajfer became synonymous with students of Jewish origin against whom a campaign was conducted with a ferocity difficult to imagine. Throughout Warsaw University campus a leaflet 'poem' was circulated in great numbers, which freely translated reads 'the Poles, stupid as always, are dazzled by the Jews', and advised them to 'grasp the Jew by his side-locks and throw him in the sea'.

The students reacted once more, this time with two separate leaflets:

FASCISM SHALL NOT PASS!

The security apparatus openly reaches out for power in the country. Its weapons are police terror, brutal provocation, strong-arm squads, lies, anti-Semitism, intimidation of the population. The moral resentment of the students' movement, provoked ... by acts of lawlessness and police terror, is presented as evidence of the alleged existence of strong reactionary forces in Poland. In order to divert popular attention from the existing troubles and their real sources, anti-Semitism is being used. The present system of government, free from any supervision by society, allows scoundrels of all sorts to feather their own nests at the expense of the people. The proof of this is corruption in the administration.

Everything shows that the people now reaching out for power are acting according to fascist principles. Repression at the universities, the pointless, rabid propaganda campaign in scientific and literary circles, show the direction of future development. We still have the possibility of resisting, although it is steadily diminishing. Without recommending any specific forms of action, we appeal to your political awareness and to your moral responsibility.

Fascism shall not pass!

There can be no return to Stalinism!

(Read this. Copy this. Pass it round for copying.)

THERE IS NO BREAD WITHOUT FREEDOM!

The fight for freedom means a fight for cuts in the excessively swollen apparatus of administration and control. The authorities unremittingly investigate how their orders are carried out.... Centralism claims to plan for decades ahead, but in fact delights in the petty-minded supervision of trifles. It ignores the people, and won't trust them. The fight for freedom means a fight for conditions which will allow all citizens to work creatively. The fight for freedom means a fight for an open economic policy, for submitting development guidelines, the state budget, and major economic decisions to the critical assessment of the people, which is now only informed of guidelines already determined and subject to no criticism. We hear about economic decisions when it is too late to change anything, we are provided with incomplete, even false, data. They go through the filter of censorship to make us believe that everything is all right. Official pronouncements make mention of errors and shortcomings. We would like to know what are the errors and who is responsible for them.

The fight for freedom means a fight for the protection of workers' interests. At present, bodies formally claiming to represent the workers are totally dependent on decisions taken by the employers. The fight for freedom is a fight for independent trade unions, for workers' self-management, for the guaranteed right of employees to make their protest. The fight for freedom means a fight for the personal responsibility of the decision-makers. We have the right to know who are the authors of guidelines and orders, to whom we owe gratitude for our achievements, and who is responsible for the errors and absurdities we see everywhere.

There can be no economic development when those who manage our enterprises keep their jobs virtually for life, when they become so accustomed to tried and familiar methods that they are reluctant to consider improvements. An apparatus which runs for too long without necessary modifications must become fossilized. The fight for freedom means a fight for bread. When the nation is unable to safeguard its right to participate in the economic life of the country, when methods of administration remain unchanged, when no new people are drawn into the decision-making process, we reach the brink of an economic crisis. Such changes, however, can only be part of a general renewal process, they can only originate with free people, the true masters of their socialist state. And therefore there is no bread without freedom!

It seems worth while to quote a rather lengthy passage from a comprehensive document circulated a couple of weeks later, at the height of the student riots, because in that document the student leaders supported their arguments concerning the economic situation with statistical evidence:

FASCISM SHALL NOT PASS!

THERE IS NO RETURN TO STALINISM!

THE WORKERS ARE WITH US!

LONG LIVE DEMOCRACY!

LONG LIVE SOCIALISM! LONG LIVE POLAND!

The March events on the streets of our capital and of other cities force us to ask what is behind all this. The press, radio and television, duly instructed, try to convince people that it all concerns rowdies, Zionists, or simply 'banana-children' from well-to-do families, free of any cares or duties. But we know that thousands of students treat their tasks at the universities seriously. There were, indeed, thousands of us, and thousands are still ready to continue the fight, although the alleged ringleaders, rowdies, and Zionists were imprisoned at the very beginning of our movement. Our movement could not have spread all over the country and included so many students, had it represented only what some political bankrupts had contrived.

What, then is it all about? It is not a question of taking this or that play off the stage or dismissing this or that professor; these are but symptoms of more profound causes. We would like to point to two such causes: the *growing economic crisis* and the crisis of certain *socio-economic* forms.

This essay is not a scholarly analysis. It consists rather of a set of examples illustrating the generally accepted assessment of the current situation in our country. We have no time for anything else; it is imperative that the people should find out as soon as possible what the situation really is.

Professor Kalecki has calculated that in 1960 the real income of a worker employed in a similar capacity as before the war was about 45 per cent higher than in 1937. Three-quarters of this increase was achieved in 1956–9, the years of the greatest successes of the working class.

In 1959–67 the price increases, both those publicly announced and those kept hidden, were the reason why workers' incomes increased only minimally. During the subsequent seven years the workers' income rose by 404 zlotys, but in 1959 the first price increases (meat) were introduced, followed in 1963 by increases in the price of gas, coal, electricity, etc., and in 1967 there was another 'adjustment in meat prices'. Meanwhile fish, cigarettes, and public transport also became more expensive. The rise in workers' wages was thus to a considerable degree neutralized by higher prices.

The difference between engineers' and technicians' incomes and workers' wages grew yearly. Why did this happen? Just because in this paradoxical system an honest job of work can only bring increased work quotas, but no higher income. All those doing piece-work know that there is no point in fulfilling, say, 200 per cent of the work quota, because in such a case the quota would after a while be raised, and it would become more difficult regularly to fulfil the new norms. Bungling is therefore more profitable, especially when it can be done during working hours, with materials and tools belonging to the factory. Industrial management, too, looks for loopholes: it will not reveal its reserves because it is easier to fulfil a more modest plan, or else only special types of goods are produced, regardless of whether anybody needs them or not.

All these are urgent problems, demanding a solution. And yet the Party leadership will not allow any economic debate, to say nothing of meeting the workers' demands. Economic decisions are made arbitrarily, without taking workers' interests into account, without asking what people think about them.

It is absurd when Polish economists prepare a five-year plan for India, but have nothing to say about their own country.

The fundamental question to be asked when assessing the nature of a social system is: *Who is the owner of the means of production?* Lawyers argue on what is property: the answers are manifold. But one can assume that the owner of a property is the man who has the right to use it and to decide its use. Who in our country is the owner of the means of production?

The real owner of the whole economy is the central Party bureaucracy. This apparatus is the collective owner, the capitalist who determines what part of the social product is set aside for workers' wages, for paying technical management, for investment, etc. In recent years, like a red thread through all the speeches of our leaders runs the statement: Our state is paying too much, it is unprofitable. To make it profitable 'price adjustments' are necessary. We ask: Where does the state find the money to subsidize prices? If our people is really the owner of its products, and the state is simply a representative of our people in its relations with other nations, then the ever-recurring refrain about 'subsidizing' is based on an absurd proposition: the people subsidizes itself.

The essay was not confined to politico-economic arguments only. In another passage its authors take the bureaucracy severely to task:

A well-equipped and most efficient police organization has been established. We have a virtual army of Party officials, more often than not mere careerists and moral nonentities. Under our eyes entire new social hierarchies emerge, from the 'infallible ones' at the top down to the workers and peasants at the bottom. When the country's economic situation reaches a critical point and an explosion becomes imminent, some enemy is invented (a method used, by the way, by the ruling party in pre-war Poland against the Moscow-financed Communists). Now such an enemy is West German revisionism. It would be foolish to ignore the revanchist sentiments in the Federal Republic of Germany. We should never under-estimate this danger. But it is interesting to note that our authorities remind us of this menace just at the moment of particular internal tension ... no doubt in order to divert popular attention from internal problems. The party élite itself is torn asunder by internal differences. Various factions within the Central Committee are engaged in a struggle for power.

Naturally enough, the banning of *The Forefathers* did not only provoke unrest and protests among students but also provided the police with an excuse for interference. Warsaw literary circles, too, gave vent to their resentment. In order to protest against the steadily growing censorship, the Warsaw branch of the Polish Writers' Union convened a special meeting on 29 February 1968. The unusually tense atmosphere was reflected in a speech delivered by the well-known philosopher, Professor Leszek Kolakowski:

It is not a question of *The Forefathers* only. The assessment of Dejmek's production is irrelevant to our discussion.... What is relevant is the fact that the political authorities, abusing their power, have usurped the right not only to prescribe rules for the correct interpretation and production, but to condemn other interpretations. We cannot but consider it a return to Zhdanov's era.... I would like to repeat – and we will have to repeat, again and again, even the most commonplace truths – that cultural life requires freedom, and that there must also be freedom for reflection on culture, on its possibilities, and its values.

Here, however, even such reflection is impossible, because every discussion inevitably leads to the principles which are fenced off with fortress-walls of prohibitions. The control by the administration of culture creates a vicious circle from which there seems to be no escape. The chasm separating cultural life from state power will inevitably become deeper, more and more energy will be wasted on sterile movement to and fro, all domains of spiritual life will suffer ever greater harm.

The administrative suppression of pent-up protests, resentment, and disillusionment ... can only lead to more and more protests. We see here a classical example of feedback: measures calculated to prevent a manifestation of resistance (no one bothers about its real causes) create a situation in which an ever greater number of such measures of pressure becomes necessary; it is an unending process....

To our disgrace, we have reached a point where the entire world theatre, from Aeschylus through Shakespeare to Brecht and Ionesco, can be regarded as an anthology of hints and innuendoes against People's Poland. The theatres are unavoidably helpless, because whenever one turns to elementary values, everything becomes suspect. We shall yet live to see the day when our light comedies become dangerous, subversive stuff. Let us recall how low the Polish film industry has sunk, what a terrible state our press has reached, the extent of restriction and harassment by which Polish scholarship is shackled. Let us recall the pitiful poverty of our debates, when nobody is allowed to say what is really at stake because everything runs into a brick wall.

Every critical voice is answered with threats, judgements are pronounced equating criticism with what is forbidden. Criticism meets with prejudice: it is considered anti-socialist and consequently aimed at the restoration of capitalism. That, however, is nothing but blackmail. If we accept that socialism can exist only when criticism is suppressed, we have also to accept that socialism is a utopia. I, nevertheless, believe some form of socialism is possible, provided it overcomes the intolerable and destructive circumstances in which the authorities consider cultural creative activity and reflexion on it as a threat which must be suppressed by the use of violence. We want to remove these circumstances in the name of socialism, not against it.

During the meeting strong-arm squads were brought by lorries and deployed at the building entrance; they claimed to be a workers' deputation and tried to get into the building. The entrance gate, however, was locked, and some younger writers stood guard.

The atmosphere at the meeting was heated. During the debate on an agreed resolution, two different groups emerged: on the one side unknown writers ready to compensate for their lack of talent with blind obedience to the prevailing Party line; on the other an overwhelming majority, including all those who enjoyed literary and moral prestige in Poland. Among the spokesmen of this latter group were Jerzy Andrzejewski, Antoni Slonimski, January Grzedzinski – immediately after the meeting an unsuccessful attempt was made to put him in a psychiatric ward – Mieczyslaw Jastrun, Leszek Kolakowski, Stefan Kisielewski, and many others. Pawel Jasienica, a well-known historian and writer, said:

The subject of our meeting is the banning of the production of *The Forefathers*. Director Balicki [representative of the Ministry of Culture and Arts], presenting the point of view of the Minister and of the Party, claimed that it was banned because of the demonstrations and – in his opinion – provocative applause by the audience, in particular by the young people. I would assert the contrary was true. During the 30 January performance of *The Forefathers* a spontaneous ovation broke out in the audience just because it was generally known beforehand that it was to be the last performance. Only afterwards, outside the theatre, did students produce a banner with the slogan 'We demand more performances of *The Forefathers!*' Was this a demand hostile to the state? Could it destroy a strong socialist régime? Of what other punishable behaviour were the young people guilty? Is it that they paid their respects to the poet at this monument?... All this was considered such a dangerous action that the police were used against boys and girls. Many were arrested, some were summarily sentenced, others are threatened with trial. We must voice from this place our most determined protest against this.

In order to insult these young people, leaflets of a disgusting anti-Semitic nature were scattered at the University campus, some even delivered at private homes. The instigators of this shameful essay attempted to slander our academic youth by insinuating that it was anti-Semitic. Who is naïve enough to believe this? The Council of the University's Department of Philosophy ascertained that the leaflets had not been produced by students; they had been brought in from outside for provocative purposes.

Colleagues, somebody would like to besmirch our nation, imputing to it anti-Semitism. Already in Voltaire's time, when our religious intolerance was denounced, lack of tolerance brought Poland great harm. I, as a historian, know it well. Nothing can do us more harm all over the world than the conviction that we are a nation of anti-Semites.

Then Jasienica read out the rhymed leaflet, quoted on page 101. He was interrupted by Jerzy Putrament, who emphatically claimed that the Party fought against anti-Semitism, which provoked exclamations of 'Where?!', 'It's a lie!', and an uproar. Jasienica's speech was unique not because he protested against the banning of Mickiewicz's tragedy and against the muzzling of Polish culture – dozens of others did the same – but because he expressly warned against anti-Semitism. Then Jerzy Andrzejewski took the floor:

No words can do justice to the whole scale of protests against the steadily growing sapping and destruction of Polish culture. The many optimistic phrases we heard last year at the Congress of Culture cannot obscure the sad reality. What the people are thinking and saying is distorted with contempt; every initiative designed to analyse our social life is rejected, every creative work boldly dealing with our wounds is banned or perverted. The present is given the lie, the past is falsified. We find ourselves in such a position that Polish writers should sound the alarm with all the might and determination we are capable of, because the very existence of Polish culture is now in danger.

It is high time for the rulers to cease to treat criticism, protests, and demonstrations, especially the demonstrations of young people, as hostile acts. I have not spoken in public for many years now; today, however, I must declare with all the sense of responsibility I am capable of, that contrary to official reports there are more and more frequent occurrences in Poland which constitute a violation of the fundamental political, social, and moral rights of man. It is not easy for me to make such a grave accusation, but I am convinced it is my duty to do so here and now, as I have no other opportunity to raise my voice in public.

Vengeance came swiftly. Some thirty authors were banned from publication, a detailed list being immediately sent to all editorial offices and publishing houses. Stefan Kisielewski, one of the courageous speakers at the writers' meeting, was attacked at night in the street and beaten up by 'unknown' individuals. Pawel Jasienica was unable to endure discrimination and isolation: after a prolonged illness he died in August 1970. Jerzy Andrzejewski spoke at his grave, and after recalling who Jasienica was, just hinted at what had happened to him:

In our graveyards rest more and more people who were once the pride of Polish contemporary literature. The last few months have claimed Anna

Kowalska, Jerzy Zawieyski, Tadeusz Breza; and outside Poland – Kazimierz Wierzynski, Witold Gombrowicz, Marek Hlasko. Today is another day of mourning for Polish literature which here, in the country of Kochanowski, Mickiewicz, and Zeromski, holds its breath, frozen into silence. We have long known the bitter truth that Polish graveyards are overcrowded; the burden of death has been increased by the burdens on the living. This funeral which we are attending today brings us special sorrow, because we are laying to rest for ever Pawel Jasienica, whose life was shaped according to his own criteria, whose life was determined by the conditions of life of his people: by fighting, glory, iniquity and humiliation.

In the most difficult period during the last war, when one had to fight, take up arms, Pawel Jasienica was a soldier, here, in our country, in the heroic Home Army. When the time came to shape new forms of life, he contributed in full with his writing and his conscience. He was one of the most outstanding and most widely read writers of the two post-war decades. He reconstructed the past, but always lived in the present. He supported with his name and his moral authority all the measures which served the well-being of the Polish Republic. As the author of major historical works he realized that freedom of thought and tolerance belong to the best traditions of the Polish nation; that culture withers, public life degenerates, priceless human values are wasted whenever freedom of expression is brutally restricted, no debate allowed, and sinister forces of deceit and concealment presume to interpret and to pass judgement on the manifold reality. Here, at his grave, it must be said that Pawel Jasienica paid a high price for his convictions and for his courage to express them. Accused of deeds he had never committed, slandered, insulted, humiliated in public, without any opportunity to defend himself, he was deprived of the right to publish his writings; his books were removed from libraries, new ones could not appear. It was hardly conceivable after all the tragic experiences of totalitarian rule, but all too true nonetheless: an eminent Polish writer, a creator of great cultural values, enjoying the confidence and respect of many thousands of readers, was banned overnight from public life and at the height of his creative powers sentenced to silence.

As a historian, Jasienica researched primarily into Polish history. His spell-binding narrative skill, his uncompromising art in overthrowing national idols and substituting for them humanist values drawn from the nation's history, brought him unusual success among the Polish reading public. But even more than a popular and best-selling author, he was a moral authority: one of those whom Poles call 'the nation's conscience'. Whenever intellectuals protested against oppression, Pawel Jasienica was among them.

After his speech at the writers' meeting on 29 February 1968 he was never again given the opportunity to appear in public, not even when Vladyslav Gomulka publicly accused him of common crimes, without of course quoting a single piece of evidence in support. Gomulka blamed him and other writers for having instigated the students' riots. But he made incomparably more serious charges against Jasienica alone: he was said to have been a mass-murderer, because the Home Army detachment in which he had served during the war continued after the end of hostilities to fight in the underground against Poland's new rulers; it had allegedly attacked, among others, the village of Narewka and slaughtered its peasant population. When Jasienica was detained by the Polish authorities together with his comrades-in-arms, he was supposed to have turned informer and betrayed them, and then – Gomulka said it with an ambiguous smile – he had been released 'for unknown reasons', while his comrades had had to stay in jail for many years.

Immediately after Gomulka's speech the mass media started a regular smear campaign against Jasienica. His flat was besieged by unidentified toughs, he was afraid to go out lest he, too, like his friend Stefan Kisielewski, be beaten up. The inhabitants of the village of Narewka, where the mass slaughter had allegedly been committed, clamoured in public for his head; schoolchildren were taught to shout in chorus: 'The intrigues of the contemptible fiend Jasienica make us sick!' Repeated day in day out in all the newspapers, broadcast by radio and television, this character assassination was closely followed by the usual 'unanimous' resolutions of various mass rallies.

The nature of these attacks can best be judged from a quotation. The following text was written by Ryszard Gontarz, ostensibly a journalist, in fact a full-time officer of the security police in active service, and one of the most zealous of Moczar's followers:

In August 1944 Lech Beynar, subsequently known as Pawel Jasienica, defected from the Polish army and joined an armed gang then active in the Bialystok province under the command of Zygmunt Szyndzielarz, alias 'Lupaszko' [Jasienica's family name *Beynar* was intended to suggest Jewish or German extraction. The same gimmick was subsequently used by Gomulka as well]. Beynar was given an alias, 'Nowina', and a lieutenant's rank, and after a few months was promoted to become Lupaszko's second-in-command. He used to incite Lupaszko's bandits to murder peasants in the Bialystok area, to burn and pillage villages. He used to indoctrinate, to teach politics, to instruct. But he would not stay content with words alone: he did not shrink from bloodshed either.

In 1949 [Lupaszko's] trial took place. Severe sentences were passed, but Lech Beynar-'Nowina' was acquitted. He then started on his writer's career. Such is the truth concerning the champion of freedom and democracy, Lech Beynar alias Pawel Jasienica. Such is the image of one of the instigators of the recent events at the University. It should also be said that many friends of Jasienica, following the objectives of the Israeli–West German propaganda, slandered our government and our nation by accusing us of anti-Semitism. Those were the circles which formed the anti-Polish propaganda centres during the Israeli aggression against the Arab countries and afterwards. Those were the circles where toasts were drunk to the aggressors' victories, and parties arranged to celebrate them. And they tried to silence honest people who told the truth in order to expose Jewish nationalism, by branding them as anti-Semites.

The truth of the matter is that in 1944 Jasienica indeed served as staff officer in the Vilno command of the Home Army, and together with his detachment took an active part in the liberation of Vilno from its German occupiers. Then, however, Soviet troops attacked and disarmed Home Army units, some of whom they deported to Siberia. Some groups of Home Army soldiers escaped into the woods and conducted a kind of guerrilla warfare. It is possible that Jasienica's former detachment was also among those groups; in any case, he was not with them, having been previously arrested by the NKVD.

Jasienica tried to exonerate himself: he wrote to the Party's Central Committee, to the Ministry of Culture and Arts, to the Prosecutor-General, to various editorial offices. He declared in a restrained and dignified manner that he had fought in the Home Army only against the Nazis, he had never heard about the Narewka massacre: if it had actually happened, he had had nothing to do with it and knew nothing about it. He had, indeed, been arrested like many thousands of others who had committed no crime other than to fight the Nazis in the Home Army, and had then been released, but he had never been told the reason either for his arrest or his subsequent release. He therefore demanded a judicial inquiry.

All his letters remained unanswered, and the newspapers suppressed his declarations. Jasienica then started to send similar letters to various private individuals, but only some reached their destination, as the police confiscated those they could lay hands on. But he still continued to fight for his honour, though doomed to failure. It was only in 1971, after the workers in the Baltic ports toppled Gomulka, that Jasienica was posthumously rehabilitated: some of his books are on sale, but no one in the new Party and state leadership has had the courage to state in public that Jasienica was slandered. Though non-Jewish he fell victim to anti-Semitism, which after all was designed to silence not only Jews but all political opponents of the police dictatorship as well; he was among the few who realized the true objectives of the smear campaign and had the courage to protest against anti-Jewish and anti-intellectual insinuations.

What began in Warsaw with the demonstrations at the end of January, and reached its climax in the students' protests and the writers' meeting, finally led to the March events, which have become as significant in Poland's recent history as the 'Polish October' of 1956. March 1968 brought about the final liquidation of all the surviving forms of liberalism that people mistakenly associated with Gomulka's return to power in 1956. At the beginning of March students' protests spread all over Warsaw, and to the Jagiellonian University in Cracow, where students adopted a resolution demanding adherence to the constitution, in particular to Article 71, paragraph 1, which guaranteed freedom of speech, of the press, of meetings and assemblies, of processions and demonstrations; proclaimed their solidarity with the Warsaw students; and organized two mass rallies in the town's Market Place.

In Warsaw, meanwhile, Jacek Kuron with a group of some fifteen students put forward a resolution demanding the readmittance of Adam Michnik and Henryk Szlajfer, dismissed because of their participation in the January demonstration. Their expulsion from the University had been decreed not by the appropriate disciplinary commission (which had twice refused to comply), but by the Minister of Higher Education, Henryk Jablonski, which, according to the rules then in force, was illegal. On 6 March a group of writers, Pawel Jasienica, Jan Jozef Lipski, Antoni Slonimski, Mieczyslaw Jastrun, Melchior Wankowicz, Tadeusz Konwicki, Jerzy Andrzejewski, Adam Wazyk and Jacek Bochenski, interceded with the Rector on behalf of the two expelled students.

Deputy Rector Zygmunt Rybicki claimed at a University Party meeting that the legal basis for the expulsion by the Minister derived from his general supervision over academic institutions. This excuse in itself gave yet further offence to the Polish intelligentsia. The students were determined to defend their illegally dismissed colleagues and called a mass rally in the Warsaw University quadrangle, to be held at noon on 8 March 1968. They did so because they were convinced that meetings inside the University campus were part of their traditional academic liberties, safeguarded by statute. Even so they attempted to obtain the express permission of the University authorities to convene the meeting, but as the acting Deputy Rector refused this, they decided to go ahead. Early that morning, long before the beginning of the rally, many students had already been arrested. The Party's Warsaw Committee dispatched one of its Secretaries, Zandarowski, to the University campus.

For twenty-four hours there were clear indications that the police had been put on alert. Specially equipped, steel-helmeted *Milicja* units from distant localities were moved to Warsaw; the police school at Legionowo near Warsaw was under stand-by orders. In the Party's Warsaw Committee building a special emergency command post was established; another was set up at the Mostowski Palace, the Warsaw police headquarters. There were many signs that the police were hellbent on a direct and violent confrontation with the students. A poster announcing the rally was allowed to remain on the University walls – a sign of unusual tolerance. Secretaries of Party organizations at the University avoided any discussion at Party meetings, claiming this should await the outcome of the students' rally. It was obvious that all the pent-up social aggressiveness stemming from general frustration was channelled to explode at a moment deemed suitable by the authorities.

On the morning of the rally, a few hours before it was due to begin, an announcement was posted throughout the University, stating that the Rector considered the meeting illegal. In spite of that some thousand students assembled in front of the library; a resolution was read out, protesting once more against the expulsion order. At a quarter past twelve motorcoaches appeared in the University quadrangle, disgorging hundreds of men subsequently described officially as workers' activists. They quickly formed a chain, pushing the students beside the library building to the doors of the Rector's office. The meeting went on in front of the Rector's building; the number of students attending the rally had by then reached some fifteen hundred. Two resolutions were adopted:

Rally in Defence of Democratic Freedoms, Friday, 12 noon

The Warsaw University quadrangle

Down with repression!

The autonomy of the University is in danger!

We will not allow anybody to trample on the constitution of the Polish People's Republic. The persecution of students who protested against the shameful ban on the production of *The Forefathers* in the National Theatre constitutes an overt violation of Article 71 of the Constitution.

We will not be deprived of our right to defend the democratic and libertarian traditions of the Polish nation. Repression will not silence us. We demand the revocation of the expulsion orders against our colleagues Adam Michnik and Henryk Szlajfer.

We demand that an end be put to the disciplinary proceedings against Ewa Morawska, Marta Petrusewicz, Jozef Dajczgewand, Marian Dabrowski, Slawomir Kretkowski, Jan Litynski, Wiktor Nagorski and Andrzej Polowczyk, indicted for their participation in the students' demonstrations after the last performance of *The Forefathers*.

We demand the restoration of the grant of which Jozef Dajczgewand has been deprived.

We demand that the Minister of Higher Education, Henryk Jablonski, as well as the Rector of Warsaw University, give within two weeks a direct reply to the student community on all our above-mentioned demands.

We, the students of Warsaw, assembled at a meeting on 8 March, express our wholehearted support for the resolution adopted at the extraordinary meeting of the Warsaw branch of the Polish Writers' Union. The writers denounced the tightening up of censorship and the banning of *Forefathers* by Adam Mickiewicz.

Students noisily demanded that the Rector speak to them, but otherwise the rally passed off without incident. Disturbances were caused, however, by the uninvited guests from the motorcoaches who all of a sudden began to beat up students, particularly girls, with deliberate brutality. Calls were then heard: 'Gestapo!', 'Freedom!', 'Down with censorship!', 'Police spies out!' The visitors formed a circle round the quadrangle but all at once found themselves pinpointed as the student leaders gave the word: 'Students, sit down!' Some five hundred men remained standing. At one o'clock the Deputy Rector Rybicki appeared on his balcony and ordered the students to disperse. Whistles, catcalls and repeated slogans were heard: 'Freedom, democracy, constitution!' but as soon as Rybicki indicated that he wanted to speak, silence was restored. He presented the students with an ultimatum: 'You have a quarter of an hour to disperse'.

The main gate was closed and locked, leaving one small exit through a side entrance at Obozna Street. Rybicki's order provoked general resentment. When he then promised to meet a students' deputation, he was asked in chorus what guarantees could he give that it would not be arrested. Rybicki replied that the rally must disperse in a quarter of an hour, as the meeting was illegal. Finally a six-man deputation entered the building and after a while a member of the delegation, Irena Lasota, appeared on the balcony and said:

We have requested that a legal meeting be allowed in the Auditorium Maximum, but this has been refused. We are therefore remaining here.

The students sang the Polish national anthem and the *Internationale*. Professors Bobrowski and Herbst tried to pacify the students, arguing that their rally had already achieved its purpose by clearly demonstrating the sentiments of the student community. Only when the students were promised that a meeting would be officially allowed on Monday was order restored, and the two professors were acclaimed. The question now was how to get rid of the men from the motorcoaches and make them leave the campus. Professor Bobrowski managed to persuade them to leave, which they did in formation, accompanied by whistles and catcalls and pelted with snowballs and small coins as payment for their infamous job; but not a single stone was thrown. Amid universal acclaim the students carried Professor Bobrowski back to the Rector's office, singing 'May he live a hundred years'.

The tension subsided and the students began to disperse, but as they approached the main gate, a large group of men armed with rubber truncheons invaded the quadrangle once more through the side entrance at Obozna Street and started to beat up indiscriminately all the participants in the rally. Obviously they were interested not in dispersing the students but, on the contrary, in herding them together. There was no escape through the various buildings, as groups of plain-clothes policemen barred all the entrances. Although the attackers behaved with great brutality, maltreating girls in particular, there was no active resistance: the students were taken utterly by surprise. After the hooligans had broken through the side entrance in Obozna Street, the main gate was in turn crashed by uniformed police detachments in steel helmets, acting with similar brutality.

Outside the University campus, too, police started to beat up passersby on Krakowskie Przedmiescie Street. Students and chance victims tried to take refuge in the Holy Cross Church, where the police did not shrink from pursuing them. A tight police cordon pushed the crowd towards the Bristol and Europejski Hotels. Around 5 p.m. schoolchildren joined the demonstration. At 6 p.m. there was a violent clash in front of the Café Dziekanka. On the streets policemen were met with shouts of 'Gestapo!' In spite of the police reprisals the crowd steadily grew: the main thoroughfare leading from the Old Town Market Place to the Party's Central Committee building remained crowded till late at night.

On that day, immediately dubbed in Poland 'the longest day of the month', the streets in the centre of Warsaw presented a picture resembling that of the SS raids during the Nazi occupation: entire street blocks were cordoned off and empty, on both sides of the roadway motorized police patrols moved warily in full combat equipment, in house entrances people were cowering, shouting and weeping. During the next few days the press, radio and television were full of vicious attacks against the students: they were accused of hooliganism, disturbing public order, attacking uniformed policemen, as well as of shouting anti-socialist and anti-Soviet slogans. The demonstrators, together with millions of other readers, listeners and television audiences, were now told that the 'riots' had been instigated by Zionist, nationally alien elements. *Slowo Powszechne*, the daily newspaper of Boleslaw Piasecki and his Pax movement, set the tone, appealing to the patriotic sentiments of Polish youth and inciting against the 'Zionists'. Its slogans were picked up by all the other papers, and *Slowo Powszechne* repeated them day after day in a slightly modified version, e.g. 'Zionism – No! Poland – Yes!'

As usually happens in the wake of such turbulent events, various accounts circulated all over the University; their truthfulness could not always be proven. Some witnesses maintained that among those who had beaten up the students there were originally some genuine workers who had been convinced the students were calling for an anti-Soviet, revisionist demonstration. It was alleged that those workers had withdrawn as soon as they realized what was really going on. Professors Bobrowski and Herbst, who had tried to restore peace between the students and the Deputy Rector and the police, were rumoured to have themselves been maltreated with rubber truncheons. Among those roughed up there was said to be a Reuter correspondent, presumably an incidental victim and eye-witness of the brawls.

There can, however, be no doubt that the unbelievable brutality shown by the police was not a matter of their being carried away in the heat of the moment, but the result of deliberate training, as was borne out by the December 1970 events in the Baltic ports. According to eyewitness accounts, including, for example, those of Scandinavian reporters who happened to be present, the police acted according to an obviously pre-arranged plan. It should be stressed that the coastal towns in 1970 were the scene not merely of scuffles: in the fight against the workers' demonstration fire-arms were used, and a peace protest ended in a bloody massacre of defenceless crowds, with troops called in to assist the police.

On 9 March 1968 students of the Warsaw Polytechnic called in turn for a protest rally. In the crowded great assembly hall of the main building slogans were shouted: 'The press tells lies!', 'No bread without freedom!' Newspapers were demonstratively torn up or set on fire. The participants enthusiastically welcomed a deputation of students from the University. Somebody put out the white-and-red Polish national flag. A procession was formed and marched towards the *Zycie Warszawy* editorial office amid shouts of 'The press tells lies!' 'Warsaw, support us!', and singing *Gaudeamus* and the *Internationale*. On Polna Street the police moved against the marchers with rubber truncheons and tear-gas grenades, and dispersed the procession. This, however, was obviously not the intended purpose of the police intervention: fleeing students were hunted down by policemen once more, some on Marszalkowska Street, some in the Polytechnic's main building and in the Electronics Department where policemen broke windows in order to enter the building, which was full of students shouting at the attackers 'Gestapo!' and 'Murderers!'

The exasperated students raised their voice once more, adopting the following resolution:

We, the students of Warsaw, assembled in this hall to fight in defence of our civic freedoms, protest against the Stalinist methods of treating students; we protest against the use of violence and against the beating of women; we demand truthful and objective information about the events of 8 March.

There was a temporary relaxation of tension over the week-end, but untrue press reports and public pronouncements, which appeared on 11 March, provoked a new wave of protests. Particular indignation was caused not only by the malicious distortion of the objectives and course of the demonstrations, but also by the openly anti-Semitic tendency of many press commentaries. The first report denouncing the riots as a result of a deliberately organized 'Zionist conspiracy' appeared, as mentioned before, in *Slowo Powszechne*; the editorial, presumably written by the notorious pre-war fascist and subsequently Soviet secret-service agent, Boleslaw Piasecki, was read out at Party meetings in Warsaw as an official guideline to Party policy.

The first senior Party official to comment on the students' demonstration in public was Jozef Kepa,[1] Secretary of the PUWP Warsaw Committee:

They [the instigators and the ringleaders] take every opportunity to make use of the bogey of anti-Semitism. They have recourse to this stratagem more and more since the Israeli aggression against the Arab countries, since Comrade Wieslaw's [Gomulka's war-time alias] speech at the 5th Trade Union Congress (June 1967), since the political campaign subsequently conducted by our Warsaw Party organization. We will not allow them to blackmail us with this bogus threat of anti-Semitism. It must not provide the instigators of the recent outrages with an opportunity to describe the measures taken against the political riots as an anti-Semitic action. . . . We will not tolerate in our country Zionist

---

[1] Jozef Kepa, First Secretary of the Warsaw PUWP Committee, was a typical representative of the second-generation *apparatchiki* who joined the Party after the seizure of power. He entirely lacked any kind of idealistic motivation, once common to Communists of pre-revolution vintage: he was ambitious, power-hungry and interested in promotion only. Kepa was considered one of Moczar's staunchest allies in the Party apparatus, and thanks to his efforts the Party's Warsaw organization, the second largest in the country, was thoroughly purged of 'revisionists' and turned into a powerful pressure group clamouring for an early change of leadership. In December 1970 Kepa supported Gierek and Moczar in their *coup* to topple Gomulka after the workers' uprising in the Baltic ports. As soon as Moczar's star began to wane, he felt no remorse in getting off this bandwagon, and was rewarded by Gierek with promotion to the Politbureau. In the summer of 1976 he was demoted from his Warsaw post and power base and appointed one of several deputy prime ministers – a move generally considered a set-back to his political ambitions.

propaganda or activity. Neither will we allow the Zionists to seek protection for themselves by accusing others of anti-Semitism. In connection with the recent events at Warsaw University, it was necessary to call upon a certain group of Party activists and use them for a political and organizational action. Our district committees, factory committees and Party organizations have discharged their duty in an exemplary manner. All comrades have shown exceptional discipline, exemplary behaviour, complete readiness to fulfil their tasks. The Executive of the PUWP Warsaw Committee expresses its thanks to all comrades. In view of this situation one can only wonder—because it is not comprehensible—that some members of high-level Party committees, reputed to be senior Party ideologists and scholars, have, to put it mildly, reacted too impulsively, protesting against the intervention of workers and the ORMO[2] and comparing this with the methods once used by the strong-arm squads of the ONR and the Falanga.[3]

Kepa's speech was printed as a pamphlet and distributed to all Party organizations in Warsaw. At the University campus, leaflets of a similar content were handed around, some of them anonymous, some issued by the Union of Polish Students. In Warsaw and in other cities, including Lodz, a leaflet was distributed designed to undermine the students' movement; it included the following passages:

Whom are you supporting?

You are supporting those who would like to dominate you, who claim to be your leaders. In order to make your choice easier, we introduce to you some of them.

Look at them closely, remember them, compare what you read here with their behaviour.

Adam Michnik, son of Ozjasz Szechter [a veteran Jewish Communist]. He was taught the art of provocation and political intrigue by Kuron and Modzelewski.... A regular and deserving informer of Radio Free Europe.

Aleksander Smolar, son of Grzegorz, the editor-in-chief of *Folks-sztyme*, the newspaper of the Social and Cultural Association of Jews in Poland. An activist of the Babel Club,[4] assistant at Professor Wlodzimierz Brus's university chair.

[2] An auxiliary police organization, composed mainly of Party stalwarts, trained and indoctrinated by security officers.

[3] A fascist organization in pre-war Poland; most of its ideological heritage was taken over by Boleslaw Piasecki and his followers in the ranks of the Pax movement.

[4] One of the youth debating clubs, which enjoyed great popularity in Poland. These clubs reached the peak of their activity during the 1956 upheavals, when there were over two hundred in the country, including the famous Club of the Crooked Circle, see page 142, n. 3. The clubs then became centres of political discussion among critically minded intellectuals, young people and students. As the influence of Moczar's police faction gradually grew, attendance declined and the clubs were infiltrated by police informers and agents.

The Babel Club (named after the Soviet-Jewish writer Isaac Babel, murdered during the great

Supported in his subversive activity by his brother Eugeniusz, student of political economy.

Henryk Szlajfer, son of Ignacy, a censor in the Main Office for the Control of the Press, Publications and Performances. On 5 June last year, he submitted a declaration of solidarity to the Israeli Embassy. Active member of the Babel Club. Highly thought of by foreign correspondents, supplier of information to Radio Free Europe.

Ewa Zarzycka, daughter of Janusz Zarzycki, former Chairman of the Warsaw People's Council. Presumably predestined for spiritual superiority as she is widely known for her exceptionally contemptuous attitude towards her fellow-students of worker and peasant stock. Expert in extinguishing cigarettes in marmalade jars.

Jozef Dajczgewand, son of Fajga and Szlomo, active member of the Babel Club; one of the chief assistants of Kuron and Modzelewski; now among the main instigators and ringleaders of the riots.

Krystyna Winawer, daughter of Wlodzimierz, Supreme Court judge, and of Alina Goldfarb, editor at the State Music Publishers.

As you can see, the élite of banana-youth,[5] born leaders recruited according to tribal principles, free from financial bother or troubles. Well dressed, with their own cars, widely travelled all over the world, after their strenuous activities they usually relax in resorts of the West.

That's what we would like to remind you of. Before you engage in conversation with them, remember who they are.

Read this and pass it on!

Another, similarly anonymous, leaflet followed virtually the same pattern:

Colleagues!

Recent events at Warsaw University, instigated and organized by political bankrupts and by certain Zionist circles, have given rise to anxiety and loathing among the majority of student youth. Diversionary reports of a reign of terror imposed by the authorities are perfidious lies spread in order to rouse among young people in other towns sentiments of vengeance or solidarity with the alleged victims. The catchwords of democracy and liberty, as well as the defence of victims of alleged injustice, serve to conceal the political aims of a small group of politicoes and adventurers! Can you support the aspirations of the Zambrowskis, Werfels, Szlajfers, Dajczgewands, Alsters, Grudzinskis,

---

purges of the 1930s) was financially supported by the Cultural and Social Association of Jews in Poland; because of its outstanding jazz group it was particularly popular among both Jewish and non-Jewish young people of Warsaw. Moczarite propaganda denounced the club as a hotbed of Zionist conspiracy, and attendance even at its non-political functions was considered a crime.

[5] A pejorative description for the sons and daughters of senior Party and state dignitaries. The Polish population considered prohibitively priced bananas an article of luxury.

and others? [Most of the names were carefully picked out not only because they were Jewish or foreign-sounding, but because the parents of these students were easily identifiable as senior Party or state officials, active during the Stalinist period.] Are they the people able to lead the youth? Those 'fighters' pretend to be dissatisfied with the opportunities offered them by our popular-democratic country, to live, to study, and to work – they prefer riots. These Zionists want to win over a part of the disoriented youth and to involve them in their political machinations. They want to organize anti-state mass rallies and demonstrations. They want to play the role of heroes whenever they brush against the rubber truncheon of a policeman maintaining public order. Colleagues! Don't let us be duped by the ringleaders of the fight against the people's power! Expose and isolate the Zionist trouble-makers and their hangers-on.

In the frenzied atmosphere the wave of protest refused to ebb. In the Warsaw University's Auditorium Maximum three thousand students, in the presence of the Senate and teaching staff, adopted a resolution condemning the brutal repressions and demanding the prompt punishment of those responsible for police intervention. A similar resolution, voted by the students of the Department of History, demanded in addition the release of their arrested colleagues and denounced the publication of anti-Semitic leaflets. The professors and students of the State Theatre School in Warsaw met and protested against press attempts to sow the seeds of discord between the intellectuals and the Polish working class. As citizens of the Polish People's Republic they expressed their determination to lead an inexorable fight against any provocation on the part of reactionaries and fascists. In the same spirit an appeal was addressed by the Department of Philosophy of Warsaw University to the Senate and the Rector. Leaflets were also distributed protesting against the growing anti-Semitic campaign:

If somebody wants to be a Jew in Poland, he should be allowed to live as a Jew in Poland. We do not want to force him to look for another country where he would be happier than here. If somebody wants to be a Pole, he should be allowed to be a Pole, irrespective of his name or his parents' origin. Our people does not want anti-Semitism. Anti-Semitism is inhuman. It is the authorities who incite to anti-Semitism.

All the protests, however, could not conceal the fact that the students did not find adequate support among the population. Attempts to contact major industrial plants failed because of indifference, apathy and fear, which soon replaced the active sympathy aroused a few days before by the spectacular student demonstrations. In these circumstances the questions submitted in parliament by the Group of Catholic Deputies ZNAK[6] merits special attention and appreciation:

Warsaw, 11 March 1968
To the Chairman of the Council of Ministers, Jozef Cyrankiewicz.

Deeply dismayed by the events of 8 and 9 March at Warsaw University and the Polytechnic, concerned about maintaining peace in our country at a time of a complicated international situation, anxious to secure appropriate conditions for the education and upbringing of young people, we ask in accordance with Article 22 of the Constitution of the Polish People's Republic:

1. What does the Government intend to do in order to curb the brutal actions of the police and the ORMO against the academic youth, and to discover those responsible for this high-handed behaviour?

2. What does the Government intend to do in order to answer the urgent questions submitted by young people? These questions also cause anxiety among the general public, and concern democratic civil liberties and the Government's cultural policy.

Arguments:

The demonstrations by student youth in Warsaw occurred because of obvious mistakes committed by the authorities in their cultural policy. The banning of *The Forefathers* was resented by young people as a painful and tragic interference, which puts our cultural life in jeopardy and insults our national heritage. We are convinced that the March disturbances at the University could have been avoided. During the rally, motorcoaches with ORMO members arrived at the University campus. This considerably inflamed the situation. On 8 and 9 March young demonstrators were beaten up with utmost brutality, which in some cases put their lives in danger. Many cases were reported of young people, including women, having been repeatedly maltreated and cruelly beaten. All this has embittered the public to an extreme degree. We ask of the Prime Minister that the Government take measures to ease tension. This requires that an end be put to violent police actions. Those who have protested against their ruthless intervention should not be treated as enemies of our social system. Neither the youth nor the population in general have shown any hostile attitude to socialism. Irresponsible outcries provoked by the ORMO and police action cannot be regarded as a criterion for judging the attitude of our youth.

We express our concern over the press interpretation of these events, which has exacerbated the situation even more. It is not the suppression of students'

---

[6] A small group of five Roman Catholic deputies to the *Sejm* (parliament) that tried to combine conditional support for the authorities with allegiance to the Church hierarchy; unlike Piasecki's Pax, ZNAK ('sign') enjoyed genuine support among believers, particularly among progressive Catholic intellectuals. The movement was split in 1976, and the present parliamentary group bearing the same name is now in fact manipulated at will by the ruling Communist Party.

manifestos, but a dialogue with the population, that can solve the present difficulties.

We appeal to you to seek for such solutions.

> Konstanty Lubienski, Tadeusz
> Mazowiecki, Stanislaw Stomma,
> Janusz Zablocki, Jerzy Zawieyski.

On the same day the students and professors of the School of Planning and Statistics in Warsaw addressed a petition to the *Sejm* of the Polish People's Republic, to the Central Committee of the PUWP, to the University authorities in Warsaw, and to the Warsaw population, denouncing the grave violations of democratic rules, demanding punishment of the culprits and the release of the detainees. The meeting also called for a repudiation of the false and insulting press reports on the demonstrations, and for making their petition public.

From other university centres all over Poland declarations of solidarity and support were sent to the Warsaw students. On 11 March the Cracow students, for example, adopted a ten-point resolution expressing full agreement with the demands for which fighting in Warsaw was still going on. But in Cracow, too, the police intervened in force, and in Upper Silesia, the bailiwick of the provincial Party boss, Edward Gierek, police dogs were unleashed against demonstrators. According to statistics suppressed by the press, on that day alone about one hundred patients were treated in hospital for bite wounds.

In the meantime hundreds of students were arrested, some of them during the demonstrations, others subsequently in their homes or on the streets. The number of students detained all over Poland was officially given as sixty, but on 19 March Gomulka mentioned one thousand, and Prime Minister Cyrankiewicz later spoke of even two thousand arrested all over the country. In spite of the mass character of the police repressions the press again and again published only the names of some thirty Jewish students, together with lengthy accusations almost exclusively against Jewish students, cunningly mixing reality with fiction. No journalist could by himself know, investigate or even invent all that was included in those reports. The material must have originated from one common source and investigations continued for months or even years. Truthful reporting was not important, but rather the slandering of deliberately chosen people; this can be seen from the fact that among those pilloried as ringleaders of the 8 March events were people physically incapable of taking part in them. This, for example, was the case of Ewa Zarzycka, daughter of the former chairman of the Warsaw People's Council[7] and

---

[7] A post comparable to that of mayor of a large city. Janusz Zarzycki, although non-Jewish

well-known wartime resistance fighter, General Janusz Zarzycki: since 1967 the girl had been studying in Paris. Her father's demands for a public and official retraction eventually induced *Trybuna Ludu* to print a short item on its last page stating that the girl had in fact taken no part in the demonstrations, even though the previous accusations had always been printed on the front page. Among the active 'Zionist ringleaders' a student named Flattau was listed, although he had been hospitalized for several months. Those accused of active participation in the riots included Adam Michnik, arrested at his flat in the early hours of 8 March, long before the mass rally in the University quadrangle; Andrzej Duracz, who on 7 March broke a leg and was in hospital; and Marta Petrusewicz, who had for some time been recuperating in a sanatorium outside Warsaw.

Particularly distressing and eventually tragic was the case of Marek Orlanski, who had been under psychiatric treatment, and for this reason in the autumn of 1967 took a one-year leave of absence from the University. Orlanski was an exceptionally gifted young man. It was said in Warsaw that he had the makings of a genius. When he was only sixteen he won the first award at an 'Olympic' contest in mathematics and physics organized annually in Poland for all school-leavers. At University he studied not only mathematics but logic and philosophy: his exceptional abilities were coupled with delicate health and symptoms of excessive nervousness. He had to interrupt his studies and in the autumn of 1967 he took a year's leave from the University, having obtained a so-called 'dean's holiday'. After leaving the University for psychiatric treatment, Orlanski kept in touch with a handful of intimate friends only. When the March protests broke out, his contacts with most of his colleagues were inevitably severed. But on 10 March, late at night, he was arrested while waiting alone at a tramway stop. The very next morning his father attempted to clear up the obvious misunderstanding, submitting to the police authorities his son's medical certificate of health and the official exemption from studies issued by the University. The boy was detained at Mokotow prison in Warsaw, although a genuine mistake on the part of the police officials seemed out of the question: the student community had for so long been diligently and efficiently infiltrated by spies and police informers that the security organs knew perfectly well the *curriculum vitae* of virtually all students considered to be Jewish, suspected of political dissent, or for any other reason kept under police surveillance. The reasons for seizing Orlanski, as well as other students patently incapable of having attended the demonstrations, can be explained only in terms of Moczar's overall strategy.

and a genuine wartime resistance fighter, was unpopular with the Moczarites because of his liberal views and personal integrity.

According to the grand design of the 'police faction', public opinion had to be convinced, by means of carefully prepared false evidence, of the dangerous character of Zionism and revisionism, the twin crimes that had long been systematically and ruthlessly denounced in the mass media and in the Party apparatus. It was part of this plan that among those detained there were relatively many Jews, a number of them the sons and daughters of lifelong Communists (including former or still active senior Party and state officials) who had spent many years in pre-war prisons or had an outstanding record of wartime armed struggle for the liberation of Poland. A veteran woman Communist who dared to protest against a house search carried out without a warrant, with the remark that the pre-war Polish police had at least bothered to keep up appearances (she herself had been several times imprisoned for her revolutionary activities), was rebuked by the young plain-clothes policeman saying 'So you didn't like pre-war Poland either!'

In the last resort students and their parents were together to be accused of preparing a sort of *coup d'état*, though this was not as simple as might be supposed – the generations had, in fact, very little in common: the parents often clung to their outmoded idealistic, Utopian belief in the cure-all of true socialism, while the children rebelled against the injustice inherent in the only socio-political system they knew from their own experience, which, in spite of its increasingly repressive character, obstinately continued to call itself 'socialism'. For example, a young university assistant, Antoni Zambrowski, ostentatiously joined the Roman Catholic Church to demonstrate his opposition to the political ideas and practices represented by his father, Roman Zambrowski, an old-time Stalinist of Jewish extraction, and until 1963 a member of the Party's Politbureau. The instigators of the witch-hunt were not discouraged by such incongruities, their script providing for a mixture of absurd and incompatible ideas: Zionism, Stalinism, revisionism, the intention to restore capitalism, and even generally anti-Polish sentiments. One and the same person could be labelled with any of these ideological 'crimes', or even all of them at the same time, which inspired the great Polish poet Antoni Slonimski, equally respected for his political courage and for his wit, to coin a dictum, repeated with relish in Warsaw: 'Now I know what a Stalinist wants – he wants to restore capitalism!'

But to come back to our story: Marek was Jewish, the son of an intellectual, a veteran Communist, later denounced as a revisionist, Mieczyslaw Orlanski, head of the philosophy department at the Party's publishing house, who had made a considerable contribution to Polish culture by bringing out a series of the classics of philosophy, including some frowned on by Soviet orthodoxy; besides, he had a reputation for being plain-spoken. Marek was put in a prison cell with criminals, beaten up and tortured. His father was unofficially told by the state prosecutor's office that he could see his son in the court building the following day, where he found his face bruised all over, scarred for life. For two months he applied in vain to the prosecutor's office and the prison authorities to arrange a medical inspection for his son: several times he was put off with a false assurance that he had been transferred to a psychiatric clinic, but found there that nobody had ever heard of the young student.

Systematically tormented by his criminal fellow-inmates and by an investigating officer called Orlewicz, forced after prolonged nightly interrogations to sign statements in a state of virtual unconsciousness, Marek succumbed to catatonia[8] and refused to accept food. On 7 May he was finally examined by doctors summoned by the state prosecutor: according to their diagnosis Marek was in mortal danger and in urgent need of hospital treatment, but it was not until nearly six weeks later that he was transferred to a prison hospital in Grodzisk Mazowiecki where the medical personnel were specially trained to detect malingering. By this time the young man, who had always been of slender build, had lost over thirty pounds, was unable to speak, and had to be artifically fed: he was in a state of total apathy. In July he was transferred to the Institute of Neurology and Psychiatry in Pruszkow with negligible chances of survival.

In spite of this the physicians managed to improve Marek's condition, but even during his convalescence the police again started to torment him with interrogations, regardless of the doctors' written protests. Only in December 1968 were the judicial proceedings against him brought to an end for lack of evidence. A month later he left the clinic, having recovered as well as could be expected, only to hear that he had been expelled from the University. Five months later the whole family emigrated to Sweden, where Marek was once more admitted to a clinic, but eventually recovered sufficiently to be able to resume his studies.

The memory of his experiences haunted him, however: he developed a persecution mania and everywhere saw police officials surrounding him, ready to torture him again. He had a bad conscience; he could not be sure whether he might not have harmed some of his colleagues by the evidence he had given during his detention – through no fault of his own, while unconscious. At the end of February 1971 he committed suicide in Stockholm.

One of the things that made Marek Orlanski's case exceptional was that his fate became widely known. Many of those then jailed still live

---

[8] Stress insanity, a particular form of schizophrenia (dissociation between thoughts, feelings and actions, frequently with delusions and withdrawal from social intercourse).

in Poland, released after an amnesty proclaimed on 21 July 1969. They maintain a prudent silence about their prison experiences, but Marek Orlanski was treated no differently from many other detainees about whom more will be told in a later chapter.

On 12 March 1968 new protest rallies took place. Scholars and technical staff of the Institute of Mathematics at Warsaw University, scientific workers of the Department of Biology and Physics, students and lecturers of the Institute of Economics, students of the Warsaw Polytechnic, repeated their protests, among others, against the anti-Semitic overtones in the press reports and official declarations. Appropriate resolutions were passed, not only in order to register opposition to an attitude considered by many to be reactionary, fascist and inhuman; the protests were also motivated by fear that the fully justified anxiety of the population over the mounting wave of terror degenerate into an unbridled, uncontrollable explosion of anti-Semitism. It is probably for this reason that a satirical leaflet was issued by students and distributed at Warsaw University:

Mein Kampf – Organ of the LEAGUE OF NATIONAL-SOCIALIST YOUTH. A spectre is haunting Europe – the spectre of Zionism. To arms against it! We [are] the nationalist and socialist youth of Poland! Our programme has two levels – that of the NATION and of SOCIALISM. Where these two levels meet we find a line. That is our line: NATIONAL-SOCIALIST ...

Who is with us?

We are not alone in our fight. With us are ORMO and the United Economic Enterprises Pax. With us is Dr Kakol.[9]

Our weapon is denunciation. Our shield – the Little Penal Code, and if this is not enough we have got:
    Dogs,
          rubber truncheons,
             gas,
                  water hoses ...

Against whom?

Our enemy is the Mafia. What is it? The Mafia consists of students and writers, of Jews and Catholics, of Czechs and Slovaks, of liberals and Encyclopaedists ... of intellectuals and cosmopolitans.

[9] Kazimierz Kakol, editor-in-chief of the fortnightly *Prawo i Zycie* (Law and Life), head of the Department of Journalism at Warsaw University and Dean of the Faculty of Social Sciences; one of the most loyal followers of Moczar. As early as 1965 he was one of the first journalists to make his organ available for anti-Semitic propaganda. Under Gierek, promoted to Minister in charge of State–Church relations.

Our slogans:
Writers, back to your pens! Piasecki, to the Politbureau! Students, out to the
army barracks! Jews, go to Madagascar!

Hitherto all we have shown to you are many contemptible agitators and
trouble-makers. Today we would like to present you with a portrait of a praiseworthy peacemaker: Mietek BONAWENTURSKI[10], an honest nationalist, an
enemy of intellectuals. As the Mafia persecuted him, for this reason he could
not get to the University. But on 8 March he did manage to enter and since
then he has stayed there on a grant from the Ministry of Internal Affairs.

On 13 March a mass rally of students from all the Cracow institutions
of higher learning was held with the participation of the Rector of the
Jagiellonian University. The students formed a procession and marched
towards the Market Place, but were soon attacked by the police and
ORMO units, armed with water cannons, tear-gas grenades and rubber
truncheons. The attackers, who according to many eye-witnesses were
under the influence of alcohol, behaved just as their colleagues had done
in Warsaw a few days earlier: they beat up demonstrators and roughed
up passers-by, even women carrying their babies and old people.

They dispersed the demonstrators and then chased the students into
the Collegium Novum, although the previous day the Cracow Party
Secretary, Czeslaw Domagala, had solemnly promised that the police
would in no circumstances enter the campus. Inside the University buildings, previously showered with tear-gas grenades, the police unleashed
a regular battle, during which some professors were beaten up – they
included the Dean of the Law Department, Professor Leslaw Pauly, Professor Karol Estreicher, Professor Konstanty Grzybowski, and Deputy
Rector Adam Bielinski. Only once before in the 600-year-long history
of the University, the second oldest in Central Europe, had its academic
autonomy been violated by strong-arm squads: in 1939, when Cracow
was occupied by the Nazis, members of the faculty, lured into a conference with the German authorities, were seized by the Gestapo and sent
to concentration camps, where most of them lost their lives.

English tourists Ken Little and Norman Steele, who by coincidence
found themselves in Cracow on that day, later reported that on their way
to the Market Place they passed several street crossings, guarded by police
assisted by civilians with arm-bands. The policemen were armed with
clubs, and many of them with pistols. The tourists were overtaken by
lorries and vans, as well as by armoured carriers, full of police. A little

[10] Reference to a police functionary Mieczyslaw Bonawentura Chojnacki who took an active
part in the suppression of students' protests, and was subsequently appointed research fellow at
the University.

later they heard explosions and saw clouds of smoke, as tear-gas had been used. They saw smoke coming out of the windows of a University hostel and heard 'a hell of a row', as if a battle had been going on inside. A moment later they saw young people jumping out of the windows, the police charging and thrashing them with rubber truncheons – several policemen ganging up to beat them one by one. The two tourists dragged many of them onto the pavement – young men, women and girls – and when they escaped into an alley there, too, they saw police chasing students, beating any they caught and dragging them into a waiting lorry.

On 14 March students of the Copernicus University in Torun called a protest meeting; the next day they were followed by their colleagues in Wroclaw and Gdansk. The Gdansk students were especially enraged, having heard that the public prosecutor's office of the *voivodship* had distributed some two hundred false student cards to plain-clothes policemen. At night the police attacked the students' club Zak and started a vicious manhunt all over the city.

On Friday, 15 March, at 4.20 p.m. [reported an eyewitness], I got off the tramway at a stop near the Polytechnic. Along the cemetery wall many police vehicles were parked, some of them with tear-gas launchers; there were several hundred policemen ready. The vehicles blocked access to the Polytechnic. Suddenly a street passage, some 200 metres long, leading in the direction of Wrzeszcz [a Gdansk suburb] was cordoned off. I heard detonations of grenade-launchers. Behind a cloud of acrid smoke, I saw policemen armed with clubs running towards passers-by and beating them ruthlessly. I did not want to run away but a few metres behind me I saw an elderly gentleman with a briefcase who, like me, refused to run away, knocked down under a shower of blows, so I changed my mind and jumped over a high fence into a small private garden. A policeman pursued me up to the house where somebody had opened a window and called me to jump in. The policeman gave up and returned to his comrades. People were running away, many shouted 'Gestapo!' I left by another way among the police vehicles in the direction of Wrzeszcz. As I passed a police command-car I saw cameramen. An officer gave them a sign, and they started to run their cameras. Then the officer ordered tear-gas grenades to be launched. The street was cordoned off and everything was repeated, the only difference being that I was by then no longer a victim but an onlooker. When I arrived at Wrzeszcz, a lot of people were standing on the pavements. Here, too, police units attacked uninvolved passers-by and beat them up. People tried to escape into shops. I saw a group of frantic people who almost trampled down a small child. Suddenly somebody shouted: 'They have killed a man!' When I looked up, I saw a police vehicle driving away: somebody was lying on the road. A little later an ambulance took him away.

In Gdynia, on Sunday morning, 17 March, the police started a brawl in Swietojanska Street, then full of students and schoolchildren. In the afternoon when Sunday walkers, including many children, strolled as usual to the top of Kamienna Gora to enjoy the panoramic view of the city and the harbour, a group of some forty policemen quite unexpectedly began to assault them and beat them up with truncheons.

Unrest continued to grow as a result of these brutalities. Student protest rallies were held in Poznan and Lodz. Young people felt they had to express their solidarity and acted accordingly, without stopping to think that they were perhaps unwittingly playing Moczar's game. In Lodz the Party First Secretary, Jozef Spychalski (not to be confused with, and unrelated to, the then Minister of National Defence and subsequently Chairman of the Council of State, Marian Spychalski), and his propaganda secretary, Hieronim Rejniak, publicly warned that they did not intend to allow 'another Warsaw' there, and closed all the cinemas. Whether they acted out of misplaced zeal or with premeditation, aiming to provoke the students into causing trouble so as to justify subsequent purges, the result was a witch-hunt against intellectuals and Jews on a scale unrivalled in any other Polish city.

An incident, funny in itself though of grave consequences for those involved, might well illustrate the political climate then prevailing in Lodz: the Party daily *Glos Robotniczy* published an article on the Zionist menace allegedly rampant among professors and students. It named, *inter alia*, two students who a short time before had allegedly arrived at a fancy-dress party in a student club dressed up as Moshe Dayan. One of the two one-eyed heroes was said to have been a man called Goldberg, though he could not possibly have attended the party as he had been called up for military service and had for many weeks had no leave; this fact was confirmed in writing by the club authorities. The club manager, Zdzislaw Hejduk, and the vice-chairman of the Lodz branch of the Students' Union were dismissed for having provided Goldberg with such a document. Moreover, when the two 'Zionist plotters' came to see an editor of the Party daily to explain that they had dressed up not as Dayan, but as pirates with an eye-patch, they were not even admitted to his presence.

A similarly sinister sense of humour could be detected during a demonstration organized by the Lodz Party committee. To the utter astonishment of onlookers on the main street a handful of African and Vietnamese students marched solemnly carrying banners with the slogans: 'We condemn the Israeli aggression!' and 'Zionists, out of the University!' The press reported a spontaneous demonstration organized by the morally sound and sensible part of the student community. At a subsequently convened mass rally of the students of Lodz University a deputation was elected, and its members were empowered to appear as the students' legitimate spokesmen. The city's Party committee then demanded from the Rector, Professor J.Piatkowski, their immediate dismissal. The Rector refused to comply, and a few weeks later he was removed from his post – as was, too, an assistant professor named Amsterdamski – and expelled from the Party.

On 15 March a state of emergency was proclaimed in Lodz which remained in force for two months. The order, signed by the Chairman of the People's Council, E.Kazimierczak, threatened especially severe punishment for anyone who caused any breach of public order. The Polytechnic nonetheless proceeded to elect its delegates, and the two schools then called for a joint mass rally, which was attended by some three thousand people, although only some two thousand participants could be *bona fide* students. Police vehicles surrounded the place where the rally was held, and here, too, there was violent beating and some fifty students were arrested. All over Poland a macabre joke circulated: people were being shot at because 'man is the ultimate target of socialism'.

For many days Party organizations in Lodz factories and offices held extra-judicial show trials at which Jewish employees were expelled from the Party and dismissed from their jobs. Among those ousted were the Deputy Rector and a number of scientific workers of the School of Medicine, the well-known film director Aleksander Ford, the manager of a film studio, R.Brudzynski, and the manager of the Ruch newspaper and book distributors. The educational film-producing company dismissed its editor-in-chief as well as two film directors, Etler and Kokesz. Etler was blamed because his films – one of them, 'The Remu Graveyard', had won an international award – dealt exclusively with Jewish subjects. A. Postolow, director of the publishing house Wydawnictwo Lodzkie, was forced to leave because his firm was blamed for dealing with 'Jewish subjects and the martyrology of the Jews', and neglecting 'peasants' strikes in pre-war Poland'. The Lodz press was purged of Jews overnight: some ten editors lost their jobs. The Internal Diseases' Clinic at the School of Military Medicine lost its chief physician, Professor Himmel; while at the Ophthalmological Clinic all physicians had to produce their certificate of baptism.

Many events closely resembled the climate in Germany immediately after Hitler's seizure of power. A sixty-two-year-old former director of the rubber industry association, M.Srebrnik, was put on trial for allegedly falsifying his school-leaving certificate. The newspaper *Dziennik Lodzki* wrote in its court report: 'The defendant behaved with an effrontary typical of people of Jewish origin.' Many Jewish veteran Communists lived in Lodz: they were deprived of their supplementary old-age pensions. A local newspaper published an article accusing a young Jewish prosecutor of having kidnapped a farmer's daughter and abducted her to Israel. The article mentioned 'old Jewish religious customs' and 'unverified stories about the use of Christian children's blood for *matzos*'. The official Party daily went so far as to print an open letter to Mrs Golda Meir; its author, P.Goszczynski, claimed that Dayan was in fact Otto Skorzeny, while she herself was hiding Martin Bormann. The journalists' club in Lodz banned Jewish newsmen from its premises. Local government officials were given confidential directives to compile a list of Jewish house-owners.

Increased pressure provoked new protest actions. Besides those mentioned earlier, there were mass demonstrations in Katowice, Olsztyn, Lublin and other cities. The overwhelming majority of Poland's 290,000 students rose up in anger against the terror, but the press continued to throw around the same Jewish-sounding names of some thirty 'Zionist plotters', blamed, together with their Zionist-Stalinist-revisionist instigators, for all the evil in the country. The authorities did not rid themselves of troublesome students merely by means of imprisonment and fines: following the example of the Tsarist authorities rebels were called up for military service and enrolled in punitive companies in the army. How many were affected by this kind of unlawful punishment throughout the country can only be gathered from the fact that in 1968 in the School of Medicine in Wroclaw alone over one hundred students were sent to such units.

In the second half of March the wave of student demonstrations began to ebb, the major reason being that the young people had not managed to draw the workers into a common fight. On 16 March the Rector of Warsaw University, Professor Turski, issued a proclamation, circulated in the form of a leaflet all over the University campus, threatening all students with immediate rustication unless they resumed their studies forthwith. Two days later the Department of Philosophy was provisionally closed, without explanation: the police searched its premises, and it was rumoured that bugging devices were installed.

At noon on 18 March a mass meeting was held in the Auditorium Maximum. Delegates of other academic institutions, some of them from other cities all over the country, read out their protest resolutions, but the representative of the Party's Central Committee who had been expressly invited by them did not appear. On the previous day the French news agency AFP reported from Warsaw that Gomulka was to make a speech on the 19th, at a meeting of party activists in the Warsaw Palace of Culture; the Polish press made no mention of this. Among the students a rumour was going round – probably deliberately inspired – that Gomulka would take a public stand on their demands. Such expectations contributed to a certain easing of tension; many students were inclined to wait and avoid any action until after this speech.

At this time the first indications of solidarity and protest actions began to appear abroad: in London Polish and British students organized a demonstration and at Charles University in Prague, and in Copenhagen, similar solidarity rallies were held. In the Federal Republic of Germany the left-wing socialist students' union SDS published an open letter to Gomulka, demanding the release of the arrested students. The general union of West German students VDS also condemned the brutal police action. French Communist students collected signatures under a declaration of protest against the persecution of the Polish students' movement, praising their 'heroic struggle'. The authors and signatories of all these solidarity manifestos made a point of protesting at the same time against the anti-Semitic campaign unleashed in Poland.

To reduce the impact of these resolutions, the Polish United Workers' Party tried hard to denounce them as additional evidence of the machinations of 'international Zionism'. But not all attempts at whitewashing were as crude as that: early in March, for example, the obituary of a girl student, Maria Baraniecka, supposedly killed as a result of police brutality, was distributed as a leaflet throughout Warsaw University. As this seemed quite plausible, the news shocked and angered public opinion, and students in particular, although nobody was able to trace the girl. Then on 16 March television broadcast a sensational item of news: Maria Baraniecka was shown on the screen alive and healthy. The reports concerning her maltreatment and subsequent death had been false, and were produced as additional evidence of Zionist provocations, to which naïve Polish students had fallen victim.

The damage caused to Poland's image abroad by the suppression of the intellectuals' and students' protests, and in particular by the anti-Semitic persecution, induced the Polish authorities to initiate a counter-propaganda drive abroad. On 12 April Jan Druto, Polish Ambassador in Paris, claimed that nobody was persecuted in Poland for racist reasons: the majority of the tiny Jewish community was deeply attached to their country. Government emissaries were sent on propaganda tours to Great Britain, the Netherlands and Austria; they held press conferences bitterly complaining against the 'fabrications' of the Western and Israeli press. These missions, however, were doomed to fail, if only because of their carefully selected composition: they included the very same people who had distinguished themselves in word and deed as champions of anti-Semitism, e.g. Zbigniew Soluba, Wladyslaw Machejek, Wilhelm

Szewczyk, Czeslaw Pilichowski and others. In some cases their record went back to pre-war active support for semi-fascist and anti-Semitic movements, and the missions could not be made successful merely by engaging the services of a handful of 'alibi Jews', such as Jerzy Lobman or Colonel Bokowiak ('Alef') who, for reasons best known to themselves, agreed to lend their support to attempts at justifying the witch-hunt both inside the country and abroad.

Zygmunt Bauman, dismissed in March 1968 together with other professors as a 'Zionist seducer' of youth, wrote that

Poland's rulers reacted with provocations and conjuring tricks. If any documents concerning these provocations did exist, they would be inaccessible to researchers, at least for the time being. Today one can at best try to collect the circumstantial evidence and describe the external phenomena. But the logic of the March events leaves no doubt that there must have been a conspiracy, reminding one of the Reichstag fire and of Kirov's assassination.[11]

[11] Sergey Kirov, Stalin's close collaborator and head of the CPSU organization in Leningrad, was murdered in 1934. His death, probably engineered by the NKVD on Stalin's orders, served as a starting-point for the Great Terror and the purges of 1935–8.

8. The Purge

BAUMAN's reference was to Moczar, his faction and his police network. Although their smear campaign against Jews, intellectuals and assorted nonconformists was originally aimed at ousting the 'undesirables' and replacing them with reliable followers of the 'police faction', this was in fact only a preliminary step towards the main goal: an assault on Gomulka himself. In March 1968 such an assault was already well under way, and it was started by a series of mass rallies in the factories, through which the entire Party apparatus all over Poland was to join in the inter-factional strife. Gomulka's closest collaborators, especially Zenon Kliszko and Marian Spychalski, were being openly attacked, though the Secretary-General himself was still spared. As a rule the mass rallies were stage-managed by Party activists who until 1956–7 had been employed in various security services, lost their lucrative posts as a result of de-Stalinization and partial democratization, and were later usually shifted to industrial plants, where they were given jobs not only in the works management, but also in the Party and trade union committees and in the workers' councils. Their zeal was spurred on by their approval of strong-arm rule and the hope of regaining their former influential and well-paid positions.

In Warsaw these groups, working together in full solidarity, were especially well represented in the Zeran car factory, in some factories producing telecommunication devices, in the Kasprzak radio-equipment plant, and in the Ursus tractor works. After the 'cultural revolution' in Mao's China they were universally nicknamed 'the *Hunveibin* movement', like their Chinese counterparts, and acted as the real driving force behind the March 1968 upheavals. Behind the scenes the *Hunveibin* movement was directed by the security organs which, however, allowed their supporters to act independently, in a manner reminiscent of the Mafia. The *Hunveibins* gained control over the mass media, claiming that they had saved the country from a revisionist-Zionist conspiracy, had warded off a *coup* against Poland's social order, and prevented the restoration of capitalism. Almost overnight they seized power in the universities and in various research institutes, euphemistically presenting their victory as the integration of Marxist scholars. Finally they won predominant positions in major Party organizations, including the Warsaw and Lodz committees. Vladyslav Bienkowski described the passive attitude of the Party leadership when confronted with the frontal assault:

Gomulka and his close collaborators in the Party leadership were taken unawares, and felt helpless in the face of a precipitate series of events. They could not but accept the inevitable, although in the light of the information accessible to them, it is by no means impossible that they swallowed the lie about the threat of a conspiracy. The whole tactics of the security organs were calculated to convince the leadership that the police alone offered the state reliable support. This, however, was only one side of the coin. There are indications that the events suited the Party leadership as well. They had to find some solution to the country's economic and social troubles, or at least to gain respite by diverting popular attention to other issues. Only in this way can one explain the zeal with which they [the Party leadership] supported the cultural revolution of the *Hunveibins*, gave them access to the scientific world and to schools of higher learning by precipitating legislative reforms and by surrendering those domains to the arbitrariness of trimphant reactionaries. Although the March events could for a short period of time distract public attention, and act as an anaesthetizing injection, this could not halt the process of disintegration; on the contrary, disintegration was speeded up and spread to other domains of public life.

In 1967–8 it was common knowledge in well-informed sources that the country was ruled by two power centres: the official one, headed by Gomulka and Kliszko, and the other led by the dyad Moczar–Strzelecki.[1] Too late, and only half-heartedly, did Gomulka attempt to reassert himself. Because of protests abroad and in several Western Communist parties, he even tried to halt the anti-Semitic campaign which had by then acquired a momentum of its own and threatened his wife as well as some of his closest collaborators. But such attempts were of no avail. When Gomulka belatedly issued detailed directives to the censors, instructing them what could and what could not be published about the Jews, they were totally ignored for the first time in the history of Communist Poland. With the exception of a handful of newspapers which still continued to hold their own in the face of Moczar's offensive – including, for example, the weekly *Polityka* mentioned earlier – virtually all the mass media had slipped out of Gomulka's control. They had long been purged of objective reporting and commentary and now assumed a shrill and aggressive tone.

[1] Ryszard Strzelecki, a veteran Communist, was rumoured to have maintained close ties with Soviet intelligence services since pre-war times; in the 1960s he was generally regarded as Moscow's chief undercover agent in Poland. Although bound to Gomulka by a lifelong friendship, Strzelecki, member of the Party's Politbureau, was presumably Moczar's sole reliable ally in the top Party leadership.

The press assumed the role of public prosecutor without bothering to verify accusations before publication. This is what was written, for example, about the meeting of Warsaw writers following the ban on further performances of *The Forefathers*:

On 29 February the Warsaw branch of the Polish Writers' Union held an extraordinary meeting convened on the initiative of a group which included such particularly active writers as Pawel Jasienica, Andrzej Kijowski, Antoni Slonimski, Stefan Kisielewski, January Grzedzinski, Jerzy Andrzejewski, and Leszek Kolakowski. During the meeting disgraceful attacks on the people's power and against socialism were made by means of demagogic slogans and hostile speeches. Many speakers did not shrink from uttering slanders and insults. ... Such scenes were obviously aimed at provoking the youth to demonstrations. Pawel Jasienica praised the activity of certain subversive elements in the University, and called for an intensification of the unrest. He passed the minutes of the meeting to the students Adam Michnik and Irena Grudzinska.

When Michnik was put on trial, in January 1969, the prosecutor read out this report as evidence to support the indictment. The defendant then replied:

The claims alleging a secret collusion between writers and students are pure invention. ... I was also not a liaison man, and although the indictment claims that Jasienica received students' reports on behalf of the writers while I got from him writers' reports, what I am now categorically stating is nevertheless true: never in my life have I spoken with Pawel Jasienica. Once, by pure coincidence, I was introduced to him, and since then I have greeted him on the street, but I have not seen him or ever spoken to him. I am very sorry that I had no opportunity to know Pawel Jasienica better, as I respect him highly as a writer.

As the trial took place almost one year after the writers' meeting, there was in any case not the slightest possibility of undoing the damage caused in the interval by the slanders and accusations deliberately put on record. Another example is an article in *Trybuna Ludu*:

In the ranks of Israel's friends there has also appeared another instigator of the riots, Antoni Slonimski. Sitting in the Café PIW in the company of the notorious 'Encyclopaedists',[2] Stefan Staszewski and the likes of him, he held

[2] The smear campaign against the 'Encyclopaedists' was unleashed by (among others) Wladyslaw Machejek, editor-in-chief of the Cracow weekly *Zycie Literackie*, and Kazimierz Rusinek; the main charges levelled against the editorial board of the Greater Universal Encyclopaedia (including the director of the State Scientific Publishing House, Adam Bromberg, and one of the editors, Stefan Staszewski, a veteran Communist who after 1938 spent several years in Soviet forced labour camps, and who in 1956 as Secretary of the Warsaw Party Committee was in charge of preparations for opposing a possible Soviet armed intervention, and in 1957 was dismissed by Gomulka) concerned the entry 'Concentration Camps' in volume VIII, written by the then chairman of the Polish

political consultations with them and instructed the spoiled sons and daughters of various erstwhile, and in some cases even present-day, dignitaries on how to provoke unrest. Jasienica and Slonimski, as well as Stefan Kisielewski, the advocate of a rapprochement with the Federal Republic of Germany in accordance with the ignominious slogan 'to forgive and to ask forgiveness' [an allusion to the Polish Bishops' Open Letter to the West German Roman Catholic hierarchy], as well as Staszewski and his cronies, those were the people from whom Adam Michnik learned the art of politics. They were the spiritual masters of Katarzyna Werfel, daughter of a Stalinist ideologist, of Wiktor Gorecki, son of the Director-General in the Ministry of Finance, of Irena Grudzinska, daughter of a Deputy Minister of Forestry, and of many others. Let us say it frankly: this did not start a few months ago, not even a year ago. As far back as 1962 a youth club of revisionist kids was founded in the House of Culture, in the Old Town. Among the club's organizers were Adam Michnik, Wladyslaw Kofman, Aleksander Perski, and Jan Gross, and among its members [a list of names follows] and other banana-kids. Most of these names can be found among the instigators of the recent incidents at Warsaw University. Then, in 1962, they were still secondary school pupils. Among those who took the club under their wings we find people like Zygmunt Bauman, Leszek Kolakowski, Wlodzimierz Brus, and Professor Adam Schaff.

The tone of this report speaks for itself. The author, however, through an excess of zeal, overlooked the fact that in 1962 Michnik could hardly have acted as the club's organizer: he was then fifteen years old, while Katarzyna Werfel was twelve.

On 14 March *Trybuna Ludu* again carried an article, entitled 'Images of Instigators', once more attacking Stefan Staszewski. The Jewish veteran Communist, downgraded long before, lived on his old-age pension, but Moczar still considered him a thorn in his side not only as one of the 'Encyclopaedists', but because, hardened in Soviet forced labour camps, he was one of the few who dared to defend themselves against Moczar's trumped-up charges. He was therefore presented in a full-page report as one of the most powerful and dangerous instigators of the students' riots. When Moczar himself demanded Gomulka's consent to

---

Commission for the Investigation of Nazi Crimes, Dr Tadeusz Gumkowski (later dismissed and replaced by a pre-war fascist and Moczarite, Czeslaw Pilichowski). The author and the editors were indicted for having insulted Poland's national dignity because they had allegedly overstated the number of Jewish victims in the German extermination camps and understated the number of murdered Poles. Rusinek argued (in *Polityka*, 11 November 1967) that it was unsubstantiated from a scholarly point of view and politically harmful to add the number of murdered Poles of Jewish origin to the sum-total of Jewish victims; that the entry in the Encyclopaedia, with its differentiation between extermination camps and concentration camps, was liable to give the impression that the German extermination policy was directed solely against the Jews, whereas in fact Jews constituted only 30 per cent of all Nazi victims.

issue a detention order against Staszewski, the Secretary-General refused and reminded his minister of police that Staszewski was a tough person whom even Stalin had not managed to break. In similar vein *Sztandar Mlodych*, the daily newspaper of the Union of Communist Youth, in an article entitled 'The Apostles', described the respected professors Bauman, Baczko and Brus as Zionist-revisionist apostles, allegedly engaged in anti-Polish activities.

In the oppressive atmosphere of slander and factional strife there was a growing feeling of insecurity in the Party apparatus and in circles closely connected with it: nobody could be sure who was ultimately going to emerge victorious. The police faction, which continued to neutralize all its potential opponents (e.g. Cyrankiewicz, Jedrychowski and Spychalski) by presenting them as Jewish, managed in mid March to achieve a decisive victory at the seventh congress of the Journalists' Union. The election of congress delegates, which had never followed democratic principles (one could only vote for a previously compiled 'unity' list), became this time a cynical farce, quite exceptional even under Communist rule. In many editorial offices journalists were urged by their editor-in-chief or Party secretary to renounce their candidature 'for the good of the cause', to absent themselves from the congress, or not to say a word there. Thanks to such pressure, those present formed a company congenial to the authorities, hand-picked well in advance.

'Whoever has the mass media under control, has power,' declared with deep satisfaction the spokesman of the police faction and editor-in-chief of *Prawo i Zycie*, Kazimierz Kakol. Later, under Gierek, he was promoted to alternate member of the Party's Central Committee and Minister in charge of State–Church relations. A powerful assault was made against *Polityka*, the only political newspaper which had managed to retain some of its reputation in Poland. A rumour was deliberately spread that it had already been decided that Kakol was to be its future editor-in chief. The congress left not a shred of a doubt as to which of the warring factions had during its Long March managed to win control over the press, and was using it most effectively in its struggle for power.

But the whole country was still waiting for Gomulka to speak out – many people, in spite of everything, were hopeful, others were sceptical but not yet totally disillusioned. The Secretary-General, they thought, could not continue to keep silent permanently in the face of the unbridled smear campaign, the growing number of student trials, the wholesale dismissal of scholars of international repute. There was, therefore, a new upsurge of hope when the news went round that on 19 March Gomulka intended to address the Warsaw Party activists. Nobody, not even the most sober people, who had long before given up all illusions concerning

Gomulka, could predict the nightmare that was to take place in the Congress Hall of the Warsaw Palace of Culture.

As the AFP reported, the Party activists were indeed summoned to a mass meeting. In the spacious Congress Hall some three thousand stalwarts appeared, including several hundred army officers, a few in military uniform, most in mufti. Kepa, as First Secretary of the Warsaw Party Committee, was in the chair. The meeting was being broadcast live on radio and television. Attentive television viewers were able to see for themselves that certain catcalls and chanting – for example 'Gierek! Gierek!' – came from identifiable groups in the auditorium: evidently the factions had taken their seats in groups. As members of the presidium appeared on the platform, for a fraction of a second their obviously astonished and bewildered faces appeared on the screens, and one could even discern whispered words: 'What's going on here? What's happened?' but the cameras were immediately turned away from the presidium and for some time showed row after row of the audience. It transpired later that the first two rows of the audience welcomed the presidium with unmistakably hostile catcalls. Only after a lengthy interval was the rostrum shown again. And, although the hall was still overcrowded, the first two rows of seats remained empty till the very end.

Gomulka spoke for several hours. His speech, reported by foreign newspapers in a shortened and expurgated version, caused a profound shock in Poland. Not only did he repeat the most absurd propaganda lies, but in addition embellished them with many details, most of them shamelessly concocted. He claimed that the performance of Mickiewicz's tragedy *The Forefathers* had been a deliberate act of anti-Soviet provocation. He made light of the petitions addressed by students to the *Sejm*, and having counted how many signatures were legible and how many illegible, he asserted that among the instigators students of Jewish origin had played a major role. Referring to the students' demands raised during the meeting in the University quadrangle, he said: 'The resolution was read out by Irena Lasota-Hirszowicz, of Jewish extraction, and by two ... well, of ours, Poles....' For the first time the leader of a ruling Communist Party differentiated in public between Jewish Poles and 'our' Poles. Throughout his long speech Gomulka never missed an opportunity to add the description 'of Jewish extraction' whenever he mentioned a Jew by name. Just like the press and the various speakers at earlier mass rallies, Gomulka, too, blamed Jewish students for the 'March events', 'bankrupt politicos', the recently dismissed Professors Brus, Kolakowski, Baczko, Bauman, Morawski, Maria Hirszowicz, as well as the writers with whose meeting on 29 February the Secretary-General dealt with at particular length. After having levelled ignominious accusations at

Jasienica (see previous chapter), he attacked other writers, including the poet Antoni Slonimski, and the Catholic essayist, Stefan Kisielewski, as Poland's enemies.

Gomulka gave his opinion of Zionism as well. It is true, he said, that Zionism was an international agency of imperialism, but in his view it would be a misunderstanding to consider Zionism the gravest menace to Poland and its socialist system. At that moment in certain parts of the auditorium hysterical disturbances broke out. Gomulka tried to restore order, he called out imploringly: 'Comrades! Comrades!' But the comrades still howled: 'Bolder! Bolder! To the very end! No half-measures!' and 'Out with the Zionists!' Once more catcalls came from easily identifiable groups in the audience, while television reporters and cameramen manœuvred so deftly that television audiences at home got the unmistakable impression that this frantic atmosphere prevailed throughout.

When he resumed his speech Gomulka divided Jews into three categories: those who felt attached to Israel rather than to Poland were free to emigrate. Here again he was interrupted by shouts: 'Even today! today!' Gomulka replied with a grin: 'They have not yet applied.' The second category, he explained, consisted of Jews who considered themselves committed neither to Poland nor to Israel, nor indeed to any other country: the cosmopolitans. They were free to stay in Poland, but must not take up jobs requiring 'national affirmation' – a vague concept, propounded by the Moczarites who, usurping for themselves a monopoly of 'patriotism', used it to denigrate their political opponents, whom they accused of not paying sufficient heed to Poland's national interests. Finally the third category were Jews who 'felt Polish', and some of them had even greatly contributed to the Polish cause: they were welcome as citizens enjoying full equality of rights. (As previously mentioned, Gomulka shamelessly plagiarized Dmowski's pre-1914 classification of the Jews, which was for years an integral component of the political philosophy of all the chauvinistic, anti-Semitic and overtly right-wing political forces in Poland, always rejected and denounced by progressive, democratic, and left-wing elements.)

By then it was clear that Gomulka had not only renounced his chance to assert himself as the leader, but was ready to join forces with Moczar and to give his blessing to the reign of terror if only he and his closest collaborators could be spared. But for all his opportunism he appeared weak and vulnerable, unable to impress even the handful of sycophants and firebrands brought to the meeting drunk with free vodka and assured that they would be allowed to go on the rampage after the rally, and to stage an anti-Jewish pogrom; fortunately the threat did not materialize.

But Gomulka's attempt to take the wind out of the sails of the 'police faction' by jumping on their anti-Semitic bandwagon did nothing to enhance his prestige: his rivals despised him even more, his potential supporters recognized his weakness and gave him up as a failure. If, in spite of everything, he managed to cling to power for another two and a half years, it was only because Moscow had by then become reluctant to run the risks inherent in a change and preferred to support the *status quo*.

Gomulka's speech was received with disgust by broad strata of the population, particularly by the intelligentsia. But Polish Jews, irrespective of their political views, were flabbergasted: for the first time since Poland's liberation they had been condemned wholesale by the ruling party's leader. They were once more outlawed, as the highest ranking politician in the country had officially sanctioned anti-Semitism. The 'anti-Zionist' campaign had already shaken them and deprived them of the feeling of security based on the sense of belonging to the Polish nation, and this speech could not fail to sound the alarm. Even those fully integrated within the Polish population gradually began to realize with growing clarity that they had been at best an assimilated but still easily identifiable minority. The mass purges had by now demonstrated the perfection with which the Party and the police had mastered the art of finding scapegoats, of pillorying them, and finally depriving them of their means of subsistence. Officially sanctioned anti-Semitism made the victims afraid of even worse things to come. Reminiscences of pogroms and extermination camps in which their parents and ancestors had perished returned, even though most Polish Jews belonged at this time to a generation which knew about those horrors only from hearsay. After the Congress Hall rally even they could not miss the ominous writing on the wall.

Gomulka, to give him his due, made a concession by opening the doors to emigration. This was, of course, a much more humane solution than sending Jews to forced labour camps, as had been planned both in the Soviet Union and in Poland during the last months of Stalin's rule. Similar proposals were now once more discussed in a sinister, matter-of-fact manner among senior officials in the Ministry of Internal Affairs responsible for the 'Jewish question'. Letting the Jews leave the country they had lived in for over one thousand years earned Gomulka abroad the reputation of a 'moderate'. But many of those directly affected were for the first time in their lives confronted with the dilemma of whether they should leave their native Poland, and they had to find an answer quickly.

Apart from the language, professional and social problems which harass the younger emigrants, the older ones also suffer from difficulties arising out of their professional specialization and have therefore diminished prospects for future adaptation, and fewer opportunities for reintegration in the labour market of a foreign country. They also lose their life insurance and old-age pensions, and, finally, must endure the emotional stress of leave-taking from a country with which they have identified themselves all their lives. The sad history of emigration, by no means Jewish only, contains countless cases of unsuccessful attempts at gaining a new identity. Franz Werfel or Marek Hlasko, Kurt Tucholsky or Thomas Mann, might be mentioned here as representatives of countless exiles, the unknown and prominent alike.

Two different motives might have prompted Gomulka's decision: on the one hand he realized that the wave of anti-Semitism could no longer be contained without a direct confrontation with the hard-liners, and he might have wished to avert a consequent threat to himself, or a loss of popularity with the exasperated population. On the other hand, he feared that a relaxation of the reign of terror, advocated and introduced by the police faction, might lead to a development similar to that which was then under way in Czechoslovakia. Motivated by opportunism, he himself preferred to help to open the floodgates and prepare the way for the great purge campaign. Moczar, then generally considered the man most likely to seize power through a *coup* following the riots, reacted immediately: on his orders the police provided various institutions with blacklists containing the names of many intellectuals – not only Jewish – active in public life. The Polish Scientific Publishers, for example, received a note listing authors whose works were no longer to be published. It included, *inter alia*, Professor Ehrlich from the Faculty of Law at Warsaw University. The University itself received another list of names of professors and assistant professors to be excluded from research and teaching; Ehrlich's name was not included there. There were many similar cases. One list, sent to the editorial offices of newspapers and periodicals, contained the names of Amsterdamski, Asserodobraj, Augustyniak, Baczko, Bauman, Blass, Brus, Ehrlich, Eulstein, Ginsbert, Gwizdz, Hirszowicz, Katz-Suchy, Kochanski, Kolakowski, Kowalik, Kerszman, Krajewski, Lachs, Litwin, Laski, Manelli, Morawski, Naszkowski, Pomian, Rosner, Sachs, Szacki, Zakrzewska and Zolkiewski.

Many other similar lists contained names apparently chosen at random, put together without any systematic guidelines. A historian of literature was alongside an economist, a lawyer together with journalists, a sociologist among civil servants. A closer look, however, revealed some of the criteria applied, each of which, or perhaps more than one, applied to a person selected for black-listing:

– a veteran Party member, often belonging to the leading cadres of the PUWP Central Committee;

- the name appeared in the authors' index of *Nowe Drogi*, including many lifelong contributors to this theoretical monthly of the PUWP Central Committee;
- membership of a team of lecturers at Party schools and assistant professors at courses of political science sponsored by the Central Committee;
- participation in the March events;
- membership of the teaching staff of universities and other schools of higher learning;
- having a reputation for championship of liberal tendencies before and after the 1956 'Polish October';
- acts of solidarity with students' strikes or protests, resistance to arbitrary relegation of students;
- open support of the March movement;
- lecturer's activity in clubs of young intellectuals, in particular in the Club of the Crooked Circle[3] or in other debating clubs.

The struggle conducted by the police faction against those who had dared to oppose them ever since the 1956 'de-Stalinization' campaign thus entered its ultimate stage, and victory of the self-styled 'Partisans' over their adversaries seemed a foregone conclusion. The Party's deplorable evolution can best be illustrated by comparing the 1968 state of affairs with the analysis made by Gomulka himself at the memorable Eighth Plenary Session of the Central Committee in October 1956, which reinstated him as Secretary-General after several years of disgrace and imprisonment. He said then:

We know the dangers arising from an insufficient supply of goods on our internal market when considerable sums of money are available. Was anything said about this at the 7th Plenary Session? No, nothing. A precise economic analysis, however, is indispensable for a correct grading of wages. Facts such as those previously mentioned should under no circumstances be passed over in silence. It must be said frankly and clearly that the costs of a false economic policy will be borne by the population, and primarily by the working class. The Party's Central Committee was unable to bring itself to take at least disciplinary measures against Party members responsible for this state of affairs. Foolish attempts at presenting the Poznan tragedy [the bloody workers' revolt in June 1956] as the work of imperialist agents and *agents-provocateurs* reveal

[3] Club of the Crooked Circle (the name derives from a street in Warsaw's Old Town where the club used to hold its meetings) was founded in 1956 and brought together many brilliant young intellectuals, and scholars of international repute. From the very beginning it was under attack by the 'police faction' as a breeding ground for 'revisionism', but was able to survive for several years thanks to the discreet support of some influential Party leaders who preferred to regard it as a safety-valve. Its closure in early 1962 was justly considered a milestone on the road to the restoration of open police dictatorship in Poland.

great political naïvety. Its roots, just as those of the profound dissatisfaction of the entire working class, lie in errors committed by the Party leadership and by the government. Juggling with figures in order to show a 27 per cent rise in real wages during the Six-Year Plan did nothing but irritate the people even more. Loss of credence among the working class implies loss of moral justification for exercising power. We can govern the country even under such conditions, but it will be a bad government which would have to rely on the bureaucracy, the abuse of law, and on coercion. . . .

And shortly after that, on 29 November 1956, Gomulka did not spare promises:

We are building in Poland a socialist system, free of distortions and abuses. We are offering the workers various opportunities for participating in the government. We are going to give to technical workers and scholars possibilities hitherto unknown in Poland for developing their creative thought.

Twelve years later nothing was left of this verbiage: the events of 8 March and their consequences, as well as Gomulka's speech of 19 March, clearly demonstrated that all illusions born in 1956 were utterly and irrevocably shattered. The student community was seething with discontent because the Party leader had maliciously distorted the nature of their protests. As early as 20 March some three thousand students of the Warsaw Polytechnic had gathered at a mass rally (banned in advance by the authorities) and proclaimed a forty-eight-hour sit-in strike. University students, too, voted to start a sit-in strike at 8 a.m. on 23 March. A leaflet issued by the students in Wroclaw declared:

The most recent statements of the Party leadership obstinately attempt to cut our movement from its social roots; they do their best to attack allegedly insignificant groups of instigators and to blur the social background of recent events. They try to sow the seeds of discord in order to divert public attention from the urgent economic problems the present leadership is incapable of solving. The example of Czechoslovakia is clear evidence that reforms carried out in a spirit of democratization are fully compatible with the principles of socialism.

In Cracow students reacted to Gomulka's speech with a forty-eight-hour sit-in strike, not even mentioned by the local press. On 21 March the rectors of all the Warsaw institutions of higher learning issued a warning, threatening students taking part in the strike with dismissal. The same day, police summary courts were introduced in Cracow by order of the local Party Secretary. In spite of the intimidation, students in Lodz and Gdansk, too, voted to join the sit-in. At the Copernicus University in Torun a mass rally was held; in Tarnow the police attacked a meeting of students and young workers – there were many wounded, and some fifty participants were arrested.

In spite of repeated threats from the Rector's office, buildings of the Warsaw Polytechnic were still occupied by striking students on 22 March. In the early morning a large crowd assembled before the entrance to the Polytechnic and, defying police attempts to disperse them, gathered again and again. There were some open manifestations of solidarity on the part of workers who had collected money in many factories to buy food and cigarettes for the strikers, and now arrived to throw their parcels over the fence into the campus. At night the crowd assembled on the streets started to light torches made of newspapers; the students reacted with loud cheers. Such acts of solidarity, in particular among the workers, although isolated, greatly alarmed the authorities. A strong detachment of riot police was therefore dispatched late at night; they broke into the Polytechnic campus and cordoned off all the exits. The Rector's ultimatum was read out on television. He strongly urged the students to put an end to the strike before 9 p.m., and threatened severe penalties for non-compliance. During the night the strike collapsed; in the early hours of 23 March the last groups of students finally left the Polytechnic's main building. The Rector ordered the suspension of lectures and banned the students from entering the campus. Their resistance had been overcome, their demands remained unfulfilled, their revolt for the time being was a failure. More than that: they had unwittingly provided their powerful adversaries with sufficient excuses to justify a radical elimination of any surviving vestiges of liberalism and democracy. The number of arrests all over the country and the number of call-ups for military service rose by leaps and bounds. Young men who had hitherto been allowed to perform their compulsory military service by taking part in periodical army exercises, which only slightly interfered, if at all, with their studies, were now punished by orders to join the army. In all major cities the Party convened mass rallies in which all employees of factories and offices were forced to participate. The press, radio and television brought extensive, detailed reports on many such meetings. Posters and placards stirred up feelings against political dissenters: 'Students, back to work!' 'We support the Party line and Comrade Gomulka!' 'We condemn the hostile machinations of the Zionists!'

As usual in such campaigns, the alleged spontaneity of the meetings was based on the sheer impossibility of holding aloof; in most cases such behaviour would have been interpreted as support for the enemies of the people. Therefore even those who were neutral or disinterested had to

reckon with serious risks, including dismissal from their jobs. A partici-
pant thus described a rally held at his place of work:

The main gate of the factory was closed, the guards were ordered to let nobody
out. The Secretary of the Party organization had previously summoned all the
heads of departments and told them he was making them personally responsible for the full attendance of their labour force. Some dozens of ready-made
posters and placards had been brought from town and distributed among
workers gathered in the hall. If anybody refused to accept them, he was intimi-
dated with threats. Selected workers had to read out speeches prepared for
them in advance. One who refused was deprived of his monthly bonus, while
an old woman who had read out a particularly militant speech was rewarded
with an additional bonus. Many workers tied the poles of their posters and
placards to their machines and left the workshop to avoid having their pictures
taken while holding the posters. After the plant manager, the Party Secretary
and some hand-picked workers had delivered their speeches, or rather read
them out, we had to vote on the text of a letter to Gomulka. Nobody bothered
to count raised hands. But we were told: 'Carried unanimously.' The letter
stated the workers had undertaken to support the Party and Comrade Gomulka
by an overfulfilment of their planned quotas; in practice this meant doing un-
paid work. After the meeting the gate was opened and everybody hurried to
get out of the factory.

All such workers' meetings were conducted according to guidelines
sent to all Party organizations ordering them to purge themselves, as well
as the local authorities and factories, of Zionists and revisionists. The
best-known victims of such purges were listed on the front page of the
Party central newspaper. In the course of a few months several thousand
people, by no means all of them prominent, but including even obscure
artisans, accountants, teachers or nurses, were dismissed because of their
Jewish origin, 'political unreliability' or simply because they had dared
to defend their slandered comrades. Refusal to follow the guidelines on
'de-judaization' – the word was never employed in print though regularly
used in conversation – was often sufficient ground for dismissal. Nobody
managed to keep count of the nameless people who had lost their jobs
and livelihood during the witch-hunt.

If normal criteria of right and wrong had been applied, and an independent judicial power in the state, there could have been no such
witch-hunt with its wretched consequences to countless people. In
Poland, however, the purge was conducted not on merits but rather
according to the criteria applied by the former head of the Soviet secret
police, Beria, who was reported to have said it was enough to seize a
man – the appropriate articles of the Penal Code could always be found.

People who had for years done their job blamelessly were now attacked on the most absurd pretexts, and deprived of their job and livelihood. In the publishing house Wydawnictwo Lodzkie, for example, the managing director, Postolow, was accused of having brought out too many books on the fate of the Jews under the Nazi occupation; J. Kutin, Under-Secretary of State in the Ministry of Foreign Trade, was forced to leave because he had allegedly allowed the duty-free import of goods sent by the international charity organizations Joint and Caritas for distribution among the poor (in fact the exemption from customs duty had previously been cleared with the government). For weeks Kutin was slandered, the victim of an orchestrated campaign of press smears, and deprived of any opportunity to defend himself. The managing director of the Era factory, Szenwald, was dismissed from his job because his daughter was pursuing her studies in London.

The following is a list of people dismissed for equally flimsy reasons: Professors Dobrowolski and Zarnowiecki (nuclear physicists); Professor Hurwitz of the Warsaw Polytechnic who later emigrated to France; Professor Antonina Klosowska; Zweben, managing director of the telecommunication works Komuna Paryska in Warsaw (who received his notice to quit while recovering from a heart attack); Nowicki, managing director of the high-tension electrical works in Warsaw; Srebrnik, managing director of the rubber industry association (who had held this position for twenty years); Rabinowicz, managing director in the knitwear industry in Lodz; the journalists Unger, Jakubowicz and Chylinska of *Zycie Warszawy*; radio editors F.Istner and A.Kaminski; Kornacki, editor-in-chief of the monthly *Polish Perspectives*, published in several foreign languages and distributed abroad. The list can be continued at will, including the gruesome case of an essayist, January Grzedzinski, who was in fact not Jewish, but in order to get rid of an obtrusive Cassandra attempts were made to lock him up in a closed psychiatric clinic.

The purge was not confined to Warsaw. In Lodz it claimed among its victims ten Jewish journalists, including Stanislaw Janiszewski, Gomulka's cell-mate in a pre-war prison, who had fought in a Communist guerrilla detachment during the war. When dismissed, he was in hospital after a heart attack; the health service administration was ordered to send him home immediately.

The film industry was singled out: film directors Aleksander Ford, Etler, Kokesz, Bossak, Brudzynski, cameramen A. and W.Forbert as well as K.Weber, were summarily dismissed, together with the Rector of the once famous Film Academy in Lodz, Professor Toeplitz. Other non-Jewish film people, including director Rybkowski, were censured because their films were not in full 'ideological' accord with Moczar's political line.

World-wide protests against the purge, which towards the end of March already assumed massive proportions, had no visible effect on the security authorities. The International P E N Club expressed its indignation, as did many universities and learned societies, associations, and prominent personalities, including Cesare Luporini, member of the Central Committee of the Italian Communist Party, and Bertrand Russell. In the Vienna periodical *Neues Forum* the following declaration, signed by 78 people, appeared in May 1968:

The signatories represent very different opinions: they include Marxists who aim at the full development of man and his creative initiative; Christians, committed to justice and peace; artists and scholars for whom freedom is as indispensable as the air they breathe; professors, academics, and elected representatives of students, who have academic freedom at heart.

All of us, regardless of our differences, watch the struggle led by the Warsaw students and professors with admiration for their courage and in solidarity with their striving for freedom. We condemn the repressive measures undertaken against them, as well as the concurrent unleashing of anti-Semitism.

We convey our greetings to the dismissed professors *Bronislaw Baczko, Zygmunt Bauman, Wlodzimierz Brus, Maria Hirszowicz, Leszek Kolakowski, Stefan Morawski,* whose significance in the creative spiritual life of their country we fully acknowledge, and whose unwavering posture we consider exemplary. The long and painful history of European movements for freedom give us the assurance that the struggles and sufferings of the Warsaw students and professors will not be in vain.

The Polish public knew hardly anything of such protests. The press only published reports about meetings of some Jewish associations abroad, presenting them as plots of international Zionist organizations to harm Poland. Apparently in this respect there was no disagreement between Gomulka and Moczar: both were bent on suppressing all protests against their inhumane policy, or on describing them as the work of Zionists or revisionists. Moczar continued to purge the Establishment and the national economy of intellectuals and even genuine Communists, dubbed 'liberals', in order to pave the way to total power for his own faction. Gomulka, unwilling to resist him and incapable of doing so, had good reasons of his own to be grateful that the Moczarites had managed to divert public attention from the pitiful economic circumstances of the country and were throwing to the lions a large number of people allegedly responsible for its misery. But eventually something resembling a stalemate between the rivals emerged: whatever served Moczar's medium-term interests also consolidated Gomulka's short-term power objective. And both presumably considered the hard-line policy an appropriate way of securing Moscow's support: without it neither could Gomulka retain the vestiges of his rule, nor could Moczar expect to achieve a decisive breakthrough in his drive for power.

From January 1968, when the old-time Stalinist Novotny in Czechoslovakia was replaced by Alexander Dubcek, who introduced the 'Prague Spring', the Moscow leadership, and the SED leadership in East Germany, relied on a tight and strict régime in Poland. The wave of liberalization in Czechoslovakia, abruptly brought to an end on the night of 21 August 1968 through the invasion of the armed forces of five member states of the Warsaw Treaty Organization, greatly affected the Polish intelligentsia as well. It was at once distressing and ironic that the desire for more freedom and democracy, which had intensified in Poland thanks to Czechoslovakia's example, fitted in perfectly with Moczar's ideas for a ruthless elimination of liberalism and democracy: according to his warped argument, any utterance of such a desire could be presented as part and parcel of a Zionist, revisionist conspiracy against socialism in Poland.

As it happened, it was just then that Moczar suffered his decisive setback. The Soviet Union evidently followed developments in Prague with such misgivings as to the future unity of its Western cordon of satellite countries that it could not at this juncture tolerate any change in the Warsaw leadership. It was therefore Moscow that tipped the balance on behalf of Gomulka as the man still able to command some obedience among the Polish public. After 28 and 29 March, when the final protests of the Warsaw students were suppressed by a brutal show of force, by mass arrests and expulsions, by the suspension of entire university faculties and university terms, and the introduction of stringent procedures for the readmission of students to graduation, order in Warsaw was restored. In an article 'Masterminds of Science or Defenders of Agitators?' *Trybuna Ludu* summed up the position and introduced a new public campaign against the purged scholars. By April the situation had so far been consolidated that Moczar was able to appear unchallenged and to address students of the Polytechnic. He told them:

In Czechoslovakia counter-revolution is at work. It will have to be suppressed. But this time there will be no repetition of the 1956 mistakes, which forced the Soviet Army to intervene in Hungary all by itself. This time the Red Army will not be left alone. We will defeat the counter-revolution by joining forces; we, too, are going to contribute our share....

Moczar said this at a time when 'friendly' negotiations between Moscow and Prague were still going on, and nobody had as yet accused Dubcek of having aided and abetted counter-revolution. Gomulka fully shared Moczar's dislike of the 'Prague Spring'. At the end of April 1968, at a session of the PUWP Central Committee, he asked those present whether they were aware what consequences the reforms in Czechoslovakia were liable to have for the Polish economy:

Thanks to their advanced technology very soon they will be able to compete with our industry on foreign markets, in particular in mechanical engineering. They will stop buying our machines and will be selling machines of their own instead; they will do a turn-about and face Western industry. This will have long-term consequences for Poland and for the Council for Mutual Economic Aid as a whole. And therefore this is not their own concern only; it is our concern, the concern of Poland as well.

With increased frequency the concepts of Poland and the Polish nation, Polish interests and the Polish cause, were now tossed around to justify a cynical police dictatorship. Nationalism and anti-Semitism became useful and consistent components of a policy which took the opportunity offered by any liberal stirring in order to make it quite clear to the entire population through massive political and police reprisals that there was not going to be any 'Warsaw Spring'. Nationalism, or rather chauvinism, requires the existence of enemies of the nation; anti-Semitism not only served this purpose, but also prevented the nationalist emotions from being turned against the USSR or East Germany. The sociologist Zygmunt Bauman, who left Poland in 1968 and now lives and teaches in England, explained why, in spite of the totally different circumstances in comparison with those prevailing in pre-war Poland, such a prescription could work:

Perhaps the rulers believed that in 1968 the Polish people was spontaneously and generally anti-Semitic, and that anti-Jewish slogans would secure popular sympathy for the government. Such calculation failed. In pre-war Poland there were quite genuine economic conditions for a 'popular' anti-Semitism, if only in the shape of a competitive struggle for market-stalls, or in the peasants' defence against exploitation by wholesale grain merchants. But there could be nothing like that in post-war Poland. The 1968 anti-Semitism was a phenomenon artificially imposed from above. But although the *provocateurs* failed in their speculations concerning the 'popular' character of Polish anti-Semitism, this does not mean that Polish Jews lacked some intrinsic qualities which predestined them for the scapegoats' role. According to recent psychological theories, a candidate for the scapegoat's part must meet at least three requirements:

(a) he must be sufficiently weak to allow aggressive instincts to be safely unleashed against him;

(b) he must be sufficiently strong, so that victory over him can restore a feeling of self-esteem and give grounds for pride;

(c) finally, he must be obviously accustomed to dealing with the current clichés used to describe the causes of frustration.

To a certain degree Polish Jews possessed all the three required qualities: they were numerically weak – 25,000 among a population of over 30 million – and in addition they were dispersed, integrated in Polish society and culture, united neither by a consciousness of national community nor by organizational ties; they seemed strong, or at least that was the impression that official propaganda, equipped with 'secret' documents, strenuously and with all the means at its disposal sought to demonstrate, by presenting them as a branch of a powerful Mafia allied with the devil in Bonn, and secretly ruling over the United States Senate, over the Pentagon, and over the world mass media, including Radio Free Europe and the Paris monthly *Kultura*; finally, Polish Jews could easily be associated with Soviet interests; Moczar, for example, spoke in a press interview about politicos who had arrived from the East in army officers' uniforms.

Bauman concludes that anti-Semitism was for these reasons the best-fitting fig-leaf for the power struggle, which was in fact the only issue in which everybody was really interested. The Jews were confronted with such a horrible choice because there was no alternative available:

I believe that some members of the party leadership, who still clung to the old Communist doctrine, accepted only unwillingly and hesitatingly the cliché they had been saddled with, that the disgusting price had to be paid for settling accounts with social protesters. In the March upheaval the Jewish issue was but a tool. The objective was quite different: the disarming of a potential opposition, the breaking down of the remaining centres of independent socialist thought, the intimidation of recalcitrants, and ... gaining favour with the new middle class, the main support of the state's power.

Such an interpretation might well explain why, even after the first great purge, the anti-Semitic campaign still continued. The notorious 'Protocols of the Elders of Zion' were published at least twice, with no publisher mentioned, and circulated as a clandestine publication. The layout, paper and print, however, all pointed to the printing presses of the publishing house of the Ministry of National Defence. As the scandal became known, a printer had to be sacrificed, but he was immediately re-employed by the printing house of the Ministry of Internal Affairs, where a second 'clandestine' edition soon appeared. The organ of the Ministry of National Defence published an article entitled 'Anti-Polish Activity on Behalf of Zionism', claiming that the Jews who in Stalin's time used to work for the security services had in fact acted to promote Zionist aims.

It is true that in the notorious UB, the Security Office, there were a number of Jewish officials. They were neither better nor worse than the obviously much more numerous Gentiles employed by the UB. All of them, however, Jews and Gentiles alike, were subordinated to Soviet 'advisers' who were at the time in charge of twelve out of the fourteen departments in the Ministry of Public Security. All of them faithfully carried out Stalin's directives. If only for this reason the argument about their allegedly exclusive role made no sense at all. The article was nevertheless reprinted in many other newspapers.

Many texts published at this time would fit in perfectly well with the editorial policy of Streicher's *Der Stürmer*, provided the word 'Zionist' were replaced by 'Jew'. This can clearly be seen from the following excerpts from a booklet, published in different versions, in many *voivodships*, in each case supplemented by some local data. In Gdansk, for example, it was circulated as the text of a 'Lecture for the Association of Atheists and Freethinkers'. It was entitled 'Zionism, Its Ideological Sources and Its Influence on Polish Medicine' and presented these grotesque ideas:

Zionism is a widespread international organization which usurps the right to rule over all Jews; for thousands of years it has been pursuing a policy aiming at the permanent economic and political disintegration of most countries of the world. Its goal is to take control over the whole globe, including all the nations inhabiting it.... The ideological sources of Zionism are derived from the monstrous double ethics of the Talmud, which divided humanity into 'the chosen people' and the so-called *goyim* (Gentiles), beasts with human faces who should be totally subordinated to the interests of the 'Supermen' – the Jews.

The anti-humanitarian Talmud-ethics of the Zionists have been adopted as a pattern and model by almost all forms of fascism, racism, colonialism, and many other genocidal ideologies, and have brought about the destruction of millions of innocent human beings. For thousands of years the double ethics of the Talmud have given the Zionists superior strength over the nations of the *goyim* because they have kept the Talmud secret. Insidiously they have won control over big capital all over the world. They have been supported by a large number of mercenaries, the so-called *shabbes-goyim*. The Zionists also invented and spread the absurd notion of anti-Semitism. In fact, anti-Semitism is a fiction, it exists no more than 'anti-Slavism', 'anti-Germanism', or 'anti-Romanism'.... Even the Nazi extermination of Jews could not be considered anti-Semitism; the Nazi criminals committed genocide.

For a long time the Zionists have considered medicine a sphere of influence through which they can gain control over the health and lives of Gentiles who might be dangerous for them. For this reason ... they would occupy, whenever possible, university chairs, posts in research institutes, clinics, hospitals, and the health-service administration. Zionist subversion in Polish medicine has assumed such enormous dimensions that in this concise study we can only present a few selected examples in a fragmentary manner. Zionist personnel policy consisted in dismissing from their posts all troublesome people – in particular those who had learned the truth about their subversive activities – or else in shifting them to minor positions and replacing them with their minions devoid of national, patriotic sentiments, as well as of political or ethical backbone. As a rule, these people did not even have the legally required professional qualifications, and therefore could easily be misused for a sophisticated disorganization of our health service, and in particular for paralysing the ideological education of our academic youth.

The main object was to train political illiterates, fully subservient to the Zionists. They persistently exploited all the state authorities under their control and turned them into veritable schools of vice and corruption, hotbeds of political subversion of People's Poland and of the Soviet Union, centres of espionage and demoralization of our academic youth. They undermined the family as a social institution with particular perfidy. They even established brothels, as well as a cult of luxury, and used to import Zionist trash under cover of 'Western culture'.[4]

A different kind of pseudo-scientific elaboration of the theory of modern anti-Semitism was pursued by a newly founded and allegedly non-party monthly review, *Miesiecznik Literacki*. Its editor-in-chief, the former Minister of Culture and Arts, Wlodzimierz Sokorski, sought to attract the country's intelligentsia. From January 1968 both Sokorski himself and other contributors published various analytical articles and essays on revisionism, Zionism and similar subjects. In June 1968 a concluding essay appeared by Andrzej Werblan, head of the Department of Education and Science in the Central Committee of the PUWP, subsequently promoted to deputy chairman of the *Sejm* and Secretary of the Party's Central Committee in charge of 'ideological' education. In a historical retrospective survey Werblan argued that national minorities (he obviously meant the Jews) were less responsive to issues of Polish patriotism, aspirations towards independence or national autonomy. He referred here to an accusation, then launched by the Moczarites inside the Party,

---

[4] The original pamphlet, signed by Professor Wiazemski of the School of Medicine in Gdansk, was unavailable to the author, who was unable to check its authenticity; excerpts were published by an Israeli Polish-language newspaper, *Nowiny-Kurier*. The author has been told that a phone-call was subsequently put through to Gdansk: somebody claiming to speak on behalf of a West European publisher inquired about copyright with a view to an eventual translation. Professor Wiazemski did not deny his authorship, and indeed entered into negotiations!

that the Jews who during the last war had occupied senior posts in the Union of Polish Patriots in the Soviet Union, and in the Polish armed forces there, had had no interest whatever in the rebirth of Poland as an independent and sovereign state. They had rather been inclined – the argument ran – to see it turned into another, seventeenth Soviet republic.

On the basis of history the author then argued that it was necessary to get rid of Jewish influence in the Party and in government. The Jews who had once been reluctant to defend Poland's independence with all their strength were now just as reluctant to do their best for Poland's advancement. Because of their crude, cosmopolitan version of inter-nationalism they failed to come to grips with national issues, and one testimony to that was that Jews occupied a much larger number of senior posts than could be justified by their proportion in the total population:

Cosmopolitanism inside the Party has provided the grounds for the false accusations of anti-Semitism against those comrades who have realized that no society can tolerate the excessive participation of a national minority in the élite of power, particularly in the fields of national defence, security, propaganda, and foreign policy. Only lack of consideration and clique solidarity of a nationalistic origin can explain the rapid promotion of people belonging to the Jewish petty bourgeoisie, not traditionally committed to Communism and mostly susceptible to Zionist influence. Experience has shown that most of them remained ideologically alien, and later easily slid into revisionist positions. Many went over to Zionism, breaking with Poland altogether and emigrating.

Although there was some resistance to Werblan's doctrine at the July 1968 Plenary Session of the Central Committee, Gomulka supported the author by saying his essay had provided a good basis for discussion. The Party ideologist, Kliszko, did not contradict him, and *Trybuna Ludu* printed excerpts.

It should be borne in mind that the present documentation deals exclusively with the output of the propaganda machine which was printed and which therefore remains accessible and quotable. Radio and television speeches made during Party meetings and mass rallies, as well as leaflets, posters and banners, supplemented the press campaign in a much more effective manner, as they appealed to a considerably larger audience. And these forms of propaganda caused no anxiety on account of possible echoes abroad, even in the Western Communist parties. It was therefore much more uninhibited, often shedding the thin 'anti-Zionist' camouflage and using crass anti-Jewish slogans; unfortunately most of this evidence has been lost. An auxiliary role was played by political cartoons.

3. Cover from *Der Giftpilz* (*The Poisonous Mushroom*), Stürmerverlag, 1938.

4. Captioned 'Taking Root', this cartoon by D. Agayev appeared in the Soviet daily *Gudok*, 15 September 1973.

When the Soviet press cartoonists after the Middle East war pilloried the Israelis in a crudely simplified manner and presented them as imperialists and militarists in a vicious *Stürmer*-like style (see cartoons 3 and 4), the Polish press followed suit with products that were no less coarse. The Polish army daily *Zolnierz Wolnosci* showed particular zeal. Long after the end of the Six-Day War its cartoonist, Zbigniew Damski, presented the war as a joint enterprise mounted by the West German plutocracy and aggressive Jews (see cartoons 5 and 6). In 1968 Damski was rewarded with a state prize in the field of fine arts for his creative activities.

Thus for a long time the Polish population was fed with texts and pictures, issued in mass editions, sometimes gross and clumsy, sometimes sophisticated. They appealed to the basest instincts – and often effectively: every nation has its share of people in a state of permanent dissatisfaction and frustration. Besides, old-time anti-Semites still lived in Poland, people who had been forced to conceal their true opinions for twenty years or more. Now their accumulated hatred could at last break out in the open. But the great majority of the politically immature were virtually defenceless in face of the systematically promoted campaign of

ŻOŁNIERZ WOLNOŚCI

GAZETA CODZIENNA WOJSKA POLSKIEGO

Polish army newspaper   22.1.1969

The former Israeli Deputy Minister of Defence announced that West Germany had made a gift to Israel of arms worth $500m.

BYŁY WICEMINISTER OBRONY IZRAELA UJAWNIŁ, ŻE NRF DOSTARCZYŁA BEZPŁATNIE IZRAELOWI BRONI O WARTOŚCI 500 MLN DOLARÓW.

— Kto kocha (wojnę...), ten nie liczy się z kosztami...

Rys. Z. Damski

He who loves (war) does not count the cost.

5.

ŻOŁNIERZ WOLNOŚCI

GAZETA CODZIENNA WOJSKA POLSKIEGO

Polish army newspaper   23.9.1968

The Israeli occupiers continued to evict the Arab population from the Gaza strip.

The experience should be used ...

(on the plan: 'Eviction plan')

6.

totalitarian propaganda. The opportunists among them hoped for lucrative jobs and power, to get at last the posts to which in normal conditions they could not aspire, lacking the necessary qualifications; now such jobs became easily accessible, provided they were ready to denounce and slander their Jewish superiors and colleagues, as well as those honest people who had rallied to the defence of the slandered. Taken together, however, the convinced anti-Semites and the frustrated, those who benefited from this campaign and the righteous with the courage to oppose it, constituted but a minority. The silent majority, in this case too, remained absorbed in its own affairs.

In spite of this, or rather because of it, it seems appropriate to recall the names of a few journalists who in those years dared to resist attempts at corruption. The correspondent of *Zycie Warszawy* at the United Nations in New York, Wieslaw Gornicki, for example, refused to file an anti-Israeli commentary, and instead sent to his editorial office a telex message justifying his attitude. Gornicki was immediately recalled to Poland and his case submitted to the Party's Control Commission. He was reprimanded, and had to work for some time as an anonymous reporter on the staff of the Polish Press Agency. Later he had his rights restored and re-emerged as one of the top columnists of *Zycie Warszawy*, but confronted once more with intensified pressure, he finally tendered his resignation, preferring to work as a free-lance writer.

Karol Malcurzynski, chief political commentator of Polish television and staff correspondent of the Party's central daily *Trybuna Ludu*, refused to comment on the invasion of Czechoslovakia. He was punished with dismissal from his television post, but was allowed to continue his work on the paper. Later he resumed his job in television as well and was subsequently elected chairman of the Polish Association of Dramatists and Composers (ZAIKS). Afterwards he was again in trouble with the authorities.

Tadeusz Szafar, foreign affairs correspondent for the Workers' (Press) Agency, refused to denounce the alleged 'Zionist' smear campaign against Poland. When he was taken to task because of this, he told a Party meeting that Middle Eastern affairs had been used by the Polish press for internal political purposes and therefore remained outside the scope of his journalistic activity. He also expressed the view that the anti-Semitic policy pursued in Poland, with the connivance of supreme Party and state bodies, was a justifiable cause for concern in the Western mass media and not an anti-Polish campaign. He was expelled from the Party, dismissed from his job, and deprived of any possibility of pursuing his profession. Szafar is Jewish, Gornicki and Malcurzynski are not: that was the reason for the different attitude of the authorities.

Official guidelines, apart from a directive signed by Prime Minister Cyrankiewicz which generally banned the employment of Jews in any of the central institutions or offices, also forbade the employment of Jews in any position with a monthly salary higher than 3,000 zlotys (approximately $300 – then slightly more than the average worker's wage). In fact Jews could not avail themselves even of this discriminatory order: whoever lost his post was virtually unable to find another job.

A number of senior officials lost their posts because of their protests against the racist campaign; they included the Chairman of the Council of State (equivalent to President of the Republic) and former First Secretary of the Party's Central Committee, Edward Ochab,[5] and Foreign Minister Adam Rapacki;[6] both were dropped from the Party's Politbureau. After a meeting at the Ministry of Foreign Affairs, marked by wild and vulgar shouting in a veritable pogrom atmosphere, several dozen of Rapacki's collaborators, both senior and junior, were in effect dismissed from the foreign service; the minister himself refused to enter his office and absented himself from Politbureau sessions. Other officials dismissed at that time included two long-serving members of the Party's Central Committee, the Minister of Finance, Jerzy Albrecht, and the Minister of Health, Jerzy Sztachelski. Neither was Jewish.

Wladyslaw Bienkowski has analysed the official statements and press commentaries on the March events. From a flood of accusations, defamations and slanders, he compiled a catalogue of arguments which can serve as the common denominator for the authorities' reaction, as the ideological basis for the fight against dissident intellectuals. The students' protests were presented by the authorities as the consequence of two different developments which had been in progress for a long time:

[5] Edward Ochab, a veteran Communist of great personal integrity, became leader of the Polish Party in 1956 with Khrushchev's express agreement, but a few months later voluntarily ceded the post to Gomulka. When the anti-Semitic campaign was unleashed, he found himself in opposition to Gomulka and Moczar. His daughters, as students, participated in the protest movement. He himself – though still Chairman of the Council of State – was placed under police surveillance. In 1968 he resigned to avoid giving in to pressure, and was replaced by the then rather senile Marian Spychalski. Later Ochab demanded the rehabilitation of the March victims, and punishment of those who had taken part in 'the struggle against Jewish Communist conspiracy with a truly fascist zeal'. His attempts were of no avail.

[6] Adam Rapacki (1909–70), as member of the supreme leadership of the Polish Socialist Party (PPS), greatly contributed to its enforced merger with the PPR and the founding of the PUWP in 1948. Until 1968 he was a member of the Politbureau of the 'United' party; in 1947–50 Minister of Shipping, in 1950–55 Minister of Higher Education, and subsequently (up to 1968) Minister of Foreign Affairs. It was in this capacity that he submitted the plan for the creation of an atom-free zone in both parts of Germany, Poland and Czechoslovakia. The Rapacki plan, put forward at the United Nations in October 1957 and later supplemented and amended several times, had until 1964 a considerable role in international discussions on the solution of the East–West conflict, although it never materialized into an international agreement.

On the one hand they were influenced by the revisionist, anti-Socialist attitude of some intellectuals who occupied responsible posts in the field of the
humanities, at universities and research institutes. Their influence corrupted
young people, germinated anti-Soviet opposition, created a climate favourable
to subversive activities. The scholars' influence was supported by a considerable number of writers who at a meeting of the Warsaw branch of their union
and under the pretext of protesting against the ban on the production of *The
Forefathers* began openly to oppose the policy pursued by the authorities and
thus supported the students' ringleaders.

On the other hand, this development can be traced back to the anti-Socialist
and anti-Polish machinations of the Zionists and of elements linked to the
world Zionist movement. The Zionists condemned the Party's policy because
of its denunciation of Israel as an aggressor; they exploited revisionist tendencies to undermine the ideology and policy of the Party and to spread both
bourgeois and Trotskyite ideas.

In such a way revisionist and Zionist influences combined and pushed part
of the unenlightened youth into participation in irresponsible demonstrations.
There were clashes and street riots in which a shady rabble, together with other
elements remotely controlled by hostile centres, took part. The security
apparatus and the forces of law and order fortunately demonstrated great skill
and determination. They soon managed to restore order, to uncover the guid-
ing centres of the plotters and to put an end to their activities.

Bienkowski went on to explain that the official analysis of the causes
underlying the riots had led to the conviction that 'the ringleaders and
trouble-makers among the students came mostly from the intelligentsia,
of which a great part was of Jewish origin, in comfortable circumstances,
and from a class which occupied responsible positions'. He then proceeded to make an analysis of his own and argued that while the student
protests had been taking place, there had also existed a strictly controlled
campaign with many facets. 'As if from underground' a number of hitherto virtually unknown ideologists emerged to propagate in the press,
radio and television their policy of toughness and renovation. Under the
following four headings Bienkowski summed up his arguments for the
emergence of a state-managed, deliberate, and in many details provoked,
conflict.

1. All the evidence of eyewitnesses proves that the first intervention by the
forces of order and security in the quadrangle of Warsaw University on 8
March was not justified by the course of events. The students' rally could not
justify it, because the intervention did not begin until the students – after meeting some professors who, by the way, were only incidentally present – started
to disperse. The professors on the spot were unanimous in stating that the

students had behaved with restraint; there had been no cause to fear outrages of any kind. The same thing happened a few days later in Cracow. The Rector of the Jagiellonian University, a member of the Council of State, asked the Secretary of the Party's *voivodship* committee to prevent police interference in the university campus; there was no need for it. A little later the police did appear.

2. The appearance of the alleged workers' detachments on the campus of Warsaw University was a deliberate, well-prepared action instigated by the security organs.

3. Many indications point to the conclusion that state executive organs intended from the very beginning to seize the opportunity for drastic intervention, and thus to provoke the desired agitation among the students and in the population at large. The forces of order would then be able to appear as victors over a widespread revolt, or even a counter-revolution.... Serious indications confirm the fact that officials of the security organs organized provocations – for example, by shouting anti-government and anti-Soviet slogans – in order to present the students' demonstrations in the desired political colouring. One of these *agents-provocateurs* was exposed by the students in the Warsaw University quadrangle on 8 March: he was one of the 'representatives of the working class' who had arrived in motorcoaches.

4. The students' protests were presented as hostile to the workers, as having been provoked by sons and daughters of the privileged groups of intellectuals. That was precisely what was needed in order to exploit the well-known fact that for various reasons, undoubtedly including a mistaken policy of mass education, the children of workers and peasants were under-represented at all schools of higher learning. Those chiefly attacked from the very beginning were 'Zionist agents of imperialism'. In various contexts the press picked almost exclusively on 'Zionist' names. All the mass media unleashed a frantic campaign in which slogans appeared borrowed from anywhere but the ideological arsenal of socialism: e.g. 'Poland for the Poles!' 'Purge the country of Zionists!' and more in a similar vein. The fact that among scholars there were many Jews (a personal union between revisionism and Zionism) facilitated the combination of different demands. To substantiate the basic claim that social order and socialism were menaced, attempts at a *coup d'état* were hinted at: a climate bordering on a state of emergency was created in order to justify severe reprisals, unpopular in normal circumstances ... on the one hand defensive measures against an imminent menace; on the other measures for an alleged revival and continuation of October [1956].

The purge and the ensuing loss of livelihood endured by thousands of families naturally brought about an increase in the number of applications for exit permits, particularly since Gomulka in his 19 March speech had expressly offered emigration as a solution. The details of official behaviour will be discussed in a later chapter; but now something should be said about the judiciary system, which had been infiltrated by members of the police faction and turned by them into a weapon of police violence, depriving the citizen of all his rights.

9. Justice and Punishment

AFTER the March riots Polish courts were kept busy. The courts should have been the place to test the veracity of often patently absurd charges, to defend the rights of harassed citizens, to restrain power-drunk officials. But this was not the case: the judiciary merely reaffirmed the correctness and the effectiveness of the measures introduced by the Party and the state administration, and in consequence no other authority remained to defend the citizen.

The trial which probably caused the greatest stir was that of Professor Parnas, a scholar well known inside and outside Poland. During the war he had fought in a Soviet guerrilla detachment, had been decorated for bravery, and promoted to the rank of major. Parnas, a microbiologist, returned to his scientific work after the war. He was engaged as an expert by the World Health Organization, he was a fellow of the Royal College of Physicians in London, and member of many other scientific bodies, including the Society for Tropical Medicine in Amsterdam. For a time he was the Rector of the Sklodowska-Curie University in Lublin. Many foreign universities awarded him honorary degrees, and his scholarly books and papers were translated into many languages.

As far back as 1963 Jakub Parnas gave up his Party membership card, and from then on was constantly harassed by Party and police authorities. He was stripped of his post as head of the Institute for Labour Medicine and Rural Hygiene that he himself had founded, he was refused a passport for trips abroad, and several times he had to endure police searches at his home. In March 1968 Parnas publicly defended the students' protests. Shortly after, on 4 April, he was dismissed from his university chair and from his other posts, and subjected to a smear campaign in the press. As a result he decided to leave the country. As a Jew he had no other choice (as we shall see) but to apply for an exit permit for Israel. But the Moczarite faction, however desirous it was of encouraging as much emigration as possible, was presumably even more interested in retaining the most prominent Jews in the country. If they emigrated their international repute and credibility might cause damaging reactions abroad. Anyhow, Parnas was arrested.

He was arraigned by the Military Prosecutor's Office, and in the spring of 1969 was put on trial by a military court sitting *in camera*. He was charged with espionage, but nobody was able to ascertain on what grounds or evidence the indictment had been based. The famous scholar, author of three hundred scientific books and papers, was sentenced to five years' imprisonment. The press did not even mention his trial. It was only after the bloody events of December 1970 that the new Party leader Edward Gierek ordered the release of Professor Parnas, thus implicitly acknowledging that the accusation had been totally groundless. In Communist states spies are not released before their term is over; at best, they are exchanged. Parnas was unobtrusively given a passport, and left Poland in October 1971 to settle in Denmark.

A purely politically motivated trial was the case of Mieczyslaw Martula, a journalist. He was in possession of the manuscript of a diary that his brother had kept under the German occupation. This very personal account of the experiences he had undergone as a Polish Jew under Nazi rule contained, together with reminiscences concerning people who had come to his assistance, certain details about Poles who had blackmailed him and threatened to denounce him to the Gestapo unless he paid their price. Martula's brother, like many other Jews in hiding, fell victim to the *szmalcowniki* gangs mentioned earlier whose existence has never been seriously questioned: indeed, some of them were executed by the Polish underground, others were put on trial and sentenced shortly after the war. Plenty of evidence of their misdeeds can be found in the book *Poles and Jews, 1939–1945*, published in 1972 by the then Minister of Culture and Art, Stanislaw Wronski. In 1967–8, however, when Martula submitted his brother's manuscript to several publishing houses in turn, such revelations were for political reasons deemed unacceptable. Martula was sentenced to three years' imprisonment. According to the prosecutor's summing-up, the mere suggestion that a Pole could have been capable of blackmailing Jews or of denouncing them to their executioners was tantamount to slandering the Polish nation: no Pole was capable of such an act! Martula, who was quietly released shortly after his sentence, under an amnesty which prevented him from securing a retrial in a court of appeal, left the country.

Premature release of those convicted might appear at a glance as a more refined way of amending wrongful sentences. In fact, it was always preceded by a period of tormenting and corrupting detention, leaving, as in Martula's case, no chance of rehabilitation. On the other hand, many victims of such arbitrary proceedings were in effect forced into a decision to flee their native country, a decision they had never envisaged before. The story of a Wroclaw student, Karol Storch, will serve as an example. When arrested in 1968 he was just eighteen. All in all, he spent fifteen months in police detention, in a military punishment camp and in a military prison. On 7 August 1969 he was pardoned, and in mid-October left for Denmark, a nineteen-year-old youngster, physically and mentally injured. His father died in the meantime as a result of unlawful detention and lack of medical care in prison.

Here follows his own account:

My father and I were arrested as Jews and Zionists. Even if we had been Zionists, there would have been nothing to be ashamed of. But I have to put things right: my father, Stefan Storch, was a Polish Jew, not a Zionist, my mother was Polish, I consider myself a Pole. I am saying this as a man driven out of Poland, slandered and humiliated by Polish authorities.

I did not go to Israel and I have no intention of going there. I have settled in Denmark. Altogether some 1,700 people of the so-called 'Moczar emigration' came to this country. In 1967 and 1968 when anti-Jewish slogans began to appear more and more frequently in the press, radio and television, as well as in speeches by official personalities, my father wrote several times to the *Sejm*, to the Council of State, and to various newspapers, protesting against and refuting false accusations. He demanded from the Office of the Prosecutor-General the arraignment of an editor. On 1 March 1968 eight police officials came to our Wroclaw flat with a search warrant. Between 7.15 a.m. and 2.30 p.m. they turned everything upside-down. They found nothing, except some carbon copies of my father's letters and articles, by no means secret. But next day he was arrested, although it was common knowledge he had a heart condition. I was arrested two weeks later, allegedly for taking part in student demonstrations.

In jail my father wrote a number of petitions and complaints, demanding his release and pointing out that his state of health precluded any suspicion of escape. At the same time he fought hard for my release. He was released on doctors' orders in mid-September but was re-arrested a month later. Shortly after that he was set free once more, and on 5 December detained yet again. The very next day he suffered a heart attack, and died.

My arrest and sentencing to two years' imprisonment had nothing to do with the Jewish issue. I was detained because as a student I was suspected of having taken part in the March demonstrations, but in all minutes, records, and court proceedings my Jewish ancestry was deliberately stressed. The indictment asserted I had at home a collection of Zionist Hebrew books. In fact, I know not a single word of Hebrew.

On the night of 14 March 1968 the police seized me in front of the Wroclaw main railway station. I had been deeply affected by the arrest of my father and had his first letter with me. As I left the station, the square in front was closely surrounded by police. On one side policemen drove passers-by from the pavements, on the other they cordoned off all the exits and side streets. Those who managed to escape in time, sought refuge in the Grand Hotel and its restaurants. Policemen armed with clubs suddenly started to beat people at random. I heard women shouting: 'Don't hit the children!' The police sealed off the railway station, only letting through those who had a valid ticket. All those arriving had to produce their identity cards. Unfortunately I had nothing on me, except a student's card: presumably they were just waiting to get hold of some students. I was taken to police headquarters. I could see police vehicles arriving, and people being pushed out of them. A girl fell with her face to the pavement, and began to scream. Policemen stationed at the gate dived for her and madly started to beat her up with rubber truncheons. I was led into a waiting-room. A police NCO, seeing my identification documents, rubbed his hands in glee and shouted at the top of his voice: 'Well, at last we've got a genuine student!' I was interrogated by two police officers in turn for four hours. I was stripped naked and searched three times, but they were still unable to come up with any definite charges. At midnight I was led to a cell intended for four detainees, but there were already eight people lying there on the floor and on the plank beds, and during the night three more were pushed in. After 48 hours' detention in the cell I was taken before a magistrate of the Krzyki city district; witnesses gave evidence to the effect that I had not taken part in the demonstrations, but in spite of their testimony I was sentenced to a 1,500 zloty fine or alternatively to 50 days' detention.

Two policemen, sworn in as witnesses, admitted that Storch had not participated in the riots: they had detained him 'just in case' because he was a student. Four days later he received a letter signed by the University Rector telling him he had been suspended. Storch continued nevertheless to attend lectures, and nobody paid the slightest attention to him.

After another week I was woken up in the morning by a telephone call: the police summoned me to their headquarters to give evidence in my father's case. I got up and washed. A few minutes later somebody rattled at the door. Policemen ordered me to get dressed and to come to headquarters with them. There . . . I was given a call-up order. On 29 March 1968 I arrived at a military unit in Zagan. I was ordered to report to a special detachment. In woods, some 20 kilometres from the town, a camp had been set up for students dismissed from universities after the March events. I heard later there were more such units scattered all over the country. We trained without weapons: prolonged, exhausting drill designed to sap our strength as quickly as possible, interrupted only by political lectures and interrogation by a counter-intelligence officer. He would ask us about our parents and friends, and naturally about our part in the March events. As I stood firm and claimed I had been groundlessly detained and sentenced, he told me angrily: 'We always say: once we have the man, we'll find the Article too.' On 5 April I was transferred to so-called 'engineers' training'; this high-flown designation covered nothing but digging trenches, first in a kneeling position, then in a lying one, finally standing upright.... Digging made me short of breath, I started to stagger and dropped my steel helmet; I had to rest a while. NCO Antoniuk, who was supervising our work, started to insult me. I said I was unable to dig any more. He ordered me to put on my gas-mask and to go on digging. I refused and was led to a counter-intelligence captain who arrested me for refusing to obey orders. To incriminate me even more, I was additionally charged with having reported to Antoniuk a few days earlier without my belt, and having insulted him in an exchange of words. The truth was that I had tried to get permission to leave because, despite stomach pains, he had forced me to crawl round the tent on my belly.

In a detention cell in Lubsko a state prosecutor called Blasiak added a third charge to my indictment – slandering the Polish nation and state: under Article 28 of the Penal Code it is a crime punishable with imprisonment of up to ten years. They were just waiting for me in a state of disturbance to say something for which they could put me on trial. After over four weeks of detention in Lubsko I had still received no letters. In order to protest I decided to go on a hunger strike and I put a notice in my meal bowl saying I was going to refuse food. Shortly after the wardens dragged me out of my cell and took me to a cellar. On the way down they hit me in the kidneys with a bunch of keys. Downstairs they put me in a so-called safety belt, resembling the belt carried by firemen, some ten centimetres [four inches] wide, with iron rings on the outside to put shafts and metal bolts in. I offered no resistance but the belt was too large for my size: I was young and very slim. One of them went out and fetched a regular strait-jacket that Sergeant Sierakowski was notorious for having used in the Wolow jail. In Lubsko they tried it for the first time on me. After the prisoner had his arms put into long sleeves and twisted so that the palms were laid on the shoulder-blades, the strait-jacket was tied up in the back; this was extremely painful. I could not stop howling, but the wardens shut the doors and nobody could hear me while they looked at me, made jokes and laughed. After a longish time a prison officer appeared and ordered them to release me from the strait-jacket. I was forced to sign an undertaking not to tell anybody about the tortures, and in addition not to attempt suicide.

Karol Storch's trial took place in three stages before a military court in Zielona Gora; the sentence was passed on 10 June 1968 after nine witnesses for the prosecution had given evidence. Officers and NCOs said on oath whatever was required of them:

Captain Galazka said I had at home a collection of prohibited Zionist books in Hebrew. He had never been to our flat: there were no such books there. Besides, I can neither read nor speak Hebrew. Colour-sergeant Wyrebkiewicz said I had demanded weapons during my stay in the military camp, presumably, together with my friends, in order to overthrow the government of Gomulka and Ochab. Sergeant Pleskaczynski, Second Lieutenant Gradziel, Lieutenant Humaniuk, Sergeant Sobocinski one after another repeated similarly ridiculous charges. The court sentenced me to six months in jail for refusal to obey orders, seven months for insulting a superior officer, and a year and a half for slandering People's Poland. The overall punishment was set at two years' imprisonment.

Storch, described in the court records (he managed to bring a copy to Denmark) as 'Karol-Maksymillian Storch, son of Stefan and Wanda née Szukszta, born on 15 November 1949 in Wroclaw, of Jewish nationality', was then transferred to a prison in Stargard, built on the site of a former Nazi concentration camp. This is how he described the place:

A lawn, flower beds, benches, even a fountain, and in the background neat small cottages, surrounded with barbed wire. The prison wardens lived in the cottages. Further on another gate, then barbed wire and a large barracks, the detention block, a place of isolation where prisoners could be beaten up and tortured, so that nobody would hear their screams. Inside there were detention cells with hard beds and all kinds of special equipment. Behind a third line of barbed wire were the living quarters. Between the lines of barbed wire ran a so-called death strip with a cord inside, to which dogs were tied at night. The whole camp was intended for 1,000 prisoners, but sometimes as many as 1,300 were there doing hard labour. Just outside the barbed-wire perimeter was an industrial plant Pomet 5, for processing metals. On the nearby state farms prisoners were employed in odd jobs; in summer the working day lasted twelve hours. Each prisoner was supposed to fulfil 100 per cent of his working quota, otherwise he was punished. For 15 months, night after night, I used to go to bed with my stomach aching with hunger. Others had to endure this for much longer. There was inside the prison a training battalion, a kind of penal company inside the jail. Its commander was Inspector Pajak, an officer of the penitentiary service with the rank of captain. He was particularly hated by the prisoners because he used methods worthy of the SS. I remember New Year's Eve of 1969 when a drunken Pajak conducted an inspection. A prisoner called through the window: 'Pajak, you are a swine!' Pajak ordered a roll-call, and then drilled us in the snow. Not all of us managed to put on our shoes and warm coats. My father died in police detention on 6 December. The prison authorities refused to give me leave of absence. Because of the officials' heartlessness I was unable to attend my father's funeral.

Karol Storch's story was by no means exceptional. Although the maltreatment of prisoners was only rarely revealed, many students sentenced to imprisonment were kept in the most sinister jails, and military service in penal camps was often imposed as additional torture. It was not only Jews who had to submit to such inhuman treatment; the number of non-Jewish prisoners was much greater, but there were many young people who, like Karol Storch, were arrested and sentenced for no other reason than their Jewish origin, even when they had nothing to do with the students' protests.

Jozef Dajczgewand, the son of poor Jewish parents, a student of philosophy at Warsaw University, known to his colleagues as a gifted young man of considerable literary talents, was arrested in March 1968. He and a non-Jewish student, Slawomir Kretkowski, were accused of being leaders of a group of 'Commandos'. It was alleged that this group had acted between February 1967 and March 1968 as a clandestine organization set up to carry out a programme detrimental to the interests of the Polish People's Republic by means of anti-government and anti-Party demonstrations; the 'Commandos' were therefore considered ringleaders of the Zionist conspiracy. Kretkowski was sentenced to a year and a half in prison, Dajczgewand to two and a half years. During his trial he pleaded not guilty to all the charges with: 'Most young Poles think as we do. No trials or sentences can hide that.'

When Dajczgewand eventually came to Sweden together with his parents, he was interviewed by Amnesty International; he claimed that the number of those arrested in March 1968 reached four thousand. He himself was at first put in a Warsaw prison, and there he was not maltreated. After his sentence was passed he was transferred to a prison in Strzelce Opolskie where there were a hundred political prisoners among two thousand criminals. He was allowed three food parcels a year and one visit a month but was deprived of books, and everything he had written was confiscated.

Among the prison wardens there was a special group of torturers. As a rule, shortly before their release, prisoners were tortured as a stern warning for the future. Three methods of torture were used: solitary confinement coupled with beating and humiliation; hanging up by a chain tied round the wrists; tying to a bench so that the blood circulation was impaired till the victim lost consciousness. A few weeks before his release from jail Dajczgewand was submitted to this third method of torture, although it was already generally known at that time that an amnesty was imminent.

Tightly tied to a bench my body became stiff all over. I experienced unbearable pain and started shouting for a doctor. The wardens burst into laughter and left the cell. As I continued to scream louder and louder, a warden came back and gagged me. I lost consciousness. As I regained my senses I could hear howling from nearby cells. I felt as if I was in a slaughterhouse. An hour later the wardens returned, untied the belts and took me to the prison doctor. He signed a statement testifying that my state of health 'allows the use of corporal punishment'. After this 'treatment' I was completely broken for a long time.

On 16 January 1969 Jacek Kuron and Karol Modzelewski were put on trial. The court proceedings were reported at length by the foreign press because the two young scholars were already well known thanks to their 'Open Letter to the Party' and subsequent imprisonment. In their evidence they denied all the charges in the indictment, but at the same time defended their opinions firmly and with dignity, and in particular denounced the racist character of the trials. Modzelewski said, *inter alia*:

The state prosecutor has mentioned the reasons which originally motivated the investigation authorities to select the defendants for this particular trial. One criterion was the social background of the co-defendants, another – and here, I, too, am involved – the Jewish origin of all the defendants, with the sole exception of Jacek Kuron. On this issue therefore I would like to dwell at some length.... What significance could my mother's maiden name have for the court proceedings? ... Has it any legal significance? Yes, there was a European state where this had legal significance, where there were such laws. But in the Polish People's Republic there are no laws – nor will there ever be – that make it legal to differentiate between citizens because of their mother's, grandmother's or grandfather's name. Therefore such a hypothesis should be exluded and I am going to exclude it ... as well as the assumption that my mother's name and the circumstance – as the state prosecutor has said – 'ascertained beyond a shadow of doubt' that all the other co-defendants were of Jewish origin constitute proof of my and their different nature in the national sense.... For the first time in my life I have encountered such an argument, and I am therefore going to refute it with an argument I have never in my life wanted to use. Well, nobody of us, here in the dock, is obliged to supply proof that he is a Pole. There was talk here of bread which, when eaten, binds a man to his country. But there is a kind of bread which, in my opinion, binds with particular force – the bread of the jail. We know the taste of such bread, we have been eating it, with a short intermission only, for nearly four years. We eat it now for the second time with the full awareness of having chosen it consciously. That is our identification, unequalled by any work-pass issued by a state authority.

Kuron, too, stressed the inhuman character of the trials:

The function of anti-Semitism in its racist form consists in replacing discussion on our country's difficult problems by denunciation of those taking part in the discussion and calling them Jews. The essence of racist anti-Semitism consists in shifting on to aliens responsibility for the misdeeds of the régime, for the defective work of the authorities.... During the investigation the interrogating officers tried very hard to find some Jewish name among my ancestors. When they failed to make a Jew out of me, they wanted at least to turn me into a Ukrainian, all in order to be able to denounce me as an alien. During the investigation there were days when I wished to admit I was Jewish, because there are circumstances when every honest man would rather be a Jew.

Most of those sentenced at that time did not make the prosecutors' task any easier, and defied all their attempts to prove punishable offences by means of threadbare inventions. Often they were brave enough to mislead the accusers, for example, when a number of them admitted to the authorship of certain leaflets even when it was obvious they had been written by one person only. But such determination did not help any of the defendants; the courts were not concerned with justice but with the interests of the authorities. In Poland there was no separation of powers: the judiciary was subservient to the state, the Party and the police; the defendants were, therefore, engaged in a struggle doomed to failure. The courage with which they openly expressed their opinions, regardless of the dangers inherent in their exposed position, was all the more remarkable. Adam Michnik, arraigned as a ringleader of the March events, said in his plea:

Our debating club was founded under the patronage of the University branch of the ZMS [the Union of Socialist Youth] which took an interest in our activity, provided us with accommodation, helped us in arranging debating meetings, professors' lectures, etc. We invited to our meetings professors of different disciplines: historians, philosophers, economists, sociologists of various persuasions and schools, also biologists. We even invited a priest, because we wanted to hear about the ideals and the modern thinking of the Church. The lectures were usually followed by discussion: we put questions – sometimes, no doubt, rather teasing questions – we voiced our opposition or approval, as young people always do. This is the whole story of the notorious 'Club of the Contradiction-Seekers'.

As civil liberties became more and more restricted, the changes could not but influence the mood prevailing among the academic youth. At the University this process was accompanied by the reversion of political and social organizations to bureaucratic methods of work. They used administrative measures instead of persuasion more and more frequently. Every critical or dissenting view was suppressed by punishment, censure, expulsion from the Party and from the Youth Union, and in recent years even by persecution on the part of the University authorities. Even for trivial misdemeanours students were summoned before disciplinary commissions and punished with a reprimand or temporary suspension from studies. I myself learned this to my cost. I was twice punished by a disciplinary commission with one year's suspension from studies, and, finally, at the beginning of 1968 I was dismissed from the University.

... A major cause for resentment and anxiety among students was the interference of security organs in the life and affairs of students and the University; such interference was then occurring more and more often. Many students were placed under constant police surveillance. Students were summoned for interrogation to the Security Office under various pretexts, and kept there for twenty-four or even forty-eight hours. And although the University authorities knew about it, they did nothing to put an end to these practices. Police officials were allowed to operate freely on the University campus.... As for the leaflet on Vietnam, I admit having written it. I don't know why Barbara Torunczyk and Karol Modzelewski confessed to being its authors.... I wrote this leaflet in connection with the Week of Solidarity with the struggle of the Vietnamese people.... The indictment claims that it contained anti-Soviet overtones, allegedly because of its concluding sentences which alluded to the 1956 Hungarian uprising. This is a terrifying confusion of ideas. Does the Prosecutor's Office really believe that a follower or friend of the Soviet Union is bound to approve unconditionally every single political act of the Soviet government? Would any critical attitude to the political measures undertaken by the USSR be considered tantamount to an anti-Soviet attitude? If so – to recall only the most recent events – the European Communist parties which have condemned the intervention of the Warsaw Pact armies in Czechoslovakia should be considered enemies of the USSR, and that is patently absurd. It seems to me that fairly often it is the critics of individual political measures undertaken by the USSR who are the best friends of that country.

Allow me to add on this occasion that I, being in jail, have no opportunity to make known my views concerning the events in Czechoslovakia, but there is not the slightest doubt that were I free, I would express – in one way or another – my condemnation of the invasion of Czechoslovakia by the Warsaw Pact armies, and in particular by our troops.

As for the leaflet entitled 'Fascism Shall Not Pass!', published in reply to the shameful rhyming leaflet containing such gems as a call 'to grasp the Jew by his side-locks and throw him in the sea', although I have neither written nor distributed it, I consider myself fully responsible for it, because I agree with it totally and in every detail. It is significant that the prosecutor described this very leaflet as a provocation, while nothing has been said about the other, to which this was a reply. I would like to emphasize that neither the investigating authorities nor the Prosecutor's Office have ever tried to discover its authors.

10. The Exodus

IF one were to believe the authorities, the emigration of the Jews as a result of pressure, terror and boycott, and encompassing the full Jews, half-Jews, one-quarter or one-eighth Jews registered in the card-index compiled by Walichnowski's department in the Ministry of Internal Affairs, was the outcome of an act of humanity. Those Jews were allegedly set on going to Israel at any price, they considered themselves emotionally attached to Israel rather than to Poland, and they were therefore given permission to leave and no obstacles were put in their way. The reality, however, was quite different.

Jews were 'encouraged' to emigrate by anonymous letters, by phone calls and menaces, sometimes by displaying in their neighbourhood small posters on walls and trees with announcements running more or less on these lines: 'Adam Weinberg, son of Isaac, because of his imminent departure for Israel, will sell his furniture and other household articles', followed by his address and phone number. In this way many Jews discovered for the first time that they intended to emigrate. In those months a new trade emerged by leaps and bounds: buyers of Jewish property could purchase household goods at ridiculous prices, as the sellers were pressed for time. Organized gangs of such buyers showed themselves eager to exploit the plight of others. But in the Party's Central Committee Moczar and his deputy Szlachcic boasted in public of the increasing numbers of applications for exit permits to Israel – in a triumphant tone, as if announcing victories won on the battlefield.

From time to time rumours were spread that the documents required for emigration, stating that their holders were not Polish citizens and were proceeding to Israel to settle there, would be issued for a limited period of time only. The fear that one day it might be too late drove many undecided people to apply for them. Such rumours were presumably circulated deliberately in order to accelerate matters. And it was not the work of individual over-zealous officials alone: on 11 June 1969 all the Polish newspapers published the following short communiqué issued by the official Polish Press Agency PAP:

In order to facilitate the departure of people who consider themselves attached to Israel rather than to Poland, a special simplified procedure has been introduced. The Polish Press Agency has been advised that the temporary procedure for issuing documents to people wishing to settle in Israel permanently will remain in force till September of this year.

As it turned out later, this, too, was false information, but it helped to persuade those who were still uncertain to apply for exit permits. It goes without saying that the communiqué revived the flagging emigration movement. The applicants, generally unaccustomed to any undue haste on the part of the state authorities in their relations with the public, now found themselves dealing with an efficient bureaucratic machine that issued emigration permits without any hitches or delay. It was obvious there was nothing improvised about it: the rules of procedure had been deliberately thought out well in advance, every detail clearly calculated to benefit the state and the Party, and in particular to prevent the emigrants from ever returning to Poland.

Many emigrants had, in fact, no intention whatsoever of going to Israel. There were many different reasons for this: some people had families in Western Europe, others hoped to use their professional skills to rebuild their lives in the USA or in some other highly industrialized country, students expected to receive grants as victims of political persecution and to continue their studies in Scandinavia or in other Western countries. All such emigrants, having rejected Israel as the country of their choice, unwittingly reduced to absurdity the charge that they were Zionists and as such committed to the State of Israel. The truth thus revealed could, of course, not receive official sanction. Appearances had to be kept up. The state and Party authorities therefore demanded from those concerned that they confirm by their own signature the validity of the propaganda thesis. This had the additional advantage of indirectly preventing non-Jewish Poles from making use of their rights which could hardly be openly refused as long as they were accorded to Jews.

As a consequence, in spite of the generous offers by Sweden and Denmark to admit large numbers of 'persons who consider themselves discriminated against in their native country' (a euphemism necessary for diplomatic reasons, but clearly meant to denote Jews), the Polish authorities insisted that Jews were entitled to apply for exit permits to Israel only. In hundreds of cases applicants for exit permit to other countries were refused passports, some of them several times over; only when they ultimately yielded and agreed to put 'Israel' instead of Sweden, France, USA, or whatever, as their destination, was the matter finally settled and their application granted.

This rule was adhered to even when it bordered on the grotesque. A Jewish employee of the Polish television network, for example, was on a business trip to France and failed to come back; his wife, French-born and non-Jewish, applied for a passport to join him in Paris together with their young daughter. Although she had never given up her French nationality, she was refused a passport. Only when she applied for permission to emigrate to Israel was she granted an exit permit for herself and her daughter.

The representation of Israeli affairs in Poland had been undertaken by the Embassy of the Netherlands, and prospective emigrants had to apply there for their visas. To be Jewish was reason enough to submit an application and the Dutch consul issued visa promises without delay. It was only afterwards that the real chase began: although people were processed with quite exceptional speed, the procedure took days and weeks, as more and more people besieged the various offices. Before a prospective emigrant was allowed to submit his application for an exit permit to the Ministry of Internal Affairs, he had to produce the following documents and certificates:

1. A certificate that his employment relationship had been dissolved. If he had not been dismissed before, he must now give notice. As many applicants had to wait several months for their permits – in at least 200 known cases even for a whole year – the risk in giving notice was considerable, and many prospective emigrants were deprived of their sources of income for indefinite periods.

2. A certificate that the applicant was not, or was no longer, a member of the Party. Party members not previously expelled as Zionists had to return their membership cards. But since a large number of voluntary withdrawals was deemed incompatible with the image of the PUWP, the Party organization or a control commission expelled them formally – and this meant another prolonged delay.

3. A certificate issued by the internal revenue office that the emigrants had no tax payments overdue.

4. Confirmation by the housing administration and the housing authorities that the emigrant's flat would be taken over, as well as a declaration of liability to hand over the flat in habitable condition, so that the new tenant would have no need to re-decorate it. A commission set up by the housing administration must make an assessment and determine the amount of money a prospective emigrant must pay for decoration and repairs.

5. A certificate from the appropriate military command that the prospective male emigrant had performed his military service or that he was exempt on health grounds.

6. In some cases, a university certificate confirming that all studies had been discontinued and all fees settled (e.g. library, laboratory, sports club, student union fees, etc.). Graduates and students had to reimburse the state for all the

expenses incurred in connection with their university education. The amount differed according to the faculties attended, but in any case it ran into five figures (in zlotys). In the case of engineers or physicians, for example, it was fixed at several times average monthly earnings; in extreme cases this amounted to two and a half years' salary.

Only when all these hurdles and delays had been overcome, and all the various stamp duties paid (which in total also came to a considerable sum), was the prospective emigrant equipped with the necessary documents and photographs so that he could finally apply to the passport department of the Ministry of Internal Affairs. He now had to fill in a very detailed questionnaire, and on this occasion, more often than not, there were fresh difficulties. Prospective emigrants who tried to enter in the blank space under 'Nationality' the word 'Polish', as they had always done, were told with cool politeness that Poles were not supposed to emigrate to Israel. Non-Jewish spouses were forced to sign a declaration that they had been informed of the religious and racist discrimination that they would encounter in Israel. This, of course, was just another example of petty chicanery; officials in the passport department were well aware that most of the applicants had not the slightest intention of settling in Israel.

These humiliations reached their climax in proceedings virtually unequalled in their cynicism and demoralizing effects: prospective emigrants were now forced to write an application to the Council of State, voluntarily asking for permission to renounce their Polish citizenship. Such an enforced declaration, invalid under international law, served a double purpose: it released the state from its responsibility for the safety, life and property of the emigrants; it deprived them of their right of return, and of their entitlement to old-age pensions. Since most emigrants were middle-aged or old people, the Polish state had much to gain by this device. On the other hand, reasons had to be given for the petitions to the Council of State. Those who tried to put 'discrimination' as the reason for their application were instructed to try again. Attempts to justify emigration with an invitation received from relatives abroad, or by the desire to continue studies or for any similar reason, including prolonged unemployment, were also not accepted. The only effective declaration was to the effect that the applicant considered himself attached to Israel rather than to Poland.

After the prospective emigrant had completed all the arrangements in the Ministry of Internal Affairs, he had to wait for the official permit, which also determined the date of departure. The waiting period would usually take up to three weeks, sometimes, however, even several months.

The uncertainty as to whether and when a permit would be forthcoming was a source of additional anxiety for all prospective emigrants who had already burnt their boats. As a rule, exit permits had only a short period of validity; people had therefore to make all their preparations for the journey and for the immediate future abroad well in advance, at the same time hurriedly selling whatever they could not or would not take with them – which was often almost all the property accumulated through hard work during the twenty post-war years. Although they were in principle permitted to take all their household goods, including furniture, no new or antique items could be taken out of the country. As this virtually excluded all furniture of value, it was as a result not worth while to bother about the rest: packing and transport were extremely expensive; besides, nobody could foresee what kind of accommodation would be available abroad.

As a result many people assumed an attitude of resigned indifference towards all their material goods, assets and objects, which – even if they had attached a great deal of importance to them in the past – seemed by now totally irrelevant in the face of impending disaster. The great sales began. Jews disposed of their property at ludicrous prices, well aware that they had been left no choice. Not only the purchasers previously mentioned, but even state-owned antique shops were eager to avail themselves of this unique opportunity. There were clear directives as to how many carpets, crystal or silver-ware, bed-linen or suits could be taken out of the country.

When the passport department finally notified the emigrant that the application had been granted, he did not receive his passport, but a small four-page travel document in blue covers, with an entry on its first page: 'The holder of this certificate is not a Polish national', followed on the last page by the statement: 'The travel document entitles the holder to leave the Polish People's Republic and to go to Israel', the date of issue, and the date by which the Polish frontier had to be crossed. The prescribed interval before departure was very short, usually between two and four weeks, and during this time people had to do everything, from packing to leave-taking, not a simple task by any reckoning.

Packing and shipping were usually done by a haulage agency. The cost of packing crates amounted to several thousand zlotys, of wood containers for furniture up to 20,000. All objects had to be listed for the customs authorities, including such details as the number of towels or socks. There were minute regulations concerning documents and books. School and university certificates and diplomas had to be authenticated not only by the Ministry of Education but by the Ministry of Foreign Affairs as well. Work certificates, membership cards of various organizations (e.g. of the Journalists' or Writers' Union), social security or health service cards, etc., could not be taken out of the country at all, and the emigrant's own literary or scientific works in single copies only.

All books packed had to be numbered, and their catalogues submitted in triplicate to customs officers (or to censorship functionaries). Titles published before 1945 were excluded, unless accompanied by a written permit issued by the National Library; as a rule, no permission was granted. Finally, the customs authorities fixed the exact date on which the emigrants must produce their luggage at the railway station for inspection; two pieces of hand luggage only could be taken on the train. The following account by an emigrant gives a fair idea of the departure proceedings:

I owned over one thousand books and I had to list them all in triplicate, in alphabetical order, giving the name of the publisher and the year of publication. Quite a bit of work. Then the hullabaloo about household goods: what were we going to do about the furniture, almost entirely made for this flat and therefore only of value to its prospective tenants? Nobody knew who was going to get the flat, and the decision could not be postponed any longer. In the meantime I asked the housing management for an estimate of the re-decoration expenses I had to cover. They amounted to nearly 6,000 zlotys. The fact that we ourselves had put in the glazed tiles in the bathroom made no difference.

Now for the curator's inspection, and we can start packing. I've never thought it possible that I would need an expert's permission to remove my own trinkets: two Meissen porcelain ashtrays, three pictures painted by friends of mine, a flower vase bought in 'Desa' [a state antique shop] for a few hundred zlotys.... All of this had sentimental value for me alone. But by now I knew better: 'The customs officer is not supposed to be an art lover. Whatever looks like a pre-war product, needs a curator's permission.'

At the Palais Blank everything was prepared for a flood of emigrants. On the wall there was a specimen of the list which had to be submitted in triplicate, each copy with the appropriate stamp. Description of an object, what it was made of, its measurements. Applicants were dealt with twice weekly. Crowded people with their pieces wrapped in newspapers reminded me of a flea-market. The official, allegedly an art historian, behaved like Lorenzo de'Medici. At least, I suppose he tried to imitate him subconsciously. He would quickly release some worthless pieces, then stop when he saw a Jugendstil vase: 'Nice, very nice, it shouldn't leave the country', he said with an almost aesthetic relish. In reply to expressions of astonishment or attempts at questioning his decision he would say with an almost ritual hand motion: 'I'm not here to argue....'

Wistfully I thought about the 'Desa' shops where foreign tourists could buy every possible *objet d'art*: at least they didn't have to deal with such a dignified art historian.

Documents, certificates, diplomas, opinions, deeds and records – that is a story apart. It was rumoured that customs officials would not release either character references or employment certificates. There were even cases when university diplomas were confiscated. This caused me the greatest anxiety. It seemed I would have to appear abroad as if newly created by our Lord. Despite everything I had the most important documents translated. People said that confiscation at the frontier could be avoided by having them officially authenticated at the Ministry. So the run-around began: the original diplomas were attested by the Ministry of Education which confirmed that the signatures of the rector and dean were genuine. The signature of the official in the Ministry of Education had now to be authenticated by the Ministry of Foreign Affairs. Finally I could submit them for translation. Once the translation was done, I had to apply to a court; its chairman would confirm by his own signature that the translator was registered as a sworn court interpreter. Now only the Ministry of Justice remained: it would in turn authenticate the signatures of the judge and the official in the Ministry of Foreign Affairs. Finally a call at one of the Western embassies which would certify the translation done by the sworn interpreter was correct. A similar procedure with certificates of birth and other documents. But this did not apply to employment certificates: the court refused to authenticate them, as they were supposed to be private documents.

Like a dancer in a nightmare, I circulated amongst the various offices with a briefcase full of stamps. Every copy needed a new stamp. Had it not been so distressing, I would have regarded it as a farce: on the way from one end of Warsaw to another, I would encounter the same people doing the rounds, just like myself looking for another official stamp. In the court I was first, but in the Ministry of Foreign Affairs the same man had just left the room. Never mind, I would arrive at the embassy before him, as I had just found a taxi.

I had a few books published before the war, so I would need a permit from the National Library. But I gave up, I had no more energy left. Finally I could start packing. They said a private company was best. It was true: on the day fixed in advance by phone only, without any payment on account, the packers came and brought the crates. They worked quickly and deftly, and incidentally offered a lot of valuable information 'straight from the horse's mouth'. Nothing must be new, everything must at least appear to have been worn or second-hand. Even if the customs officers wouldn't notice anything, in case of doubt they could order an additional inspection at night or in the early hours of the morning: a special commission would come to the customs warehouse and crates would be reopened. I would have been most happy to leave with a briefcase only, but who knew when and how I would start work again? And the books, these would be an irreparable loss.

At last the piled-up crates stood in our flat. During the packing we had made a list of things; now it had to be typewritten in triplicate. Once that was over I went to the railway station to fix the date for customs clearance. The lists were no good; a week before new specimens had been issued. I was supposed to specify what went into which crate, and separately what I was going to take as hand luggage. Besides, I needed a certificate from the housing administration as to how many rooms I had occupied, as well as an authorization issued by a curator. Once all this was in order, they would fix the dates. So I had to rewrite them once more. Two days later (the administration was not open every day!) I returned to the customs office.... By now there was a new specimen on the wall, different from the one I had compiled. From now on six copies were required. Fortunately, I managed to convince the officials that two days before the new regulations had not yet been in force, so I was unable to conform. They accepted my list and fixed the date. But I had to add a note that the objects listed represented the totality of my assets.

The customs office was overcrowded, the atmosphere on both sides nervous. I met a former colleague of mine. She was on the verge of tears; she was to leave that night, but her customs clearance had already lasted three days. She was not sure whether it would be over in time for her departure. People had with them a copy of *Monitor* [the official gazette] containing the regulations setting out the conditions of the 're-settlement'. Now I understood why I had been unable to procure this issue of the *Monitor*: provident people had bought it all up. But even this would not help them: the official customs officers were still more important than the document, and in any case there was no time for appeal. In principle, one was allowed to take 'everything', but the concept of 'everything' was restricted by the *Monitor* regulations, and those in turn by their interpretation by the customs officers. I was told the customs office had found a way to circumvent the law stating that personal goods of the 're-settlers' were duty-free: they levied a duty on the crates in which the things had been packed. Five zlotys per kilogram, and the crates were large and heavy; they had to be shipped on trucks.

At last the day of the customs clearance arrived. As I did not want to put my irascible temper to the test, I sent my wife to attend the inspection of our things. I myself appeared around noon only, bringing vodka and sausages: according to those in the know, that helped to speed up the customs clearance procedure. And, indeed, the customs officers readily disappeared behind a crate where the bottles were – they did it very discreetly, taking turns. Besides, to tell the truth, they were in need of refreshment. The hall was icy cold, and the spectre of an additional verifying inspection obliged them to be painfully thorough. They glanced through every book very carefully; then their attention was drawn to the bed-linen: they counted it thoroughly. But still it proceeded quite quickly, and around 4 p.m. we were through. I was happy; the prospect of freezing here for another day was not very tempting. Besides, now more than ever it was a pity to waste time. On the table lay a handful of confiscated objects: a map of Warsaw, *Reflections on the Jewish Question* by J.P.Sartre, some numbers of a scholarly review with my articles. It was not important; abroad I would be able to procure them through a Polish press distribution agency. Discreetly I pressed 200 zlotys in the customs officer's hand – I was really grateful to him for having made haste. He took the money and presumably considered himself bound by a debt of gratitude: next day I was told one crate had been passed through duty-free.

The writer of this account had little enough reason to associate pleasant memories with the period of his leave-taking from Poland, but it is remarkable that in spite of all the harassment by the authorities he still mentioned, here and there, his good fortune amidst misfortunes. The emigrants often told of unexpected kindnesses and small gestures. They were usually grateful to the petty officials who in spite of constant anti-Semitic indoctrination on the part of their superiors put decency and humanity above official regulations. This should be gratefully recorded here because in general circumstances were not conducive to any display of gratitude towards those who retained their dignity and decency in this poisoned atmosphere. The benefactors were either unknown or else must not be 'compromised' before their colleagues.

As previously mentioned, emigration was an expensive and even a ruinous undertaking. A family of four, for instance, had to pay 5,000 zlotys each for travel documents; this alone comes to 20,000 zlotys. Stamp duties for various documents, translations and certificates amounted to another 2,000 zlotys. Re-decoration of the flat, paid for before departure, would cost up to 6,000 zlotys. Add on top of that sundry travel expenses incurred during multiple trips to various offices and authorities, the transportation of objects for which a curator's permits were required, and of furniture which had to be moved by taxi or hired van – and an estimate of another 2,000 zlotys would not seem excessive. All this does not include the ludicrous prices charged for a *lift* (wooden railway container) for the crates, for packing and transportation to the railway station. A family of four might well spend up to 75,000 zlotys, at a time when average monthly wages amounted to about 2,500 zlotys.

The disproportion was obvious: in any case the Polish state drew all possible benefits; those unable to find the money on their own were assisted by such organization as the Jewish Agency, Hebrew Immigrant Aid Society, or the American Joint Distribution Committee. The state, therefore, not only confiscated all the assets left in the country, but was paid in hard currency for the virtual expulsion of all those who were too poor to pay their own expenses.

The so-called super-inspection, carried out by the security police rather than by customs officers, was not only an additional harassment of the emigrants, but chiefly served propaganda purposes. Television, film and photo reporters were duly invited, and a little manipulation was enough to fish out of the crates belonging to many different families some choice silverware or china, and to display it as evidence of the wealth that Jews were taking out of the country. There were a number of press reports as well: after the Jews had been vigorously persuaded to leave the country, it was now claimed that they were emigrating because they preferred to live wherever there was more money to be gained.

Once all the difficulties had been overcome there still remained the hardest experience of all: for the last time they found themselves on Polish soil at the Gdanski railway station in Warsaw whence trains left for Vienna. Day in, day out, large crowds gathered there, even though the secret police did not bother to conceal the fact that they were taking pictures of those present. Tears, kisses, words of hope, flowers, leave-taking for ever.... Here it became obvious anti-Semitism was not a popular cause. The Nestor of Polish scholarship, Professor Tadeusz Kotarbinski, missed no departure of a fellow-scholar. There were heart-breaking scenes when parents saw off their children, when lovers, brothers and sisters, friends were torn asunder; even married couples: it happened that a wife left and her husband decided to stay 'in spite of everything'.

Families could accompany the emigrants to Katowice: there the customs officers and frontier guards boarded the train and on its way to the frontier, or directly on the border, there was another customs control, often a humiliating body search as well. Some families were taken off the train by night, merely because they had too many pieces of hand luggage: many had their documents and certificates taken away at the last moment. Polish money had to be left behind: the emigrants were to name relatives to whom such sums were to be sent, but often the money never reached its destination.

The next morning at 7 a.m. the emigrants left the train at Vienna's Eastern railway station with $5 per person (that was all the foreign currency they had been permitted to buy before leaving Poland) and with a travel document stating they were not Polish nationals.

In 1969 the monthly review *Kultura*, published in Paris by exiled Poles and widely respected for its intellectual integrity, sent out a questionnaire concerning the background of Jewish emigration from Poland, and published its findings in its November 1970 issue. The reasons most frequently mentioned by the respondents, and the most often repeated points of criticism against the state and the Party, fall under the following headings:

1. Intellectual terror: mendacity and persistent dealing with half-truths; demagogy; terrorization of conscience; discrimination against the intelligentsia; increasing restrictions at universities; falsification of history; slandering of the critically minded; suppression of criticism and opposition; growing restrictions on individual freedom; censorship; uniformity (*Gleichschaltung*) of the press; diminishing opportunities to publish.

2. Intimidation and physical terror: arrests of people of similar views to one's own or of relatives; one's own experiences in prison or detention; political trials; encouragement to inform on others to the police; total absence of judicial security as a result of a partisan judiciary and executive; control over all domains of public life by the security apparatus of the Ministry of Internal Affairs.

3. Ideological contradiction between theory and practice: humanism reduced to a meaningless slogan; power politics preferred to ideology; totalitarianism; lack of social justice; Stalinism as an immanent component of the dictatorship.

4. Abuse of power by the state apparatus: faked elections and fictitious character of popular representation; lack of democracy; rise of a power élite; domination by bureaucracy.

5. Economic disarray: permanent supply shortages; low productivity coupled with high labour quotas; mismanagement of economy; lack of confidence in future development.

6. Social corruption: career-hunting; bribery; negative selection at all levels.

7. Lack of sovereignty: dependence on, and subservience to, the USSR.

In addition the *Kultura* inquiry produced interesting conclusions, showing what events had convinced the contributors that the hopes awakened in 1956 would not be fulfilled by the new political leadership. Here, too, several groups of problems can be traced.

1. Revival of spiritual terror: closing down of *Po Prostu* [a weekly journal of students and young liberal intellectuals which played a major role in the 1956 upheavals]; tightening up of censorship; closing down of debating clubs; propaganda campaign against liberalist literary weeklies; slandering of scholars and writers; regimentation of all spiritual and educational institutions; *The Forefathers* ban.

2. Re-emergence of police terror: continued growth of the security apparatus; renewed violation of civic rights; intimidation of society; political trials, e.g. of Kuron and Modzelewski.

3. Ideological confusion: inter-faction in-fighting within the leadership; con-

demnation of all critical utterances as anti-Party revisionism; propagation of outdated reactionary and nationalist ideas as official ideology; anti-Semitic campaign.

4. Institutional issues: no forces capable of internal revival in the Party; secretiveness of political life; lack of democracy in Party and state.

5. Economic misery: absence of promised reforms; failure of workers' self-management; dissolution of the Economic Council.

6. Personnel merry-go-round: the earliest promotions strengthened the anti-reformist faction; return of Stalinists to their posts; alliance with Piasecki.

7. Doctrinaire foreign policy: growing dependence on Russia; reaction to the Hungarian uprising.

Gomulka and Moczar, in following a policy determined by their own narrow interests, inflicted incalculable damage on their own country. In an age when the world is only too familiar with the horrors and inhumanity of expulsion and banishment, they uprooted thousands of people, robbed them, killed some of them, drove many to their deaths. With various degrees of success the emigrants have tried to adapt themselves to their host countries, but the Polish population continues to live, after the expulsion of the Jews, in miserable conditions that have not changed. In the summer of 1969 Gomulka delivered a speech at the Zeran car factory in Warsaw where a worker asked him:

Comrade Gomulka, the last price rises have hit us badly.... Well, we know now it was the work of the Zionists, but since the Party and the government have got rid of the Zionists, will prices now go down?

At about this time Bienkowski wrote to Gomulka: 'Surely you are not under the illusion that it was all the fault of the Jews, of the "Zionists" (a pre-war commentator once wrote: "The Jews will do for breakfast, but what about lunch?"). You can perhaps sleep better at night than I do, since nobody tells you what is really going on in the country.'

In the middle of 1970 the then Deputy Minister of Internal Affairs, General Franciszek Szlachcic, summed up the situation. He referred to the number of emigrants and of Jews still waiting to leave the country, and in one breath added: 'We' – meaning the police – 'have liquidated the opposition both among the youth and among adults.' He was convinced the Party's control was by then unassailable.

A few months later it became clear how wrong he had been: Gomulka, faced with the totally dismal state of the Polish economy, was forced to introduce drastic price increases together with higher work quotas. By then no ready-made scapegoat was available, no prospect was in view that might divert the workers' wrath from the political leadership. The great foreign-policy success, the agreement with the Federal Republic of Germany over the recognition of the Oder–Neisse frontier, had lost significance in the face of the basic internal difficulties: workers in the Baltic ports took to the streets. This time Gomulka had to call in troops against the allegedly ruling class. He was immediately toppled, together with several other members of the Politbureau.

He was replaced by Gierek, not by Moczar who lost his game as far back as 1968. When the Red Army, together with the troops of other Warsaw Pact states, invaded Czechoslovakia in August 1968, the Soviet leaders considered Gomulka, rather than his ruthless and ambitious security minister, capable of safeguarding peace and order in the rear of their military operation. This was despite Moczar's good friends among the Soviet hawks, Shelest and Shelepin. Any doubts about this shift in the internal balance of power were removed at the November 1968 PUWP Congress: Brezhnev publicly took Gomulka's side. Moczar did not make it to the Politbureau, although there were three vacancies. He was passed over in favour of two new men, party functionaries who had hitherto not even been alternate members of the Politbureau.

In mid 1971 Gierek finally got rid of the troublesome and ambitious climber: Moczar lost his influential post in the highest Party decision-making body. The new Party leader did not, however, purge all Moczar's old cronies – on the contrary, he won over most of them by promoting them to higher posts and honours.

Every day, new injustice is perpetrated throughout the world, power is outrageously misused against defenceless people. Yesterday's injustice fades away, other nations forget. In any case, the Jewish exodus did not have a lasting effect either on Poland or the world at large: several thousand people in Poland obtained better-paid jobs; several thousand people occupied flats abandoned by Jews; nobody knows how many oppressed and persecuted people preferred suicide or in other ways fell victim to official harassment. Probably some 25,000 people were expelled – nobody bothers to ascertain their exact number – and have had to make themselves new lives in foreign countries. The gains and losses in this game of power politics have been forgotten. The handful of Jews still living in Poland will soon die out. The 'problem' has been solved, the one-thousand-year-old history of the Jews in Poland has drawn to its end.

Today Poland is virtually free of Jews (*judenrein*), though by no means free of anti-Semitism. This is not meant as a paradox: it is a simple statement of fact. Modern Communist anti-Semitism has no need of Jews in the flesh – a fictitious image will do quite as well, indeed better, as there is no opportunity to compare the image with its alleged model. As though shadow boxing, the Polish mass media and the official Party propaganda continue to pursue a campaign of systematic character-assassination against the ghosts of the once proudest and most illustrious Jewish community in Europe.

In the 1960s anti-Semitism in Poland served its purpose as a smokescreen to cover a cynical struggle for power inside the Party and state establishment. It can no longer play this role, though it can still be of use as a necessary part of the prevailing doctrine drummed into the entire population to make up for the loss of independence and sovereignty, for the subservience to foreign rule, for economic misery and backwardness, for cultural stagnation and oppressive censorship. The new function of present-day anti-Semitism as part and parcel of the ideological make-up of Communist-ruled Poland is the subject-matter of the final chapter.

11. Endo-Communism

ON 8–9 July 1968 the Eighth Plenary Session of the Central Committee of the Polish United Workers' Party was held in Warsaw. Its agenda provided for confirmation of the so-called Theses, or platform, of the already overdue Fifth Congress, held later that year. In fact, though neither Gomulka's report nor the stenographic minutes of the ensuing discussion have been published in full, the session provided a kind of *post-mortem* examination of the turbulent developments during the preceding months, commonly referred to as 'the March events' – i.e. the attempt to seize power by a well-organized faction inside the Party riding on the crest of an unprecedented wave of anti-Semitism. Even the emasculated reports published in the official *Trybuna Ludu* left no doubts that for the first time in over ten years the deliberations of the supreme Party body failed to follow faithfully a carefully pre-arranged scenario: there were a number of discordant voices.

Amazingly, dissent was voiced not by the liberal intellectuals, who had by then been thoroughly disciplined, cowed and silenced, but by some hard-liners, tough *apparatchiki*, who had started their political careers in the pre-war underground Communist movement and in later years acquired a well-earned reputation as incorrigible Stalinists. But somehow some of them had retained a modicum of personal integrity. For all their conscious life they had been taught that anti-Semitism was a poisonous weapon of diversion, used by the reactionaries to corrupt workers and to distract them from their class struggle, that in no circumstances was it compatible with revolutionary ethics or even with left-wing (or 'progressive') convictions. It seemed that now at least two veterans, Julian Tokarski and Boleslaw Ruminski, both former members of the government and heads of economic ministries, were too old and too naïve to come to terms with the new ideological trend in vogue – the odd marriage between Communism[1] and anti-Semitism.

It is, of course, impossible to say how many other Communist veterans shared their aversion. In any case, only a handful had survived the wholesale slaughter of Polish Communists during Stalin's great purges in the late 1930s, while the Second World War and the Nazi terror had also

---

[1] The problem of how much ruling Socialist parties have deviated from their initially humanistic ideals is beyond the scope of this book. We use the terms 'Communist' and 'Socialist' with reference to movements and countries that style themselves as such.

taken their heavy toll. Besides, to speak out against the official Party line required by then much more courage and independence of mind than was usually displayed by burnt-out, disillusioned, aging men well in their sixties, as a rule interested rather in retaining their veterans' privileges than in keeping faith with the ideals of their youth. So, most of them remained silent, though one cannot help wondering what they really thought about the irony of fate.

For a thousand years Jews had lived together with their Polish compatriots on the banks of the Vistula river in a country unfortunately devoid of well-defined, natural frontiers, squeezed between the expanding landmasses of Germany and Russia. In pre-war Poland one inhabitant in ten was Jewish: Jews constituted the second largest religious and ethnic minority. The thousand-year-old symbiosis of Poles and Jews had its ups and downs: enlightened Poles were proud of the hospitality and tolerance extended to Jews persecuted in and expelled from medieval Western Europe, while Jews were grateful for the protection granted to their ancestors by the powerful kings and magnates of the old Polish–Lithuanian Commonwealth and repaid it with their generous contribution to the country's economic welfare and culture. In popular etymology the Hebrew name for Poland was believed to have derived from God's commandment 'po-lin': here you will find rest. Vilno, the ancient capital of Lithuania and the northernmost and easternmost outpost of Polish (i.e. Western, Roman, European) culture, was compared to Jerusalem. Adam Mickiewicz, Poland's greatest national poet – author of *The Forefathers*, whose production became the excuse for launching the most shameful hate campaign in post-war Poland – had spoken of 'Israel, my elder brother'. In the mid nineteenth century the barriers of religion, language and culture, previously almost impenetrable, began to crumble: the modern intelligentsia, which, in the absence of independent national statehood, assumed the role of guardian of Poland's cultural heritage and the pioneer of its future, had its antecedents not only in the impoverished Polish, Roman Catholic gentry, but also in the urban middle class of partly Jewish and German origin. Intermarriage and conversion became so common that it is not surprising that Moczar's researchers into people's ancestry found their task so strenuous and so rewarding at one and the same time.

Anti-Semitism as an economic, political and cultural phenomenon did not appear until the turn of the century, although the earlier Polish–Jewish relationship had not been free from prejudice and discrimination: noblemen scorned people engaged in commerce and money-lending, the middle classes envied their enterprise, and the largely illiterate, ignorant and devout peasants not only hated the 'Christ-killers', but tended to ascribe their misery to 'alien' middlemen, shopkeepers, and usurers rather than to the absentee landowners of their own faith, or to the remote rulers who had partitioned their country.

The first and most influential modern political party in Poland, the *Endecja*, representing the interests and the aspirations of the burgeoning middle classes, regarded the Germans as Poland's main enemies. This was not only because Prussia was one of the country's oppressors which, moreover, was engaged at the time in a savage drive for enforced Germanization that threatened to exterminate native Polish elements in the western parts of the country, but also because Germans, descendants of ancient settlers and relative newcomers, constituted a considerable part of the urban population. By the same token *Endecja* preached anti-Semitism: a demagogy best suited to influence the middle classes and the professions anxious to get rid of their competitors, both German and Jewish, and at the same time to win acclaim among the xenophobic section of the peasantry and the most conservative part of the Roman Catholic hierarchy. *Endecja* also sought accommodation with Russia as the greatest Slav nation and as a natural ally against German encroachment; in those years before the First World War the Tsarist autocracy and the Greek Orthodox Church in Russia began to recognize the usefulness of anti-Semitism as an antidote to the revolutionary ferment which shook the Russian Empire. Jew-baiting thus provided an additional link between the notorious Black Hundreds in Russia, and Polish nationalism, a common ground stronger than the Poles' traditional hatred of their Russian oppressors and the Russians' fear of the Polish Western heritage, stronger even than the perennial rivalry between Roman Catholicism and Greek Orthodoxy. Not surprisingly, in Polish, just as in English, the word *pogrom* is a direct borrowing from the Russian.

The Polish labour movement – both its revolutionary, 'internationalist' wing which later became the Communist Party of Poland (KPP), and the moderate, national-oriented variety, which subsequently split into the Polish Socialist Party (PPS) moulded more or less on the Western European, social-democratic pattern, and the Pilsudski camp which ultimately shed its socialist protective colouring and became the ruling party in the independent Polish state between the two world wars – always regarded *Endecja* as their main enemy. For this reason, too, in addition to the abhorrence in which democrats, liberals and socialists of every persuasion traditionally held all kinds of national, religious or racial discrimination, the left-wingers (in the broadest meaning of the term, from Communists to the followers of Pilsudski) condemned and fought anti-Semitism.

As mentioned above, this changed to a certain extent in the last pre-Second World War years, chiefly under the impact of the world economic crisis and of the rise of Nazi Germany, when the ruling Pilsudskiites (*Sanacja*) introduced semi-fascist, dictatorial methods of government and tried to steal *Endecja*'s thunder by borrowing their nationalist and anti-Semitic slogans. However, people who considered themselves progressive continued to regard anti-Semitism as the preserve of sinister social re-action and chauvinistic obscurantism. The Communists were especially vociferous in their condemnation of anti-Semitism and of every other kind of discrimination or persecution, although they did not always act from the purest of motives; *Endecja*, on the other hand, avenged itself on them by coining the phrase Jewish-Communist conspiracy and by pre-senting Communism as a Jewish plot, directed against Poland and her national interests.

The accusation should not be dismissed lightly – though not because of the allegedly dominant role played by Jews in the Polish Communist movement – because it was one often made both before the war and in recent times, and is sometimes uncritically repeated even by *bona fide* con-temporary Western scholars. In all multinational states – and pre-war Poland with its ethnic and religious minorities constituting a third of the country's total population certainly belonged to that category – those discriminated against tend to support revolutionary movements rather than to advocate the maintenance of the *status quo*. In Poland this was true not only of Jews, but also of Ukrainians, Byelorussians and even Germans (before Hitler). According to recently published statistics, based on Party archives only partly disclosed in Moscow, the proportion of Jews among members of the Communist Party in ethnic Poland (i.e. excluding the Eastern borderlands, the so-called Western Ukraine and Western Byelorussia) oscillated around 22–24 per cent; at a glance this might seem excessive by comparison with their 10 per cent of the total population, but it should be borne in mind that Jews lived mostly in towns where Communists were relatively strong. Among leading Party activists Jews were probably over-represented, but even this can be explained by their disproportionate share in Poland's intelligentsia, the stratum which supplied most of the Party activists, notwithstanding all the doctrinaire slogans about its proletarian origin. There was, however, some justifica-tion in the charges concerning Communist neglect of Polish national interests, but the reasons must be sought elsewhere than in the percentage of Jews in the Party. As long as this cardinal question was freely discussed in the Party, the dividing lines never conformed to national, ethnic or racial criteria. In other words, Jewish Communists were neither better nor worse than their Gentile comrades.

There is no denying that before the First World War the forerunners of the Polish Communists, the SDKPIL (Social Democracy of the

Kingdom of Poland and Lithuania, the party of Rosa Luxemburg and
Feliks Dzierzynski) were hopelessly wrong in their under-estimation of
national and patriotic feelings: they regarded the restoration of an independent Polish state as impossible under capitalism and irrelevant under
socialism, and believed that the struggle for national liberation would
only distract Polish workers from their revolutionary struggle, fought side
by side with Russian (and German) workers. They were not alone in their
illusion: their point of view accorded with Marxist teaching and was
shared by virtually all European social democracy. It was the Polish
Socialist Party (PPS), with its stress on the indissoluble link between
national and social liberation, which was then considered a maverick.
That is why the outbreak of the First World War in 1914 caused such
a shock to socialist opinion, and almost put an end to the Second International. Suddenly it turned out that one of the founding fathers of German social democracy, August Bebel, himself son of a Prussian NCO,
had been right all along in claiming that socialism stops at the barrack
gates: workers who voted for social democracy and repeated slogans of
international brotherhood started, without protest and enthusiastically,
to kill each other in defence of their countries. Patriotism proved stronger
than socialism, and the Bolsheviks were the first to draw the proper conclusion and to encompass nationalism within their ideology.

There is no reason to doubt that Polish Communists would have been
capable of imitating the new masters without delay and of discarding
their sectarian approach to the national question and their negation of
the independent, albeit 'bourgeois' Polish state, established thanks to a
fortuitous, almost simultaneous defeat of all the three partitioning
powers. The fact that they failed to do so, that in consequence an overwhelming majority of Poles continued to treat Communists with extreme
suspicion as indifferent or even hostile to Polish national interests, as
potential and actual agents of foreign powers, was due not to the disproportionate participation of ethnic minorities (on the contrary, this was
the effect rather than the cause), but to a blind subservience imposed by
the Russian Bolsheviks, victorious in their own country, on all Communist parties, to a domination exercised formally in the name of world
revolution, but in fact in order to safeguard the interests of the newly
created Soviet state. Even in Lenin's lifetime independent Poland was not
only expendable but considered an obstacle to be removed – by force,
if necessary – in order to enable the Bolsheviks to join hands with the
West, and initially with Germany, where a revolution seemed imminent
immediately after the war. In consequence Polish Communists could
never outgrow the ambiguous, if not downright traitorous, role they had
played during the 1920 Polish–Soviet war. It was much worse under Sta-

lin, when Soviet Communism began to identify itself with the Great Russian-Tsarist tradition – anathema to all patriotically minded Poles. Polish Communists had to support not only Soviet (in popular feeling, *Russian*) claims to the Eastern borderlands, inhabited for the most part by Ukrainians and Byelorussians, but also, at least till the mid 1930s, German demands for revision of the Versailles peace treaty at Poland's expense. Most of them, Poles and Jews alike, obediently complied, but they still remained suspect in Stalin's eyes; future historians will have to assess to what extent this influenced his decision to dissolve the Communist Party of Poland and to exterminate virtually all its leading cadres. But attempts to put the blame for its unfortunate policies on the preponderance of 'non-Polish' (i.e. Jewish) elements among members and activists of the KPP are tantamount to ignoring Soviet or Stalinist pressures – apart from which such attempts are unsupported by historical facts. This, however, was the gist of the 'theoretical' essay by Werblan, mentioned in an earlier chapter: its aim was to provide justification for the 1967–8 anti-Semitic campaign, and at the same time to keep the Russians happy.

The KPP's successor, the Polish Workers' Party (PPR), was officially proclaimed in Nazi-occupied Warsaw in January 1942; in fact, its foundation was meticulously prepared, in both political and organizational aspects, on Soviet territory by a handful of veteran Communists who had escaped the Stalinist purges either because they had been in Polish jails or in Soviet forced labour camps. Rounded up by the Soviet authorities, they were then told to compile a brand-new programme which – in accordance with Stalin's grand design of an anti-fascist coalition – would place emphasis on patriotic, 'National Front'-type slogans, play down their links with the pre-war KPP and indeed scrap all the traditional revolutionary demands that went beyond parliamentary democracy and rather modest economic and social reforms, in any case long overdue in Poland. The 'new' party was to be *plus catholique que le Pape*, to outbid all its rivals in patriotic and nationalist demagogy, provided that nationalism was directed against the Germans only, and by no means against Poland's other traditional foe, Russia.

The New Look imposed by Stalin and his henchmen did not please some of the KPP veterans in the Soviet Union, among whom there were a considerable proportion of Jews. But when it was transmitted to Communist underground groups inside Poland, it encountered even greater opposition among the 'natives'. To a certain degree this paralleled the defiant stand of Tito's partisans in Yugoslavia. The resistance did not last long – hatred of the German invaders was so fierce and spontaneous that it overcame all objections to the suppression of traditional internationalist slogans, while Stalin's moral authority made up for the enforced renunciation of a clearly defined socialist revolutionary programme. Contrary to legends concocted *ex post*, the differences of opinion never coincided with ethnic divisions: it was a Jewish former leader of the KPP, Alfred Lampe, who joined the Communist movement after a split in the Poalei-Zion party, and who in his *Thoughts on New Poland* first demanded the extension of Poland's Western frontiers to the Oder and Neisse rivers, without, of course, mentioning that this would compensate Poland for the loss of its Eastern borderlands in favour of the Soviet Ukraine, Byelorussia and Lithuania. Among Comintern emissaries sometimes parachuted into Nazi-occupied Poland to form an underground party and to convince ex-Communists of the need to assume patriotic, or even nationalist, camouflage, there were a considerable number of Jews (including one of the wartime Secretaries-General, Pawel Finder), although their usefulness would appear rather questionable at a time when the Nazis had already started to send ghetto inmates to the gas chambers of Auschwitz and Treblinka. It is not difficult to understand that Polish Jews, as well as Poles of non-Jewish origin, were apt to subscribe to the new patriotic slogans wholeheartedly: the Nazi 'Final Solution' was in its penultimate stage and the only ray of hope lay in a speedy victory of Soviet arms. It was then that Julian Tuwim, one of the most eminent Polish contemporary poets, himself a Jew but by no means a Communist, wrote in his New York exile a passionate prayer for a 'good-neighbourly frontier in the East and eternal chasm on the West' for his people 'squeezed between German savages and a new nation of a hundred nationalities'.

It needed a most perspicacious political mind to discern at this early stage that Polish Communists, having adopted the pseudo-patriotic, nationalistic slogans with the gusto and zest typical of all neophytes, would be ready to surrender to their Soviet masters the essence (as distinct from the tenderly nursed external trappings) of sovereignty and independent nationhood. But they also appropriated a considerable part of the vocabulary previously associated with the right wing of the political spectrum, headed by the *Endecja*. Anti-Semitism, for obvious reasons, was discarded – in words, if not always in deeds: Polish military units formed in the USSR under Communist tutelage could not dispense with Jewish activists, especially in their political apparatus, but officers were actively encouraged to Polonize their names and to conceal their origin in order to enhance the new 'national' image of the army, staffed as it was largely by Soviet regular officers, often of vaguely Polish ancestry and trying to 'pass' for Poles; needless to say, all such clumsy attempts at camouflage were counterproductive.

PROCLAMATION

Re: Death Penalty for assistance to Jews who have left Jewish residential areas without permission.

Numerous Jews have recently left the Jewish residential areas to which they were assigned without permission. They are still for the time being in the Warsaw district.

I hereby declare that by the third decree of the Governor-General concerning residential restrictions in the Government-General of Oct. 15, 1941 (UBL GS p.595) not only will Jews who in this way have left the residential areas assigned to them be punished with death but that the same punishment will also be imposed on any person who knowingly harbours such Jews. This does not only include shelter and food but also any other sort of assistance, e.g. by conveying Jews in any sort of vehicles, by the purchase of Jewish goods, etc.

I hereby instruct the population of the Warsaw District to inform the nearest police station or police command post immediately of any Jew who stays without authorization outside a Jewish residential area.

Any person who has enabled a Jew to receive assistance or is still at the present time doing so but who informs the nearest police authority of this by 16.00 hours, 9 September 1942, will not be punished by the law.

In the same way, no punitive proceedings will be taken against anyone who reports to 20 Niska Street, Warsaw, or the nearest police station or police command post any goods acquired from a Jew.

Warsaw,　　　　　　　　　**THE SS AND POLICE CHIEF,**
6 September 1942　　　　　　　　*Warsaw District.*

A previous chapter has already mentioned the ambiguous attitude of the Polish population in the face of Nazi extermination of Jews: acts of supreme heroism in rendering assistance to victims of the Holocaust, often punished by the death of the 'culprit', his next of kin and even his neighbours, alternated with indifference, glee and active complicity. But pre-war political divisions and affiliations were not always a guide to subsequent behaviour: there were known cases of convinced anti-Semites who remained true to God's commandment of loving thy neighbour, and of Communist guerrilla detachments which murdered Jews hidden in the woods, either for fear of German reprisals or from greed, pure and simple. Some such partisan commanders later rose to senior posts in the Party and state apparatus, and only those who had fallen out with current policy on quite different grounds were ever brought to trial for wartime crimes against Jews – and even then the public was not supposed to glimpse the truth. Such was the case of General Grzegorz Korczynski, veteran of the Spanish Civil War: in the 1950s, on suspicion of supporting Gomulka-ite deviation, he was tried *in camera* for the treacherous slaughter of a Jewish guerrilla group. But after a few years in jail he was set free without a full inquiry into all the circumstances of the case, rose to be First Deputy Minister of National Defence, then as an active Moczarite was downgraded by Gierek and exiled as ambassador to Algiers, where he conveniently died.

Nevertheless in the first post-war years anti-Semitism in Poland was associated usually with armed underground and political opposition to the new Communist régime, while those among the Jewish survivors who had decided to throw in their lot with 'People's Poland', and to eschew emigration, as a rule regarded the authorities as their protectors and loyally contributed to the work of post-war reconstruction. The notorious pogrom of 1946 in Kielce even today raises many puzzling questions: according to the official explanation it was provoked by the anti-Communist underground, but serious indications pointed to the complicity of the security organs, interested in creating diversion and in compromising the political opposition. Generally speaking, however, in the early post-war years there was no official discrimination against Jews, who for the first time were able to engage in careers previously barred to them by custom if not by law (civil service, armed forces, security service, heavy industry, etc.). But the ruling Communist establishment, including its Jewish members, did not dare actively to combat latent anti-Semitism for fear of alienating backward strata of the population, and of marring its recently acquired 'national' image. The indiscriminate mass influx of new members into the ruling Party (membership rose from a few thousand at the end of the war to over one million four years later, to reach about two and a half million today) did not help either: even if one discounts the careerists and climbers attracted by the rulers' lavish patronage, some of those who joined for more or less commendable reasons were motivated by patriotism and nationalism. Nobody bothered to eradicate the prejudices they had brought with them to the mass Party; on the contrary, official propaganda tended rather to aggravate them even more, and as the new generation rose in the Party and state hierarchy, and step by step constituted itself as the New Class – to use an apt phrase coined by Milovan Djilas – it marked the whole nation with its own stamp.

Let us take an example. The Golden Age in Polish history and culture coincided with a multinational Polish–Lithuanian Commonwealth, which unfortunately for the country's future just failed to develop into a threefold entity by granting full equality of rights to the Greek Orthodox Ruthenians (Ukrainians). Thanks to its periods of religious and national tolerance Poland was able to absorb priceless values contributed by alien but loyal elements, and at the same time its cultural influence radiated far to the east and the north, bringing voluntary assimilation and the Polonization of entire social strata and even nationalities. In the inter-war period Poland's weakness derived less from its multinational character than from a policy of discrimination which gave rise to centrifugal aspirations among the ethnic minorities. In any case, there is nothing in Marxist theory which explains the alleged superiority of a nationally homogeneous socialist state; the Soviet Union, after all, to say nothing of Czechoslovakia or Yugoslavia, is in theory at least a multinational state, and none the worse for it. The fact that the post-war Polish state was almost (though not quite) free of minorities could by no stretch of imagination be presented as a result of the conscious policy pursued by the country's new rulers. But of the real causes nothing or little has been said: the extermination of over three million Polish Jews by the Nazis and the emigration of the overwhelming majority of the survivors; the surrender of the Eastern borderlands to Russia, followed by the compulsory 'repatriation' or resettlement and enforced Polonization of the remaining Ukrainians; the expulsion of several million Germans from recently acquired so-called Recovered Territories, carried out at Stalin's command and sometimes according to his ruthless methods – these subjects are still strictly taboo. But official propaganda, starting with the indoctrination of schoolchildren, presented the legacy of war as an unprecedented success and victory for Polish *raison d'état* and as a source of strength, thus playing up to obscurantist megalomania (which was, in fact, the façade for an inferiority complex kept alive by permanently harping on dark plots hatched by alleged enemies of Poland), coupled with the xenophobia of a part of the semi-literate peasants who, in the post-war decades, migrated to the cities, found employment in the rapidly expanding industries, and educated their children to form the new middle classes, bureaucracy and intelligentsia. An exiled Polish writer, K.A. Jelenski, has called contemporary Poland, with its frontiers shifted to the west, with a nationally homogeneous population, without Jews, allied to Russia, and ruled by an authoritarian government, 'a paradoxical realization of the dream of Roman Dmowski', the founding father of the *Endecja*. Dmowski, who, for all his rabid nationalism and obsessional anti-Semitism, considered himself a democrat and a liberal, would probably have rejected a Communist one-party dictatorship but would have felt quite at home in the chauvinistic climate of present-day Poland where the blame for all the country's troubles is being laid at the door of 'aliens' – Germans and Jews. His disciples, influenced in the 1930s by the apparent successes of fascism in Italy and Germany, would find fault neither with totalitarianism in a police state nor with the demagogic populism and pseudo-egalitarianism which have replaced the socialist ideals of the past. At a glance this might seem paradoxical, but then Boleslaw Piasecki, for over three decades an unfailing supporter of the most repressive faction inside the Polish Communist establishment, began his political career on the extreme wing of the *Endecja* camp, and his implicit claim that he has remained true to the ideals of his youth can easily be substantiated. Irony of fate with a vengeance: for it was the *Endecja* that coined the phrase Jewish-Communist Conspiracy (Judeo-Communism) and for many years reaped political benefits by its skilful linking of the two incongruous (but equally unpopular) notions. The present régime in Poland can with much more justification be dubbed *Endo-Communism* (Endo- from *Endecja*), as it has encompassed successfully the most heinous qualities of two political doctrines which had hitherto seemed totally incompatible.

And this brings us back to the question of anti-Semitism and its place in the Communist system of government. There is a natural tendency to regard present-day Communist anti-Semitism as a direct continuation of the pre-war variety; hence it is but one step to attributing to all Poles, irrespective of their convictions or political affiliation, an innate hatred of Jews. Libellous myths and sweeping generalizations die hard, and it would be quite futile to try to refute them by quoting countless proofs to the contrary, drawn both from the past and the present. But still it is important to realize that there is a fundamental difference between pre-war and post-war anti-Semitism, otherwise neither the events of 1968 nor their prehistory and subsequent development can be properly understood. To quote Professor Zygmunt Bauman, a well-known sociologist, himself a victim of the 1968 witch-hunt:

The anti-Semitic campaign which had been growing underground in Poland for several years, and which swept to the surface in the early spring of 1968, had nothing to do with the activities or the social and economic role of Polish Jews. A clear distinction must be made in this context between conditions in pre- and post-war Poland. Before the war the Polish petty bourgeoisie and intelligentsia had to face the problems of economic competition, aggravated by the general economic backwardness of the country, and these provided a basis for the spread of the so-called popular anti-Semitic sentiments. But nothing of the sort existed in post-war Poland. In a socialist Poland where, moreover, there were no numerous Jewish communities, there were neither Jewish industrialists nor Jewish street-traders to compete against the rest of the population. What is more important, however, Polish Jewry after the war, and in particular after the mass emigration in the years 1957–8, could neither politically, economically, nor culturally be regarded as a cohesive community, conscious of its separate identity and of its distinct group interests. Within Polish society Jews were active only as individuals, representatives not of Polish Jewry but of the separate professional and regional bodies which form part of the Polish nation as a whole. The new wave of anti-Semitism was therefore neither a natural nor even a perverse reaction to the part played by the Jews themselves in the economic and political life of Poland. The mainsprings of this anti-Semitic campaign must be sought elsewhere than in any specific Jewish problem. They must be sought in the internal situation in Poland, or more specifically, in the social conflicts and contradictions which can in part be blamed on the present leaders [this was written in 1968] and which threaten these leaders with an explosion of incalculable consequences. The 1968 anti-Semitic campaign, as distinct from all the pre-war anti-Semitism, is a purely political phenomenon, in which the Jews are playing the part of a scapegoat to attract the whole accumulated aggressiveness and frustration of the embittered and disillusioned mass.

Here we have the heart of the matter. The pre-war economic and social anti-Semitism, to which August Bebel's old adage about anti-Semitism being the socialism of fools would be applicable, died out together with three million Polish Jews murdered by the Nazis. For a few years after the war traces of 'folk' anti-Semitism still lingered, mixed with compassion for the innocent victims of the unprecedented slaughter, but fed by fear that the survivors, or the victims' next of kin, might reappear and claim the property seized in the meantime by neighbours. It was also fed by the old *Judeo-Communist* stereotype which transferred the almost universal hatred and mistrust of the new rulers and their Russian masters to the handful of 'aliens'. But by the mid 1950s even this was on the wane, and, given a few more years, a new generation might have emerged, by

7. 'The seductive Jewish snake lures the deluded to their doom', *Der Stürmer*, no. 47, 1941. The caption inside: 'I enjoy devouring the world.'

8. 'Song of Peace', from the Soviet publication *Agitator*, February 1970.

and large free from racist bias. But this was not to be: there were forces interested in rekindling the dying flame for purposes of their own. Anti-Semitism reappeared therefore in Poland as primarily a political weapon, and the people who wielded it were undeterred by the fact that their alleged target was virtually non-existent: an abstract image of the Jew even then had already largely replaced the flesh-and-blood Jews, almost totally assimilated in the population of the nationally homogeneous state.

Where the new wave came from is by no means a mystery: *Ex Oriente Lux!* Polish Endo-Communism was not unique. Although it has developed distinctive traits of its own, it can (but will not!) claim among its antecedents the curious blend of fossilized orthodox Marxism, of oriental despotism, and of Great-Russian[2] chauvinism and expansionism, which went under the name of Stalinism. The Russified Georgian, like the Frenchified Corsican or the Germanized Austrian, went to the

[2] It should be stressed that anti-Semitism and chauvinism are not innate traits of the Russian people, in whom the sense of justice and tolerance is no less developed than in others. Negative feelings are constantly stirred up and kept alive, at no little effort, by the interested power groups.

extreme in bowing to the traditions of his adopted country. Anti-Semit-ism had always played a major role in the Great-Russian or Muscovite heritage, but in the tyrant's old age it became an obsession which *cannot be rationally* explained. Jew-baiting applied in moderation had already proved its usefulness during the interfactional struggles in the Soviet Communist Party during the 1920s and 1930s, especially as a corollary to Stalin's Great Purges, and then again in the fight against 'rootless cosmopolitans without a fatherland' in the late 1940s. On the other hand, the planned mass resettlement of Soviet Jewry, epitomized in the case of the 'Kremlin doctors' ('murderers in white gowns') but fortunately thwarted by Stalin's timely death, not only indicated that the senile dicta-tor was by then mentally unbalanced but that there was inherent insanity in the entire edifice of the régime built to his orders: the future was to show that this had not been a passing aberration or perversion, but part and parcel of the system.

Anti-Semitism had by then become an exportable article, with the East-ern European satellite countries its chief recipients. There were, to be sure, significant quantitative variations. The frenzy which accompanied the Slansky trial in Czechoslovakia – a country, by the way, exceptionally free from 'folk' anti-Semitism – was unsurpassed anywhere else. Poland escaped relatively unscathed: there were some purges of Jewish staff in the armed forces, in the security and Party apparatus, even in state admin-istration and economic management, but those were pursued quietly, without noisy propaganda. Preparations for the mass internment of Pol-ish Jews never went beyond preliminary planning, and were dropped im-mediately after Stalin's death and the liquidation of the 'Kremlin doctors affair' in Russia. The reasons for such restraint, all the more astonishing in the light of subsequent development, are not easy to guess. The tiny proportion of Jews in the total population would not account for it: con-ditions were more or less the same in Czechoslovakia. Neither would the presence of some Jewish Communists at the top of the Party or in the security service make any difference: they were much more numerous and influential in Hungary, or even in Rumania. It is of course quite poss-ible that had Stalin lived a few years, or even months, longer, Jakub Ber-man would have met with Slansky's fate, and Polish public opinion would have been treated to a similar smear campaign against Zionists, Trots-kyites and cosmopolitans. Why, then, was Poland spared such a shameful spectacle? The fact that only a few years earlier it had been the scene of unprecedented slaughter might have had something to do with it: East Germany was another country where for obvious reasons anti-Jewish overtones were at this time rather muted. But sometimes the simplest answer happens to be the true one: there was, as yet, no organized faction inside the Polish Party ready and able to use anti-Semitism for its own purposes. The number of Jews, their influence, the role they had played – all this was irrelevant. Whenever and wherever the wave of anti-Semitism mounted, it was for reasons over which Jews, or even Jewish Communist dignitaries, had little or no control.

Paradoxically enough, there was an upsurge of official anti-Semitism in Poland, but in 1955–7, at the height of a process described as de-Stalinization, democratization or 'the Polish October'. The issue was raised by a powerful faction inside the Party, called 'Natolin'; their adversaries used to brand them as Stalinists or neo-Stalinists, but in fact they were ardent supporters of Khrushchev, who, for all his settling of accounts with the dead dictator and his methods of ruling the state and the empire, did not lag behind Stalin in the cynical exploitation of anti-Semitism. There is ample evidence that the Natolin faction embraced anti-Semitism under direct Soviet prodding (though they did not need too much encouragement). Russian diplomats, 'advisers', even casual visitors, were quite uninhibited in spreading anti-Jewish propaganda in Poland, eagerly seconded by the Natolin faction.

This bid for power on the crest of an anti-Semitic wave backfired badly and brought its instigators more damage than gain. The masses remained impervious to Jew-baiting not only because they vehemently rejected whatever bore the imprint 'Made in the USSR', but because Natolin had miscalculated and over-estimated the extent of latent traditional, or 'folk', anti-Semitism. On the contrary; this was the one and only period in the post-war history of Poland when mass media, staffed almost exclusively by Natolin's rivals, advocates of 'reform Communism' (shortly to be branded as 'revisionists'), reflected the general mood in the country, in the Party's rank-and-file, and in particular among the intelligentsia, and waged open warfare against anti-Semitism and against other aspects of *Endo-Communism*. The April 1957 circular letter of the Party's Central Committee on the need to combat anti-Semitism, quoted at length in a previous chapter, was the crowning achievement of this campaign. Soviet-inspired anti-Semitic demagogy employed by the Natolin faction appealed only to the New Class of Communist bureaucracy, but twenty years ago this was still a thin layer, as yet far removed from the omnipotence it acquired in the later period. Still, the introduction of the Jewish issue into an inter-party struggle was ominous enough to convince most of the remaining Polish Jews (including those repatriated from their Siberian exile) that there was no future for them in a Communist-ruled country. Gomulka did not put any obstacles in the way of their emigration. He was quite happy to be rid of those who for all their ostensible assimilation continued to mar his beloved image of a 'nationally homogeneous state'. By 1958 probably no more than some thirty thousand Jews, or rather, in most cases, Poles of Jewish descent, remained in Poland – less than one per thousand of the total population.

Fourteen years of Gomulka's second period of rule (October 1956 to December 1970) might be considered an exercise in moderate *Endo-Communism*. Public opinion, in Poland for a relatively short time, in the West for much longer, tended to regard Gomulka as a sincere Polish patriot, a statesman who for all his Communist orthodoxy had his country's national interests at heart. Usually overlooked, however, was the one-sided slant assumed by his 'patriotism': while stressing motifs of national unity, with the traditional vocabulary of revolutionary socialism and class warfare to a large extent abandoned, it was attuned from the very beginning to the voluntary restriction of Poland's sovereignty in its relationship with the Soviet Union. The main difference, compared with the Stalinist period, consisted in the ideological justification of total subservience to Russian supremacy: Polish *raison d'état*, instead of 'the international solidarity of the working class' or the 'leading role of the first socialist state'. All attempts at increasing the country's independence *vis-à-vis* its powerful neighbour to the east were parried with the argument that the Soviet alliance remained the sole reliable safeguard of Polish statehood and of its Western frontiers, allegedly threatened by West German revanchism, the spearhead of American imperialism. As time went on the German bogeyman was used with increased frequency, as this was perhaps the most important common ground of agreement between the Communist rulers and the largely anti-Communist, or politically indifferent, population of Poland. Since the consensus was of limited scope only, this – in addition to the unfulfilled promises of 'October 1956' and to growing economic difficulties – made for the increasingly authoritarian and repressive character of Gomulka's régime. The dreaded security service, virtually dismantled in 1956, was thus able to stage a spectacular comeback. Placed under General Mieczyslaw Moczar, whom Gomulka, in spite of all the evidence to the contrary, obstinately considered his staunch supporter, the secret police quickly exceeded its pre-1956 total as regards both officials and informers, and began to yearn for a political role of its own. By the early 1960s the Moczarite 'police faction' emerged as a serious contender for power: professing to represent the most consistent and radical wing of the Gomulka-ite camp and to aim for the achievement of the 1956 programme, it was in fact a rejuvenated offshoot of the disintegrated Natolin faction, most of whose leaders and followers had rallied to it.

If the surviving pupils of Roman Dmowski could regard Gomulka's

Poland as an embodiment of the traditional dream of *Endecja* – they would not be happy with the Communist social system but would tend to discount it as a necessary evil justified by the supreme interests of national survival, or as a protective colouring required by Soviet Russia – the Moczarites began to resemble closely the young hotheads of the 1930s who, impressed by Italian and German fascism and its social demagogy, had split the Polish nationalist movement: Piasecki had no inhibitions about joining forces with Moczar. In order to outbid the incumbent Party leader they went one better, replacing nationalism with outright chauvinism and xenophobia.

It was a dangerous game requiring great skill. Soviet leaders were deeply suspicious of every kind of nationalism – except, of course, the Great-Russian variety which since Stalin's times had served them as a means to legitimize their internal and foreign policy, at the expense of the earlier Marxist variety. Their experience with Communist nationalism had been most unfortunate: one has only to recall Tito's Yugoslavia, Mao's China or even Ceaucescu's Rumania. Poland was an exceptionally delicate case, not only because of its strategic position in Europe, but also because of its profound distrust of all things Russian, vengefully reciprocated in Russia's sentiments towards its Western neighbours and one-time enemies. In 1956 Khrushchev had proved himself an exceptionally perspicacious politician, seeing through Gomulka's nationalist demagogy and trusting him for what he really was – a loyal Communist who in any case would be compelled to rely on Moscow's support to maintain his rule in Poland in the face of quasi-total opposition to a Communist régime (though it was most difficult to sell the idea to the rest of the Soviet Politbureau). An open challenge to Gomulka from more extreme nationalist positions would certainly incur disfavour with the Russians, who had not given up their commanding positions in Poland: for an imprudent politician it might have been suicidal.

Moczar ultimately did not make it to the top, but he came near enough to dispel any doubts that he enjoyed at least a considerable measure of support in the Kremlin. His master-stroke consisted in having wholeheartedly embraced anti-Semitism. Whether he himself was tainted with anti-Jewish prejudice, or even whether he sincerely believed a handful of Poles of Jewish origin in senior Party and state positions could actually bar his road to power, is totally irrelevant. But he rightly recognized anti-Semitism as the master key which would open to him various locked doors by removing people (whatever their origin) apt to oppose his rise, and would also – even more important – supply him with a credible alibi *vis-à-vis* the Soviets, explaining away his otherwise inadmissable harping on nationalist themes.

The origin of Stalin's anti-Semitic policies can be traced back to the obscurantist tradition of Tsarist autocracy and of the Greek Orthodox Church, and to his morbid suspiciousness and conviction that even the most innocent, sentimental attachment of Soviet Jews to the State of Israel or to their co-religionists abroad, in particular in America, constituted a mortal danger to the cohesion of the totalitarian state. Both reasons have retained their validity under Stalin's successors, but they have been further strengthened by foreign policy considerations. Unlike Stalin, Khrushchev and Brezhnev saw their chance in the Third World, especially in the Middle East: anti-Semitism, under the guise of anti-Zionism, came in handy in wooing Arab favours. The book mentioned earlier, *The State of Israel*, by K. Ivanov and Z. Sheynis, appeared for the first time in 1959, thus giving the lie to the claim that the Soviet anti-Israeli and anti-Zionist campaign was sparked off by the 1967 Six-Day War. On the contrary, its purpose was to prepare Soviet public opinion and to make Moscow's anti-Israeli stand palatable. Its secondary, but for all that not less ominous, aim was to convince readers that all Soviet citizens of Jewish origin were potential Zionists, that is, as Zionism was an instrument of imperialist intelligence services, potential spies.

In Poland the book was immediately followed by similar literature, partly translated from the Russian, partly written by native imitators. Apparently this played into Moczar's hands, as his Jew-baiting could now convincingly be made to fit into the mainstream of Soviet propaganda, his own particular goals being conveniently camouflaged and forgotten. But one should not miss the point: no such book, even translated from the Russian, could conceivably have appeared in Poland without the Party's general *placet*.

This need not surprise us: anti-Semitism, especially in its more moderate version, wholly conformed to the doctrine of *Endo-Communism*. Gomulka did not shrink from making use of it in his fight against 'revisionism' both inside the Party and among the intelligentsia. As relatively many of the intellectuals, writers, scholars, etc. who had opposed his increasingly authoritarian rule were of Jewish origin (or could be labelled as such), people soon began to identify 'revisionists' – as in the case of 'cosmopolitans' a few years earlier – with Jews. Gomulka was ill-placed to emphasize the point (his Communist past would hardly allow for open anti-Semitism), there were still some Jews among his closest collaborators, and many others (including, as we know, he himself) had Jewish wives. He was therefore content to fight 'revisionists' and 'Zionists' in the name of Communist orthodoxy and of Polish *raison d'état*. But he neither could nor would restrain his over-zealous young men. For a long time he did not apparently fully realize that they were not hitting at his real or imaginary adversaries ('revisionists'), but at himself and his team.

Here, at last, we reach the crux of the matter. In the mid 1960s Gomulka's Poland was in the throes of a deep crisis. Workers were dissatisfied because in spite of slogans and promises the national economy stagnated and the standard of living, pitiful by all comparisons, would not rise, while the ruling élite unashamedly feathered its nest. Students, and young people in general, could not help comparing the Utopian formulae they were being indoctrinated with, with the surrounding drab reality, imposed by aging leaders out of touch with the times. Intellectuals were frustrated and dismayed by censorship, not only oppressive but stupid to boot, and by the stifling climate of parochialism which had replaced the period of relaxation which in the second half of the 1950s had contributed to the short-lived flowering of creative activity. Catholics were alienated by the sudden revival of the anti-Church campaign in connection with the millenary celebrations of Poland's conversion to Christianity and of its statehood; patriots were fed up with chauvinistic, anti-German slogans used as a cover to conceal the effective loss of sovereignty. Even the New Class of Party and state bureaucrats, managers and officers grumbled and complained that their chances of promotion were held up by a handful of senile worthies, retained in office not because of their professional skills but because of real or imaginary performances in the distant past. It was an authoritarian régime blended with everyday muddle: not oppressive enough to stifle all opposition by terror, too oppressive to allow even limited freedom of expression. The call for a change became general.

The Moczarite 'police faction' was the only one to provide a simple diagnosis and an equally simple solution. All Poland's troubles, both in the past and in the present, were attributed to her external enemies and 'alien' elements inside the country: Poles, left to themselves, would always manage to bury the hatchet, to settle all their differences, and to work in harmony for the common good of the whole nation. The police minister who had gone on record in the early post-war years as proclaiming that the only good soldiers of the Home Army were the dead ones – and had not shrunk from translating his words into practice – had by then managed to put all the blame for the excesses of the Stalinist period of terror on a handful of Jewish security officials – assiduously avoiding, at least in public, all reference to his own achievements, as well as to the role played by Soviet 'advisers'. He had also succeeded in rallying around himself a respectable proportion of convinced anti-Communists, former members and followers of right-wing political parties, including even fascist and semi-fascist groups. Under his guidance an ex-servicemen's league, ZBOWID, ceased to be an insignificant organization of army and resistance movement veterans, interested chiefly in the welfare of its members, and became a powerful political body that sometimes competed directly with the Party in stressing its 'patriotic', so-called nationalist character. Thanks to virtually unlimited financial resources and skilfully dispensed patronage, ZBOWID quickly acquired a membership of well over a quarter of a million. For some time there was even talk of forming a separate youth movement under its aegis. Like some other ex-servicemen's organizations in various countries, especially in Germany between the two World Wars, the ZBOWID, with its rabid nationalism and authoritarian inclinations, in addition to its emphasis on 'soldierly values', can be regarded as a fertile breeding-ground for fascism. When necessary, however, it continued to pay lip-service to standard Communist slogans.

While trying to woo the workers with crude egalitarianism, the Moczarites concentrated their attention on winning the favours of the class they rightly regarded as decisive in a Communist totalitarian society – the New Class, the main beneficiary of all the social upheavals of the last decades. To a large extent of peasant[3] stock and peasant mentality, the New Class was, generally speaking, the most satisfied with the régime which had given it a chance to leave the wretched villages, to acquire a rudimentary education, and to climb the social ladder. At the same time the New Class was ambitious, impatient with too slow a rate of promotion (in its own eyes), and envious of the old intelligentsia, whether of gentry or urban origin. The New Class consisted not only of the proverbial *apparatchiki* – Party bureaucrats of limited intelligence and no professional skills, who enjoyed virtually uncontrolled power in their home areas – it comprised, too, civil servants and regional officials, economic managers, engineers and technicians, army and police officers, teachers, doctors and scientists. As a rule they were not interested in ideological issues, certainly not in the ideals of socialism. They were inherently conservative because the *status quo* safeguarded their social privileges, suspicious of dissent because they still felt insecure in their freshly won position, conformist, narrow-minded and intolerant, full of prejudice and superstition.

The New Class formed the mainstay of Gomulka's rule; he himself, for all his past Communist record, epitomized it in a perfect manner. Moczar was shrewd enough to realize he could not win its support in a frontal attack against Gomulka: he would do much better by outflanking him and presenting another target and hate object. An external

---

[3] The term 'peasant' in this book refers to the East European peasant strata who, as a result of the backwardness of their countries, partly lived in semi-feudal conditions or continue to do so.

enemy would not do: the German card had been played for all it was worth by Gomulka himself; the Russians were taboo and could only be obliquely hinted at. The most convenient substitute was, however, provided by the internal foe: the intellectuals ('revisionists'), never satisfied with what they had, always grumbling and bent on disturbing the existing social order, and of course the Jews, dimly remembered from a distant childhood in the countryside as the 'Christ-killers' and bloodsuckers, or from the war years as subhuman outlaws, robbed and killed at will. It did not matter that there were so few of them: the image of 'the Jew' was much more important than the physical presence of Jews, especially since every adversary could safely be branded as Jewish and fitted into the overall notion. Besides, the actual Jews in Poland, some of them, for sure, in the highest positions and systematically poisoning the mind of the faithful but gullible and undecided leader, were but a tip of the iceberg, of the world-wide conspiracy against Poland, mounted by American imperialism and West German revanchism, and using 'Zionists', both in the country and abroad, as their Fifth Column – a household word in Poland since the last war, with all its pejorative connotations.

To such witch-hunting Gomulka could hardly object: he himself had made use of anti-Semitism to get rid of his rivals in the internecine struggle inside the Party, while anti-Semitism in the guise of anti-Zionism had been made respectable by the Soviets and accepted by the ruling Communist parties in Europe. Judicious Jew-baiting allowed Moczar and his henchmen to pretend to act in the best interests of Gomulka and the country, as being responsible for overall security he was only doing his duty, unmasking and rendering harmless Zionist agents who had managed to infiltrate even the highest posts of command. And as a fervent patriot he was only strengthening national unity by getting rid of an alien and disruptive element – true to the spirit of Gomulka's own guidelines. Of course, if the leader were to hesitate and vacillate, this would only confirm the vague suspicion that he had grown old and senile, and should therefore be replaced by a younger, more dynamic and vigorous man of heroic wartime record, who would not let any sentiments and past reminiscences stand in the way of national revival. For the time being, however, the battle was being fought in Gomulka's name – even if the goal consisted all along of paving the way for a contender. The change of leader was finally achieved – after a delay due to an unforeseen international complication (Czechoslavakia) – in December 1970, at the cost of several hundred workers massacred during strikes in the Baltic ports. Moczar's triumph, however, proved very short-lived indeed, but that is an entirely different story.

In previous chapters we have tried to present the 1967–8 events from the point of view of their victims. We have quoted at length eye-witnesses' reports. But ten years have passed since, and one cannot help asking the question: Why? What wrong had the victims done to merit brutal expulsion from a country which some of them, wherever they happen to live now, still continue to regard as their own because of their ancestors' ten-centuries-old attachment and because of their own contribution to Poland's reconstruction after the Second World War.

The only rational answer we have been able to arrive at is summed up in this chapter. The transformation of Communism into national-communism has effectively taken place everywhere, in all countries where Communists have seized power and probably in most parties still fighting for power. The new ideology has served different, sometimes even antagonistic, objectives: in the Soviet Union it provides a rationale for Great-Russian chauvinism, for the oppression of other nationalities, and for world expansion. Among other peoples of the USSR, and in particular in the so-called satellite countries, it made resistance to enforced Russification easier, and even contributed to maintaining the vestiges of sovereignty (e.g. Yugoslavia or Rumania, and of course China); in those cases it has something to recommend it, even though it does not always contribute to relaxation of internal oppression. But elsewhere the incongruous marriage of Communism and chauvinism has only disguised total subservience to Moscow; such is the case in what we have called *Endo-Communism* in Poland, though parallels can be found in other countries too, such as Czechoslovakia and East Germany. That, with great-power imperialism, is one of the most serious distortions of socialist ideals which may well have been Utopian but had at least sprung from noble intentions.

In the mid 1960s the Polish *Endo-Communist* régime was undergoing a deep crisis. The ruling clique was clinging to power, afraid of any significant changes; another faction sought to unsaddle it and to usurp its place. With equal cynicism, though to a different extent, both had recourse to chauvinistic demagogy and its corollary, anti-Semitism, to stave off a hopeless outburst of students in support of intellectual dissent. The price of this struggle, ultimately won by a *tertius gaudens* but within the same New Class, was paid by many thousands of Poles of Jewish origin who had not even been a party to the quarrel: they were forced to emigrate and to disperse all over the world. The Jewish community in Poland virtually ceased to exist. But we are not at all sure whether even a higher price has not been paid – and still continues to be paid – by the Polish nation as a whole: the March 1968 revolt of students and intellectuals failed because it found no support among the workers; it found no support because the rulers had managed to convince the workers that the students' cause was no concern of theirs. A plot had been hatched by a handful of enemies of Poland and socialism, by 'Zionists', a nationally, ethnically and racially 'alien' element. It was foiled thanks to the vigilance of the Party and of its faithful security organs, and followed by a widespread purge of the perpetrators and their allies – Jews or Jewish flunkeys to a man. No wonder that when the riot police and army, two and a half years later, fired at defenceless shipyard workers at Gdansk, Gdynia and Szczecin, the intellectuals and students did not stir. This, too, was part of the price paid for succumbing to the poison introduced under the guise of anti-Semitism.

And the same poison continued to trickle even after the immediate political aims had been achieved. Only in 1976, after the serious workers' riots and strikes, was a bridge built between the proletariat and the progressive section of the intellectuals. People who maintained a modicum of personal integrity and independence of mind disappeared from public life or were reduced to silence. Gomulka was finally toppled by workers' protests, Moczar disgraced and put in honourable semi-retirement, Gierek's new team – to which an overwhelming majority of Endo-Communists of both Gomulka-ite and Moczarite factions had eagerly flocked – sat secure in the saddle, but not a single victim of the 1968 witch-hunt has been rehabilitated or reinstated, not a lie exposed, not a slander withdrawn. Anti-Semitic propaganda has never ceased to appear in the mass media.

To a large extent the persistence of anti-Semitism in a country which had become virtually *judenrein* (free of Jews) is due to the blind imitation of Soviet patterns: in Russia the Jewish question is still very much alive because anti-Zionism is intended to ingratiate Moscow with the most reactionary Arab states (*vide* support of all Communist-ruled states for the UN resolution equating Zionism with racism) and also because two or three million Soviet Jews (their exact number still very much in doubt) courageously fighting for human rights, including their right to maintain their cultural identity as a nation or their right to emigrate, constitute today quite a potent factor of political struggle in the USSR. Hence the steady flow of openly anti-Semitic literature, published in Russia and unfailingly translated into Polish, Czech, etc. Polish hard-liners, unable to follow Soviet anti-Semitic practices for lack of their own Jews, expelled in 1968, at least demonstrate their unwavering loyalty in the propaganda domain.

Nor do they limit themselves to translation alone: while Zionism continues to supply the Polish mass media with an all too easy target in foreign policy, especially when Middle Eastern affairs are concerned, there is an insidious anti-Jewish propaganda in trashy novels, thrillers or non-fiction reports, printed in mass editions for semi-illiterate readers. Here all the negative heroes, whether seducers of virtuous Polish maidens, embezzlers, profiteers or smugglers, or else American spies, wreckers or agents of West German intelligence, bear distinctive Jewish names or display other qualities which make instant identification possible. In the 1970s most such publications were brought out by the Ministry of National Defence Press, but other publishing houses were not far behind. A blatant example is provided by a four-volume autobiographical novel, or rather *roman à clef, Waiting for the Final Word*, by Vladyslav Machejek, editor-in-chief of a Cracow weekly, a rabid Moczarite and anti-Semite; it is probably the most coherent exposé of *Endo-Communism* ever printed. Not only are all Poland's misfortunes directly attributed by the author to Jews who had infiltrated top echelons of the Party bureaucracy and the security services (historical personages usually appear under thinly disguised and easily recognizable pseudonyms), but a ready recipe for improvement was supplied as well: Poland had to be ruled by native Poles, whatever their political affiliation. Censorship, as a rule exceptionally sensitive to the slightest hints of 'anti-Sovietism', in this case made an obvious exception by allowing for the discreet criticism of 'foreign' interference, though admittedly this was limited to the Stalinist period.

Another current of barely concealed anti-Semitic propaganda is to be found, curiously enough, in scholarly publications addressed mainly to intellectuals. Marxist dogmas notwithstanding, anti-Jewish slanders are being borrowed literally from the well-known *Endecja* arsenal. A few examples, selected almost at random, provide ample evidence that these are not isolated cases.

In 1969 a literary magazine, *Poezja*, devoted to poetry and printed and published in Warsaw, reprinted, without any explanation or introduction, an essay written by a brilliant young writer, Gajcy, who did not survive the war. The original had been published in a clandestine sheet brought out under Nazi occupation by an extreme right-wing anti-Semitic organization a few months after the Polish Holocaust. The author, referring to Polish poets of Jewish origin, entitled his essay 'We Do Not Need Them Any More'. He claimed that Polish poetry between the two World Wars had been three-quarters alien to Poland and to the soul of its people, because of the racial origin of the poets. Contemporary Communists have appropriated this thesis as one of their own, without a single word of acknowledgement.

Eugeniusz Duraczynski, a historian known for his obedience to the Party line, in a report submitted to the Congress of Polish Historians in 1969, and subsequently published in *Miesiecznik Literacki*, a literary monthly, not only repeated the slanderous statements that Jews had always been hostile to Polish statehood, but utterly denied any significant Jewish contribution to Polish armed resistance under the Nazi occupation, and even a specifically Jewish armed struggle – as though there had never been an uprising in the Warsaw Ghetto, to take but one outstanding example. This unprecedented falsification of history provoked many letters of protest by readers; the editorial board printed only one of them, signed by Tadeusz Holuj, as well-known writer, himself an ex-inmate of Auschwitz extermination camp, together with an evasive reply by the author. The journal promised to continue the polemics, but never did – in this case the undeniable historical facts left no place for any further elaboration of anti-Semitic lies, so long as no refutation of them was forthcoming.

In 1974 a book on society in inter-war Poland, by Janusz Zarnowski, a Polish historian of Jewish origin, was reviewed by another historian, Jan Borkowski, in a scholarly monthly, *Przeglad humanistyczny*. Most of the review was devoted to the Jewish question and to anti-Semitism, and would make any Nazi organ proud, although it was written by a Communist graduate of an academy of the Party's Central Committee. Once more Jews were presented as an 'anti-Polish element' who had not only exploited their fellow-countrymen but systematically pushed them out of the better-paid jobs – at the time when anti-Semitism was being adopted as the official policy of the then ruling Party. Well-known cases of pogroms and anti-Jewish excesses at the universities were dismissed as 'brawls' between Jews and Gentiles, more often than not provoked by Jews, while most of the casualties were non-Jewish. Protests from other scholars were ignored by the editors, and extracts from the slanderous review were published by some other papers, including a weekly owned by the Pax movement.

Finally, Polish Scientific Publishers in 1976 brought out a one-volume *The History of Poland*, compiled by a team under the editorship of Professor Jerzy Topolski; 140,000 copies, beautifully produced and lavishly illustrated, provide the general reader with a comprehensive survey of his nation's past, from pre-historic times to the present day. The book has been unreservedly praised by the reviewers, and the Party's theoretical monthly *Nowe Drogi* devoted a special scholarly symposium to its publication. It may therefore be justly regarded as an official exposition of the views held by the current rulers of Poland.

This is hardly the place to engage in polemics on the merits of the case presented by contemporary Polish Party historians; one would have to explain at length how Szczecin, cut off from the Polish state and Polish cultural influence in the early Middle Ages, receives much more preferential treatment than Lwow or Wilno, cities which for centuries had been lively centres of Polish culture but were recently incorporated into the USSR; or why Tsarist Russia is meticulously cleansed of any responsibility for Poland's past misfortunes, the partitions included; or why the savage slaughter of thousands of defenceless inhabitants of the Warsaw suburb of Praga in 1794 is dismissed with a few words ('whereby the civilian population also suffered...') because the Russian troops were commanded by Alexander Suvorov, regarded by Stalin and his successors as a great soldier. As might be expected, the number of distortions, falsifications and outright lies increases as the authors start to deal with recent events, and history is replaced by crude politics, but this aspect can be safely left to *bona fide* scholars who are sure to tear it to bits. But one cannot help wondering what the average Pole will learn about his Jewish fellow-countrymen.

The answer is – as good as nothing. He will not be told that Jews lived in Poland from times immemorial, that the first authenticated mention of the new kingdom was found in an account left by a Jewish traveller from Spain, or that coins minted by the first historical ruler of Poland bore Hebrew letters. He will learn nothing of the history and culture of the Jewish community in Poland, and next to nothing of its contribution to the economic and cultural development of the country as a whole – except that Jews were usurers and therefore enjoyed the protection of kings and magnates. Not a single word is said about the Jews who over the last two centuries had voluntarily given their lives for Poland's freedom – and if there are some whose names cannot be omitted, then nothing points to their origin. If Jews are mentioned at all, it is only as an alien element, hostile to the Polish cause and a factor of the nation's weakness. *Endecja* gets its share of praise for having realized the German danger and the need for alliance with Russia (later with the USSR), and if the fact cannot be concealed that it had fanned the flames of anti-Semitism (e.g. during the 1905 revolution) the author hastens to add: 'This did not prevent collusion between the *Endecja* and the Jewish upper bourgeoisie'. In the historical rivalry between *Endecja* and Pilsudski's camp the author's sympathy is clearly with the former, perhaps because Pilsudski's régime 'managed to win over wide strata of the Jewish bourgeoisie', but both parties are said to have been in agreement on the Jewish question: the government 'supported ... the emigration of the Jewish population to Palestine', while *Endecja* called for 'the boycott of Jewish trade and a restriction on the number of Jewish students'. 'None of these slogans', concludes the author with unmistakable regret, 'led to a solution of the overpopulation issue.'

A solution of a kind was provided by Hitler, but, for obvious reasons, the author is most reticent when dealing with the Holocaust. In two different chapters he fleetingly touches upon the fate of Polish Jewry: his description fully deserves to be quoted verbatim:

Population of Jewish origin had to submit to particularly harsh discrimination. They had been forced to wear special yellow armbands and stars of David on their breasts to distinguish them from other inhabitants. Assets of the Jewish population were seized, and Jews were collected in special ghettoes or camps, and from there led to work. They received starvation rations. All attempts to help them were severely punished by the occupiers. In spite of this the Polish population opposed the occupiers' policy towards the Jewish population and came to their rescue.

And some thirty pages further on:

In March 1942 the Nazis started to carry out the so-called final solution of the Jewish question, i.e. the extermination of the Jews confined in the ghettoes. In the summer of 1942 [22 July to 13 September] they liquidated the Warsaw ghetto; part of the people were murdered on the spot, part were transferred to camps in Treblinka, Majdanek and elsewhere. During a short time some 300,000 people were killed. The final extermination of the Warsaw ghetto came in the spring of 1943. Part of the population, led by the Jewish Fighting Organization [ZOB] and PPR [the Polish Workers' Party – Communists], put up armed resistance [19 April to 8 May] that was bloodily crushed by the SS. In the same period ghettoes in other towns were also liquidated. The Polish population *en masse* opposed discrimination against the Jewish population and rendered them considerable assistance in their armed struggle.

And that is all. Even the number of Jewish victims was not considered significant enough to mention; total war casualties in Poland were estimated at over six million, without specifying that half of them were Jewish – over three million – out of a pre-war population of three and a half million. One will seek in vain to learn the fate of the survivors: the last chapters, dealing with post-war Poland, after stating with satisfaction that 'the population of Poland underwent a process of national homogenization' because 'immediately after the war the non-Polish population in principle returned to their native countries', do not see fit to mention Jews at all. By the same token there can be no question of anti-Semitism: the events described in this book are here summed up in two short sentences:

In the spring of 1968 the Party was confronted with another assault by various anti-socialist forces, including revisionists. With the support of the working class these forces were routed.

Endo-Communism

The History of Poland appeared in print several years after the final expulsion of the Polish Jews, as if to remind us that anti-Semitism can well flourish even without Jews. It is still needed as one of the props on which the whole edifice of *Endo-Communism* is based, and to a limited extent it can still serve some purpose whenever a scapegoat is needed. In December 1970, during the workers' uprising in the Baltic ports, a pamphlet was hurriedly printed, putting the blame for the shipyard workers' discontent on a handful of Polish Jews who had found refuge in the Scandinavian countries; it was only Gomulka's ignominious downfall which prevented the distribution of this honest effort by some zealous Party stalwarts. In June 1976 when workers again downed tools to protest against price rises, there were no more Jews to blame, but security officials still beat up strikers to make them confess they had been paid by 'the Jews', presumably from abroad, while the mass media engaged once more in Jew-baiting and looked for 'alien' blood among the intellectuals who had rallied to the defence of the workers. And so it goes on and on.[4]

You cannot treat the Jews like Spain once treated the Moors. Whenever any Spaniards oppress any Moors, the Moors fare badly, but the Spaniards fare even worse.

This was written nearly a century ago by Eliza Orzeszkowa, the great Polish novelist. The events taking place in some countries today prove that her words have lost none of their relevance.

[4] The display staged for the benefit of the West in connection with the thirty-fifth anniversary of the Warsaw Ghetto uprising did not in any way reveal a change of attitude.

HISTORY teaches that virulent smear campaigns do not always lead to the extreme of genocide, but without such campaigns the latter would be impossible. This makes the systematic incitement of hatred against any minority so dangerous and its consequences so unpredictable.

J.B.

Abbreviations

KPP	Communist Party of Poland
MKK	Little Penal Code
ONR	National Radicals
ORMO	Polish Voluntary Police Force
OZON	Camp of National Unity
PAP	Polish Press Agency
PPR	Polish Workers' Party
PPS	Polish Socialist Party
PZPR/PUWP	Polish United Workers' Party
SDKPIL	Social Democratic Party of the Kingdom of Poland and Lithuania
UB	Polish Security Service
ZBOWID	Union of Fighters for Freedom and Democracy
ZMS	Union of Socialist Youth
ZOB	Jewish Fighting Organization
ZSP	Union of Polish Students

Index

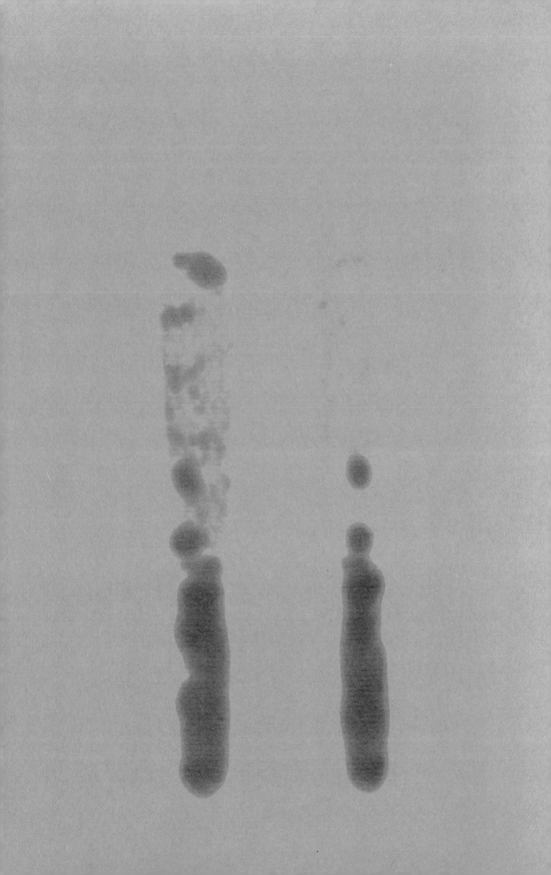